TERRORISM:
A PHILOSOPHICAL ANALYSIS

PHILOSOPHICAL STUDIES SERIES

VOLUME 101

Founded by Wilfrid S. Sellars and Keith Lehrer

The titles published in this series are listed at the end of this volume.

TERRORISM

A Philosophical Analysis

by

J. ANGELO CORLETT

*San Diego State University,
San Diego, U.S.A.*

KLUWER ACADEMIC PUBLISHERS

DORDRECHT / BOSTON / LONDON

A C.I.P. Catalogue record for this book is available from the Library of Congress.

ISBN 1-4020-1694-8

Published by Kluwer Academic Publishers,
P.O. Box 17, 3300 AA Dordrecht, The Netherlands.

Sold and distributed in North, Central and South America
by Kluwer Academic Publishers,
101 Philip Drive, Norwell, MA 02061, U.S.A.

In all other countries, sold and distributed
by Kluwer Academic Publishers,
P.O. Box 322, 3300 AH Dordrecht, The Netherlands.

Printed on acid-free paper

Printed in the Netherlands.

TABLE OF CONTENTS

Key Words/Names: civil disobedience, Joel Feinberg, humanitarian
intervention, indigenism, Immanuel Kant, Martin Luther King, Jr., Karl
Marx, John Stuart Mill, legal obligation, moral duties, moral rights, Native
Americans, non-violent direct action, pacifism, political violence, John
Rawls, retribution, revolution, secession, Socrates, terrorism, Michael
Walzer.

For Joel Feinberg,

A person of excellence in both mind and moral virtue,
and whose kindness seems to know no bounds.

PREFACE

This book is the culmination of over 15 years of research on terrorism, secession, and related concepts such as the obligation to obey the law, pacifism, civil disobedience, non-violent direct action, political violence, revolution, and assassination. It is sincerely hoped that the content of this book is construed as an ethical and philosophical attempt to advance human understanding of some of life's most intractable problems, namely, terrorism and more generally, political violence. This book is proffered as a propadeutic to further study of these issues and is not to be interpreted as the author's final word on them. For the pursuit of truth and avoidance of error is never wholly complete, but at best a life-long process of continual reflection, analysis and argument. And it will please the author of this book if it brings even a modicum of knowledge to the difficulties it investigates.

Some of the chapters of this book have been published or have otherwise experienced the critical assistance of various public academic forums, and I am sincerely grateful to those who have shaped my thinking about terrorism and its related concepts. Among those who have provided critical and helpful insights concerning various sections of the contents of this book are: David Copp, Richard Falk, Joel Feinberg, Richard W. Miller, and Thomas Pogge. I am grateful also to those who have provided incisive comments on an earlier draft of this book: Virginia Held, Aleksandar Jokic, Al Spangler and Burleigh Wilkins. And I am tremendously indebted to the invaluable insights of the Publisher's referee for this book, the Philosophical Studies Series Editor-in-Chief, Keith Lehrer, and to Kluwer Academic Publishers for having the courage to publish it.

I would like to acknowledge that the content of Chapter 2 is a revised version of my article, "What is Civil Disobedience?" *Philosophical Papers*, 27 (1997), pp. 241-59. Chapter 4 is a greatly expanded version of my article, "Secession and Native Americans," *Peace Review*, 12 (2000), pp. 5-14. Chapter 5 is a revised version of my article, "Can Terrorism Be Morally Justified?" *Public Affairs Quarterly*, 10 (1996), pp. 163-84. I am grateful to each of the journals and their respective Publishers for use of the articles in revised form.

Finally, at the time of completion of this book, I accessed a copy of Professor Ted Honderich's illuminating book, *After the Terror*. I regret that due to considerations of time, Honderich's book is not herein given the attention it so richly deserves.

INTRODUCTION

Recent years have been plagued by incidents that often eventuate in political violence such as terrorism and secessionist movements. A rather few examples of recent terrorist acts include the "Unabomber" Theodore Kaczinsky's acts of violence against various individuals from the 1970's through the 1990's in the United States, the 1998 bombings of the U.S. embassies in Nairobi and Tanzania, the 21 December 1988 bombing of Pan American flight 103 over Lockerbie, Scotland, the 1996 abortion clinic and gay nightclub bombings in Atlanta in the year that followed the 1996 Olympic bombing (an act that is rather difficult to classify as genuinely terrorist), the constant bombings of Occidental Petroleum oil pipelines by FARC in Colombia during the past decade of its nearly 40-year civil war with the Colombian government, the 19 April 1995 bombing of the federal building in Oklahoma City, OK, and the 11 September 2001 attacks on the World Trade Center and U.S. Pentagon buildings. It must be kept in mind, however, that such well publicized incidents of terrorism tend to overshadow in the minds of many the fact that more regular terrorist acts occur in countries like Israel (by Israel and Israelis against Palestinians, and by HAMAS against Israel), Great Britain and Spain, just to name a few. Examples of secessionist movements include the Colonists secession[1] from the British Crown in 1775, the peaceful secession of Brasil from Portugal in 1822, the southern states in the U.S. and their united secessionist attempt from the U.S. northern states during the U.S. Civil War, the secessions of various former USSR republics into independent states during the early 1990's, Quebec's recent attempts to peacefully separate from Canada, Macedonia's success in seceding, the recent creation of an independent Slovakia, as well as the current Basque separatist's move to secede from Spain, and the civil wars that erupted in recent secessionist movements in Croatia, Bosnia and Herzegovina.

It is particularly important to understand terrorism and secession, not only because their occurrences are increasing in numbers globally, but because of the violence that typically, though not always, accompanies such political movements. Philosophically, we want to know precisely what are

---

[1] If some are correct in thinking that the Boston Tea Party and other incidents of political violence by Colonists against the British constituted acts of terrorism, then the U.S. seems to be founded on its committing terrorist-secessionist acts against the British Crown. This would seem to imply that U.S. patriots, then, are not in a moral position to condemn outright either terrorism or secession.

terrorism and secession, and can they ever be morally justified? What is the difference between a truly terrorist act and one that seems like one but is not? What makes them terrorist acts as opposed to, say, the mere hijacking and bombing of an airliner? And does the distinction matter? The philosophical analysis of the nature of terrorism that I provide and defend answers the former question, and in so doing it provides the law good reason to distinguish between merely criminal behavior and genuine terrorism. Such a distinction is important in that it serves as a good reason for courts to sentence one kind of behavior more harshly than the other, other things being equal. Perhaps what most distinguishes the respective kinds of behavior is motive or purpose. But what *kind* of motive or purpose distinguishes terrorism from terrorist-like criminal behavior?

Moreover, at first glance, it might seem that, though secession might be justified on moral grounds, it would be ludicrous to think that terrorism could *ever* be morally justified. For, it might be argued, how could an act, event, or state of affairs which is so indiscriminately violent be morally justified?

In order to bring rational reflection to bear on matters of terrorism and secession, it is essential that a series of inter-related questions be addressed. For the questions of whether or not terrorism and secession are ever morally justified are contingent on the answer to the question of whether or not political violence (of which terrorism is a species) is ever morally justified. And the question of whether or not political violence is ever morally justified is dependent on the answer to the question of whether or not violence more generally is ever morally justified. Yet the answer to these questions presupposes an answer to the question of whether or not it is ever justified, on moral grounds, to break the law, and if so, whether one must in such cases do so non-violently. This book considers each of these queries in reverse order.

Chapter 1 is devoted to a philosophical investigation of the question: Is there a moral obligation to obey the law? If so, what *kind* of obligation is it? As we shall see, Immanuel Kant avers that it is an *absolute* moral obligation, always to be upheld, while Socrates does not give a clear answer to this question. Perhaps Socrates thinks we have a *prima facie* moral obligation to obey the law, as is considered in Chapter 2. If we do *not* have an *absolute* obligation to obey the law, under what conditions and in what ways are we morally justified in disobeying it? Pacifism is one way to disobey the law. What is *pacifism*, and under what conditions is it morally justified? Civil disobedience is yet another way to disobey political authority. What is *civil disobedience*, and is it ever morally justified? Intuitively speaking, it would seem that if neither pacifism nor civil disobedience is ever morally justified, then political violence would not ever be morally justified. For if non-violent modes of political disobedience are not morally justified, then it would appear that violent methods of political change would not be justified. One assumption here is that in general violent methods of social change require a special moral justification that non-violent ones do not require. This is because, it might be argued, violence holds the potential for innocent lives to be lost. And this is especially true of violence that targets groups many of the constituents of which may be morally innocent.[2] On the other hand, what if both pacifism and civil disobedience are at least sometimes morally justified as means of challenging the law?

Chapter 3 centers on the question: What is *political violence*, and is it ever morally justified? More specifically, what is *terrorism*, and is it ever morally justified? What is *secession*, and and is it ever morally justified? Whether or not terrorism or secession are necessarily violent means of political challenge, it is clear that they *are* ways of confronting political authority. By "confronting political authority," I mean, for example, a terrorist and/or secessionist act that addresses a particular political power structure, whether by sending it a message that expects a cooperative response, or by simply striking out in retaliation for a perceived wrong doing, or in some other way that is based on something that the targeted political regime did, failed to do, or attempted to do unjustly. And it is important to understand not only what each of these methods of confronting political authority is, but under what conditions each might be morally justified. By "morally justified" I mean, briefly, that a practice is supported by the balance of human reason, all things considered. Moreover, if one is morally justified in doing something, then one has a moral right to the exercize or enjoyment of it. Of course, that one is morally justified in and has a moral right to this or that hardly amounts to a moral duty to the same, though it does (generally) imply a moral duty of others to not interfere with the exercize or enjoyment of the right.[3]

In Chapter 4, I provide a philosophical analysis of the nature of secession and the conditions under which it is morally justified. Unlike any other philosophical analysis of secession, mine sets forth and defends an indigenous perspective on secession that is at the same time based on generally accepted principles of the recent discussion in analytical philosophy. In the end, it is only those (typically groups) that have valid moral claims and/or interests to (the occupation of) certain lands that have

---

[2] This is not meant to imply that either pacifism or even a failure to act for social change does not require a special kind of moral justification. For in either case, such action or inaction, as the case may be, might well eventuate in the harming or taking of innocent lives because of the failure of certain folk to act in saving the lives of self or others.

[3] This notion of a moral right is borrowed from Joel Feinberg, *Freedom and Fulfillment* (Princeton: Princeton University Press, 1992), Chapters 8-10; *Problems at the Roots of Law* (Oxford: Oxford University Press, 2003), Chapter 7.

moral rights to secede, given the content of the generally-accepted "Territoriality Thesis."

The nature and moral status of terrorism is analyzed philosophically in Chapter 5. But at the outset it is important to delineate, in anticipation of the later discussion of the nature and moral status of terrorism, the sorts of terrorism there might be in light of the current state of international politics, science and technology. One reason for this discussion is to raise awareness as to how Herculean the challenge of terrorism is nationally or globally. And one reason for this is that even if political and economic coalitions are sought in order to combat terrorist groups worldwide, smaller, less powerful countries and allies against such terrorists might well find themselves far more vulnerable than the relatively few more powerful states, thus exposing themselves to an even greater risk of terrorist attacks in order to thwart their participation in any kind of anti-terrorist coalition.

The threats of specific terrorist activities might take a number of horrific forms. First, there is the *terrorist act of taking hostages*, perhaps leading to violence against those kidnapped and those to whom the terrorists appeal in bargaining for their respective positions. An example of non-violent form of terrorist hostage-taking is the 1996 seizure of the Japanese Embassy in Lima, Peru, by the MRTA, while an example of terrorist hostage-taking that led to violence is the famous 1972 Olympic Games in Munich, Germany where some members of the Palestinian Liberation Organization took as hostages several Israeli athletes, a series of actions that ended in the deaths of both parties. Another example of violent terrorist hostage-taking but as a means to ending the civil war in Russia is the group of armed Chechen rebels who, on 25 October 2002, took and held hundreds of hostages in a Moscow theatre, a terrorist act that eventuated in the deaths of dozens of terrorist rebels and hostages after negotiations broke down between the rebel terrorists and Russian officials. Second, there is the *threat of bombing of targets by terrorists*, which of course is more of a direct militaristic tactic. Examples of this sort of terrorism abound, as there are numerous such threats on airports and other buildings throughout various parts of the world. Third, there is the traditional threat of *terrorist hijacking of airplanes*, usually of the commercial variety, containing passengers who are citizens of the regime with whom the terrorists seek to deal or "punish". One such example is the terrorist bombing of the Pan Am airliner over Lockerbie, Scotland, in 1988.[4] Moreover, what the world has learned from the 11 September 2001 attacks on the World Trade Center and the U.S.

---

[4] On December 21, 1988, Pan Am Flight 103 left London heading for New York. Including the crew there were 259 people on board. Over the village of Lockerbie, Scotland the plane exploded and pieces fell into two rows of houses, killing 11 people on the ground. The final toll was 270 dead.

Pentagon buildings is that terrorism may well take the forms of hijacking commercial jets containing passengers, but for the purpose of attacking suicidally specific targets which will eventuate in tremendously adverse effects such as deaths, significant physical and/or psychological harms, economic upheaval, etc., of the terrorists' target(s). But even if a country decided to devote significantly increased funding in airport security and other related security, terrorists might, fourthly, resort to *chemical methods of terrorist attack*. This might take the forms of poisoning air or water supplies in a specified country, or it might take the form of using such harmful chemicals or substances in the forms of "dirty" bombs. But terrorists might, fifthly, *gain access to heavily guarded domains such as nuclear missile silos in order to commit terrorist attacks*. After all, they might gain such access by having inside "plants" or by some strong arm tactic at a time of lapses in security. Sixthly, terrorists might attack rail transportation by either planting bombs in railway cars, passenger or cargo, or by simply targeting the rails. Other forms of terrorist violence include the typically easier methods of poisoning food and water supplies. These methods are particularly problematic in that food and water supplies are so vulnerable and so costly to secure against such acts. Of course, terrorists might rely simply on credible *threats* of violence, especially if there is an adequate track record of political violence sufficient to ground the fear of its target(s). Obviously, terrorism can (and often does) employ more than one of these sorts of threats or acts simultaneously.

The point of this discussion is not to be alarmist, but rather to simply outline some of the various ways in which terrorism has already occurred, or might take form. For those societies seeking to guard themselves and others against terrorist attacks must first have some basic ideas of the forms terrorism might take if they have even a reasonable hope of succeeding in thwarting it.

The primary task of this book is to provide a moral and philosophical assessment of terrorism and secession, respectively. The significance of this book is that it provides new philosophical analyses of the natures of terrorism and secession. Understandings of the nature of terrorism herein do not fall prey to the question-begging definitions that currently plague most, if not all, recent accounts of what terrorism is. Moreover, new analyses of the conditions under which terrorism and secession are morally justified are proffered and defended. In the case of terrorism, the conditions require a rather conscientious moral agent to engage in morally justified terrorism. In the case of secession, an indigenous perspective is given, one that is grounded in the well-acknowledged "Territoriality Thesis." But this indigenous perspective, absent from all recent philosophical accounts of secession, is not found only in my discussion of secession. Rather, it is articulated and defended in terms of how certain acts of terrorism might be justified against significantly oppressive political powers. Thus while thoroughly grounded in the mainstream analytical philosophical discussions of obedience to the law, pacifism, civil disobedience, and political violence, this book represents a dramatically new way of understanding terrorism and secession. For perhaps the first time in the history of analytical philosophy, indigenous rights are brought to the *forefront* of discussions of terrorism and secession. This move is made without apology, and until there is sufficient reason to think that certain experiences of historical injustice against indigenous peoples or indigenous rights somehow fade over time in their importance.[5] That my Indigenism focuses on Native North Americans is a reflection of my knowledge of the history of indigenous experiences in that region. Perhaps what is argued herein concerning Native North American moral rights might well apply to other indigenous persons and groups throughout the world, though I am careful to not extend my arguments globally.

Along the way, various critical discussions are presented concerning what certain well-respected contemporary philosophers have argued about the nature of civil disobedience, humanitarian intervention, political violence, and more specifically, about terrorism and secession (Indeed, the book ends with an argument that, given what John Rawls says about the nature of humanitarian intervention, terrorist intervention might well qualify as morally justified humanitarian intervention in some cases). For instance, Chapter 3 provides not only a counter-example to Rawls' analysis of the nature of civil disobedience, but it explains for the first time in philosophical literature on civil disobedience that civil disobedience and non-violent direct action differ from one another, and why. So while the book contributes to philosophical analyses of terrorism and secession by setting forth and defending an indigenous account of these realities, it does so by building its case on the backs of recent philosophical discussions of terrorism, secession, and their related concepts. This book provides and defends what promises to be a reasonable and informative philosophical analysis of the nature and moral justification of terrorism. That is, it sets forth and defends a notion of what terrorism is, along with an analysis of the conditions that, to the extent that they are satisfied in a given case, would justify terrorism on moral grounds. Furthermore, it provides a guiding principle that would delimit (or not, as the case may be) the kind(s) and duration(s) of terrorism that are justified given the facts of each context of terrorism. For the most part, my analysis of terrorism intends to address revolutionary/retributive brands of it, with the proviso that both state and non-state terrorism fit well under such categories. By "revolutionary terrorism" I mean terrorism that is aimed at

---

[5] I have discussed such matters in J. Angelo Corlett, *Race, Racism, and Reparations* (Ithaca: Cornell University Press, 2003), Chapters 8-9.

bringing down or otherwise replacing a particular government. By "retributive terrorism" I mean terrorism that aims at giving a person or group what they "had coming to them," e.g., giving them what they deserve. Of course, on my analysis of the nature of terrorism, revolutionary terrorism ought to be but is not always retributivist, and retributive terrorism is not (nor ought it be) always revolutionary in any deep sense. However, on my analysis of the moral status of terrorism, revolutionary terrorism must always be retributive in the sense mentioned, though I do not address the matter of whether or not retributive terrorism ought to be revolutionary in a deep sense.

Moreover, though this book links uniquely the problems of terrorism and secession, it is not argued herein that only terrorism that aims at secession is (or could ever be) morally justified. As just mentioned, there are varieties of terrorism that are in no way linked to secession, just as secessionist movements need not engage in terrorist activities. The conceptual link between some acts of terrorism and secession is meant to demonstrate how complex both problems are, and to suggest to philosophers and others who take seriously such phenomena that indigenous rights and experiences of racist oppression help to provide a heretofore unarticulated perspective in analytical philosophy. Thus the main points of this book about terrorism are meant to apply to terrorism moral generally, quite apart from secession. Likewise, the primary arguments concerning secession are meant to apply to secession quite unrelated to terrorism.

With much confusion about what counts as terrorism and secession, and even more confusion regarding the matter of whether or not they could ever be morally justified, it is especially crucial to develop rational and reasonable theories concerning these problems. And in both cases, this book articulates for the first time (in analytical philosophical literature) indigenous perspectives on these matters. By the end of the book, it becomes obvious to the reader how significant the adoption of this perspective is for discussions of the natures and moral statuses of terrorism and secession. One aim of this book is to make plausible the adoption of the indigenous perspective on these matters that so importantly effect our lives. Another purpose, of course, is to begin to explore philosophically ways in which the goal of peace can be achieved and sustained throughout the world.

A final set of introductory notes concerning the ethical perspective from which the content of this book is argued. Since this is a book about some of the ethical dimensions of terrorism and secession, and not a book about ethical theory itself, it would be unreasonable for readers to expect a defense of the moral philosophy adopted herein. Nonetheless, it is appropriate to at least outline without defense (though not without reason) some of the most important ethical assumptions with which I work in developing my analyses and arguments concerning terrorism and secession.

I adopt a moral realist perspective according to which moral concepts, at least some of them, have real content and are not, as an emotivist might claim, unreal or mere expressions of personal feelings having no informational content whatsoever. This realist perspective is important in that it cautions against the view that a terrorist is morally justified if she *believes* she is justified in engaging in terrorism, and against the equally misguided claim that whatever response to terrorism is *deemed* right is indeed right, regardless of what is reasonable to think about the matter.

Moreover, I assume an admixture of deontological and consequentialist approaches, one that would seek to guard against a purely consequentialist standpoint, on the one hand, or a purely deontological perspective on the other. Mine is an ethical standpoint that seeks to be sensitive to the foreseeable results of an act while holding to the most reasonable moral principles that would and should guide our actions. Against those who might argue that such putative moral principles have no content apart from considerations of the consequences of an act, I would respond by noting that certain principles *must* guide our actions lest the ends of our actions are believed to "justify" the means to those ends. Thus I adopt certain moral principles relative to the matters of terrorism, secession, and political violence more generally. Some such principles are that only those guilty of wrongdoing should ever suffer harm or retribution; that the harm or retribution suffered by the morally guilty should always be in (albeit approximate) proportion to the amount of harm caused by the guilty; that unrectified evil or injustice is evil or unjust still (that there is no moral statute of limitations on injustice); that moral rights and duties are "real" and carry at least *prima facie* weight in ethical deliberations. *To the extent that* either of these principles is violated in performing act having moral import, then that act is morally unjustified.

Whether or not an act of terrorism or secession is morally justified is not only a matter of degree, it is contingent on the extent to which a reasonable case can be made for a genuine act of terrorism or secession satisfying the conditions that would justify them on moral grounds. And the same is true concerning the possible moral justification of terrorists and secessionists, respectively. If such a case can be made, then the burden of argument shifts to those who would deny that such acts of terrorism or secession, or their respective agents, are morally justified. In any case, moral principles are needed to guide our reasoning about such volatile problems.

Yet our moral principles must be context sensitive, e.g., sensitive to how the actual world functions: how humans think; what is reasonable to expect of humans under this or that set of conditions, etc. Such principles ought to be sensitive to the overall consequences of actions. But consequences of actions are not all that matter. Justice, rights, and historical experience also provide meaningful moral contexts with which our complex ethical deliberations must cope. Here I assume, with Joel Feinberg, that, for instance, a world without rights (and justice), "Nowheresville," is seriously and morally deficient to one in which persons are accorded moral and legal rights that provide at least a *prima facie* case for non-violation,[6] perhaps some of which serve as what Ronald Dworkin calls "trumps" over the temptation to subsume, in a purely consequentialist manner, rights under considerations of utility.[7]

---

[6] Joel Feinberg, "The Nature and Value of Rights," *The Journal of Value Inquiry*, 4 (1970), pp. 243-57.
[7] Ronald Dworkin, *Taking Rights Seriously* (Cambridge: Harvard University Press, 1978).

CHAPTER 1

IS THERE A MORAL DUTY TO OBEY THE LAW?

There are a variety of positions that might be taken concerning the question of whether or not there is a duty to obey the law. First, there is the view that there is an absolute legal obligation to obey the law, one which holds that we ought always to obey the law no matter what because the law is the law and it ought always to be obeyed. This naïve legalistic notion of the duty to obey the law has few, if any, takers. But a legalistic view that has proponents is the one that states that there is a *prima facie* legal obligation to obey the law because the law is the law and it ought to be obeyed except in circumstances where the law permits disobedience. In either case, it is a legal duty to obey political authority that we have. A position equally extreme to that of the naïve legalistic one is the skeptical legalistic position that denies that there could ever be a legal obligation to obey the law. One reason why this position is problematic, if not nonsensical, is that it seems to hold that no legal system or body of law would bind citizens to it by way of obedience. Yet it appears that most, if not all, legal systems do precisely that.

This book is about the possible *moral* justification of certain acts of political violence such as terrorism, and this chapter is concerned with questions, not so much of legal duty, but of *moral* duty. So the questions with which we are most concerned along these lines are the following: Is there an absolute moral obligation to obey the law? By "absolute" here I mean a duty which accrues at all times and in all circumstances, no matter what. If so, then political violence, insofar as it breaks the law, is impermissible, and the argument stops here. Let us investigate, then, this question in light of what Immanuel Kant had to say about it.

KANT AND THE ABSOLUTE MORAL DUTY TO OBEY THE LAW

Of all of the ingenious sorts of arguments that Richard Wasserstrom[1] considers for there being an absolute moral obligation to obey the law, he does not consider the following one. In *The Metaphysical Elements of Justice*, Kant argues that:

> It is the people's duty to endure even the most intolerable abuse of supreme authority. The reason for this is that resistance to the supreme legislation can itself only be unlawful; indeed it must be conceived as destroying the entire lawful constitution, because, in order for it to be authorized, there would have to be a public law that would permit the resistance. That is, the supreme

---

[1] Richard Wasserstrom, "The Obligation to Obey the Law" in Joe P. White, Editor, *Assent/Dissent* (Dubuque: Kendall/Hunt, 1984), pp. 29-44.

legislation would have to contain a stipulation that it is not supreme and that in one and the same judgment the people as subjects should be made sovereign over him to whom they are subject; this is self-contradictory.[2]

Thus for Kant no disobedience to the law is justified: no pacifism, no civil disobedience, no non-violent direct action, no terrorism, no secession (or any other form of political violence).[3] From his words just quoted, it would appear that Kant has set the stage for our philosophical discussion of terrorism. It is, he argues, self-contradictory for the law to permit disobedience to it. For according to Kant, disobedience to political authority destroys the state's constitution. On Kant's view, there is a social contract wherein citizens consent to be governed. Under such an arrangement, Kant argues, it is self-contradictory to then have the law permit disobedience to political authority. This amounts to the law's admitting that it is not supreme in that there are instances where it might legitimately be disobeyed. It is a self-contradiction, Kant argues, for the law to contain within itself a law permitting citizens to disobey it. After all, did they not consent to live under its rule? Kant's Argument for the Absolute Moral Obligation to Obey the Law looks something like the following:

(1) The law must contain no contradictions;
(2) The law's permitting disobedience to it in any form implies self-contradiction in the law;
(3) Therefore, disobedience to the law in any form is unjustified.

It would appear that Kant makes an assumption to the effect that (1) is true, and we might be willing to grant him (1). It is difficult to imagine a case where we would want the law to contradict itself.

However, the truth-value of (2) is less secure, it would appear, and for the following reason. It is not obvious that even if the law requires its own consistency, that disobedience to the law is always a contradiction for it. Kant might well beg an important question here. Is there something obviously self-contradictory in the law's assuming that, although it is supreme in the sense that it rules its citizens who consent to be governed by it as a matter of social contract, that the law is also imperfect and might well need revision in light of its errors and imperfections? Perhaps Kant would be

---

[2] Immanuel Kant, *The Metaphysical Elements of Justice*, John Ladd, Translator (Indianapolis: Bobbs-Merrill, 1965), p. 86.
[3] I do not mean to suggest that either terrorism or secession are necessarily violent. Indeed, mere terrorist threats are not physically violent, nor are all secessionist movements violent (Notable examples include Brasil's peaceful secession from Portugal, noted in the Introduction, and more recently, Quebec's attempt to secede from Canada).

correct if the law was perfect and contained no errors, and contained all of the answers we need for the problems we face. Then to disobey the law would seem to logically entail doing the wrong thing, morally speaking. For the law and morality would coincide perfectly. But what of the real world, where the law and morality at best coincide *sometimes*? As Ronald Dworkin (and others) have pointed out, the law is as fallible as those who make and interpret it.[4] Moreover, to prosecute at least certain forms of disobedience to the law (e.g., civil disobedience) would in many instances amount to prosecuting/punishing society's most patriotic and even finest citizens.[5] Even this important distinction might not be needed to interpret Kant's words here. For recall that he argued that we are to "endure even the most intolerable *abuse* of supreme authority." This means that Kant admits that supreme authority can be abusive, and I take it that he would agree that such abuse constitutes morally impermissible or even condemned behavior. Thus Kant would be implying that no matter what, it is self-contradictory to disobey the law. If Joel Feinberg is correct, then such a position on disobedience to the law is congruent with that of legal positivism.[6]

But let us appeal to Kant's own moral philosophy in order to see if his argument for there being an absolute moral obligation to obey the law is coherent. Of course, Kant's own Categorical Imperative states that we are never to treat anyone as a mere means to an end, but as an end in herself only, and that this version of the imperative is linked also to Kant's notion of human dignity, rights and self-respect. Now imagine a self-proclaimed democratic regime where race-based slavery obtains, or where genocide obtains, or where some other obvious instance of a violation of Kant's Categorical Imperative obtains. Would Kant, in light of this, suggest that even under such circumstances, the "most intolerable abuses of supreme authority" ought to be "endured?" Surely this runs counter to our moral intuitions. Not only would we think that any regime that engages in such brutality and human rights violations is hardly one worth having, we would do so *largely on the basis of part of the core Kant's own moral philosophy!*

Now in defense of Kant, he also states that "No one can bind himself by a contract to the kind of dependency through which he ceases to be a person, for he can make a contract only insofar as he is a person."[7] But what if the state abuses its citizens nonetheless? Kant's answer is that "There can therefore be no legitimate resistance of the people to the legislative chief of

---

[4] Ronald Dworkin, *Law's Empire* (Cambridge: Harvard University Press, 1986).

[5] Ronald Dworkin, *Taking Rights Seriously* (Cambridge: Harvard University Press, 1978), Chapter 8.

[6] Joel Feinberg, "Civil Disobedience in the Modern World," in Joel Feinberg and Hyman Gross, Editors, *Philosophy of Law*, Fifth Edition (Belmont: Wadsworth Publishing Company, 1995), p. 133.

[7] Kant, *The Metaphysical Elements of Justice*, p. 98.

the state; . . . there is no right of sedition, much less a right of revolution, and least of all a right to lay hands on or take the life of the chief of state when he is an individual person on the excuse that he has misused his authority."[8] So here we have as complete a denial as perhaps there can be of the idea that it is ever justified to disobey political authority.

However, we are still assessing (2) of Kant's argument, challenging the notion that it is *always* self-contradictory to disobey the law. Whether or not we assume a perfect regime or set of laws, is it really a self-contradiction for a set of laws to entail or include a rule of law which permits disobedience to the law under certain circumstances? In an imperfect legal system, it might well be the aim of the law to perfect itself over time. And if it is a truly democratic regime and set of laws, would it not want citizens to assist in the perfection of the system of political authority? This might be motivated by citizens' desire for moral and political and legal rightness. Thus a legal system might contain a rule, call it the *Morality Trumps Legality Principle:*

> MTLP: Citizens are justified in disobeying the law if and only if their disobedience to the law is supported by reasons which outweigh, all things considered, the reasons in favor of obedience to the law in question.

The very disobedience to the law might well eventuate in the betterment or change of the legal system, disobedience to the law might well better promote obedience to Kant's own moral values of self-respect and human dignity. Thus we have Kantian moral reasons in favor of legal disobedience, and (2) of Kant's argument seems to be weakened considerably. And if (2) is dubious, then Kant's argument seems not to support there being an absolute moral obligation to obey political authority.

Now if Kant is wrong and there is no *absolute* moral obligation to obey the law, it does not follow straightaway that there is *no* moral obligation to obey political authority. For there might well be a *prima facie* moral obligation to obey the law. A *prima facie* moral obligation is one that stands as valid unless there exist overriding moral considerations that would, in certain circumstances, render the obligation null and void. Obviously, a *prima facie* moral obligation to obey political authority is weaker than an absolute one. If my assessment of Kant's position about there being an absolute moral obligation to obey the law is correct, might there nonetheless be a general *prima facie* duty to obey the law?

This takes us to the arguments of Socrates and John Rawls in favor of there being some *prima facie* moral obligation to obey the law, and Feinberg's objections to there being such an obligation.

---

[8] Kant, *The Metaphysical Elements of Justice*, p. 86.

SOCRATES AND OBEDIENCE TO THE STATE

In studying Plato's *Crito*, we find that Socrates, in his few remaining hours to live after having been convicted of corrupting the youth and sentenced to die, articulates at least two arguments for their being a *prima facie* moral obligation to obey the laws of the state. The first is the Argument from Gratitude and the second is the Argument from Fidelity to the Law. Let's examine each of these arguments in turn.

The Argument from Gratitude may be couched in the following way:

(1) Those who accept the services of the state owe to the state a debt of gratitude, and this gratitude precludes disobedience to the state;

(2) Citizens of the state accept the services of the state;

(3) Therefore, citizens of the state owe to it a debt of gratitude, and this gratitude precludes disobedience to the state.

One concern with this argument pertains to (1). For it is unclear whether citizens accept or merely receive benefits from the state. One can *receive* something from another without accepting it, where *acceptance* entails, among other things, a kind of voluntary, knowing and intentional receipt of it and for certain understood purposes. Receiving something might not be voluntary, knowing, or intentional. It might not even be explicit. But my accepting something seems to imply all of these things. If this distinction is reasonable, then we can reject (1) in that we as citizens hardly accept the state's services, we merely receive them. At least, this is true of many of them, such as roadways and their maintenance, police protection, and so forth. While we might accept some of the state's services even explicitly, intentionally, etc., we do not seem to accept them all. Thus it seems that at best the argument at hand would imply a *limited sense* in which citizens accept the state's services and are bound to obey the laws of the state.

Secondly, let us assume, for the sake of argument, that citizens *do accept* services from the state. As Feinberg argues, whatever gratitude generated by this acceptance is a feeling. Yet as he points out, feelings hardly generate duties! So there might at best be a feeling of gratitude but not a duty to be grateful.[9]

Thirdly, even if there were a duty to feel grateful to the state for accepting its services, what is the plausible argument in favor of the claim that that would mean citizens would have a duty of reciprocation in the form

---

[9] Feinberg, "Civil Disobedience in the Modern World," p. 126.

of even *prima facie* obedience to the laws of the state? Feinberg dismisses, then, this argument for there being a *prima facie* obligation to obey the law.

The second argument that Socrates articulates is the Argument from Fidelity to the Law, and it can be rendered thusly:

(1) Once a person has given her consent to be governed by the state's authority, she assumes a duty of obedience to the state;

(2) All citizens have granted consent to be governed by the state's authority.

(3) Therefore, all citizens have a duty of obedience to the state.

(1) appears to be unproblematic, as stated. So the strategy in assessing this argument might revert to an attack on (2). One basic objection to this argument runs as follows. (2) is false since, as Feinberg points out,[10] many citizens have not given their consent to be governed by the state's authority. Although naturalized U.S. citizens have done so, few other citizens have.

In reply to this objection, it might be argued, along with John Locke, that we can infer *tacit consent* of all citizens to be governed by the state's authority. This move would be to invoke the famous social contract theory of Locke's political liberalism in order to preserve (2). In rebuttal, however, Feinberg argues that Locke's notion of tacit consent was that our consent is implied by our acceptance of governmental benefits and by our continued residence in the country. Note that the Lockean point about citizens' accepting government services harkens us back to the previous argument and its problems with that claim. Recall that even if we do *accept* and not just receive such benefits, this hardly generates our duty to reciprocate in the form of obedience to the law![11] So the mere fact that we accept benefits from the state hardly justifies, lacking some further and plausible argumentation to the contrary, a duty to obey the state's authority.

Moreover, the mere fact that we accept benefits from the state does not generate our duty of obedience, not even *prima facie* obedience, to the law. For had we known that our acceptance of governmental benefits would bind us to a lifelong fidelity to the state's authority, perhaps we would have declined the benefits. This argument for a *prima facie* duty to obey the law reminds one of the man who buys a woman a dinner and a gift and then tries to make her feel as though she has a duty to sleep with him, e.g., obey his insistence that she engage in sex with him. Had she known that those were his intentions in giving her dinner and the gift, she might very well have declined his advances. So the state, by analogy, cannot rightly expect us to

---

[10] Feinberg, "Civil Disobedience in the Modern World," p. 127.
[11] Feinberg, "Civil Disobedience in the Modern World," p. 127.

obey it simply because it provides us services, however helpful those services might be.

Furthermore, what of the Lockean rejoinder that takes tacit consent to be based on continual residence in the country? As Feinberg argues, continued residence in a country hardly means that you realized that in doing so you incurred a lifelong debt of obedience to the state.[12] It might have been the only place you could have lived, realistically speaking. Not everyone has the financial means to leave a country, and so continued residence therein hardly serves as evidence of an intentional, voluntary, and knowing commitment to the state's authority. Such residence, however permanent, might be accidental.

Thus the Lockean notion of tacit consent does not seem sufficient to bind our allegiance to the state's authority, and (2) fails to establish a *prima facie* duty to obey the law based on fidelity to the law. The Argument from Fidelity to the Law is unsound. So not only is Kant's argument for there being an absolute moral duty to obey the law problematic, so are Socrates' arguments for there being a *prima facie* moral obligation to obey the law. For both the Argument from Gratitude and the Argument from Fidelity to the Law are dubious.

RAWLS AND THE *PRIMA FACIE* DUTY TO OBEY THE LAW

Rawls articulates two arguments in favor of our having a *prima facie* duty to obey the state's laws.[13] The first is the Argument from Fair Play, and can be set forth as follows:

(1)   Justice requires fairness;
(2)   Disobedience to the law is unfair;
(3)   Therefore, disobedience to the law is unjust.

This is a simple argument, and it is meant to establish that there is a *prima facie* duty to obey the law. As we will see, Rawls himself has given us a rather sophisticated theory of civil disobedience. Thus we should not construe the Argument from Fair Play to be one meant to establish the existence of an absolute moral obligation to obey the law. Nonetheless, is Rawls' argument in favor of there being a *prima facie* moral obligation to obey the law plausible?

Rawls argues that breaking the law requires special justification since it might well be that in disobeying the law the citizen is "free riding" on the

---

[12] Feinberg, "Civil Disobedience in the Modern World," p. 127.
[13] John Rawls, "Legal Obligation and the Duty of Fair Play" in Joe P. White, Editor, *Assent/Dissent* (Dubuque: Kendall/Hunt, 1984), pp. 45-56.

legal obedience of others. In other words, those who break the laws of the state do not play fairly. But as Feinberg argues, even if there is a *prima facie* duty generated from the Argument from Fair Play, it is a duty to other citizens, *not* to the state! More precisely, it is a duty to not take advantage of other citizens in a "harmless" way. But Feinberg argues that not even this is implied or follows from the Argument from Fair Play. For there are various unlawful acts that neither harm nor take advantage of even other citizens, much less the state: victimless crimes such as cohabitation or running a red light on empty streets under perfect driving conditions. Feinberg argues that we do not have any *moral* duties to obey *these* sorts of laws.[14] Thus since there are some laws that require not even a *prima facie* duty of obedience, then there is no general *prima facie* moral obligation to obey the law and Rawls' Argument from the Duty of Fair Play is problematic.

Rawls also provides the Argument from the Duty to Uphold Just Institutions as support for his claim that we have a general *prima* facie obligation to obey the laws of the state: We each have a moral duty to establish, support and maintain just institutions. Feinberg concurs with Rawls to some extent on this matter. It is obvious that we have such a moral obligation. Yet Feinberg doubts whether it would follow from this point that we have a *general* moral duty to obey valid laws. For much lawbreaking does not at all threaten just institutions or undermine democracy and its ideals. Consider the case of running a red light with no one else on the road and in perfect driving conditions. Does this and certain other lawbreaking really undermine the bases of just institutions? These actions of disobedience to the law do not threaten just institutions because they are done without witnesses, harm no one, and thus do not disrespect the law. As Feinberg argues, there could be a *prima facie* obligation to obey the law only if, of necessity, every instance of deliberate disobedience to the law were a violation of a basic *prima facie* obligation, but that seems to be no more true of the *prima facie* obligation to uphold just institutions than of those of gratitude, fidelity to the law, and of fair play.[15]

So Kant provides us with insufficient reason to think that we have an absolute moral duty to obey political authority, and Socrates and Rawls (respectively) fail to give us unproblematic arguments in favor of there even being a *prima facie* moral duty to obey the laws of the state. But if Feinberg is correct and we have not even a *prima facie* moral obligation to obey political authority, then this implies that it is morally justified to disobey the law. Yet there are a variety of ways in which one might disobey the law. And surely not all of them are justified. So how do we discern which ways of disobeying the law are morally justified, and why?

---

[14] Feinberg, "Civil Disobedience in the Modern World," p. 129.
[15] Feinberg, "Civil Disobedience in the Modern World," pp. 129-30.

Let's begin with an analysis of the nature of pacifism given that, intuitively speaking, it would seem that if anything is morally justified, pacifistic disobedience to legal authority would be. Then we will consider the nature and possible moral justifications of civil disobedience and non-violent direct action, respectively. Subsequently, we will examine critically the natures of political violence, secession and terrorism, and the conditions under which they would be morally justified means of confronting political authority.

CHAPTER 2

CONFRONTING POLITICAL AUTHORITY
NON-VIOLENTLY

If the previous line of argument is plausible, then it follows that some form of legal disobedience is morally justified. But since there are a variety of such ways to disobey the law, then it is important to examine philosophically some of them in order to better understand which ones, if any, are morally justified. Let us consider each of the following forms of legal disobedience: pacifism, civil disobedience, non-violent direct action, and in subsequent chapters, political violence in general, including secession and terrorism.

PACIFISM

Jan Narveson argues that pacifism is faced with a contradiction. It is, more precisely, self-contradictory. In so arguing, Narveson construes the nature of *pacifism as not only the view that violence is evil but also that it is morally wrong to use force to resist, punish, or prevent violence.*[1] One point of philosophical and moral significance here is that if pacifism thusly construed is plausible, then it would seem to follow that no form of political violence would be morally justified. This would imply that instances of political violence such as the Soviet revolution, the Cuban revolution, the allied forces defeating of Nazi Germany, etc., were not morally justified. It would also imply that the attempt on Adolf Hitler's life, along with the various forms of self-defense and defense of others which would involve violence, would not be morally justified. Yet intuitively speaking, to deny the moral rightness of such actions would be problematic.

M. Jay Whitman construes Narveson's argument that pacifism is self-contradictory in the following way:

> Narveson concludes that the pacifist can deny the right of self-defense consistently only if he denies the right of defense in general. For, when we claim that violence is morally wrong, we are claiming that a person *has no right* to indulge in it. But a right *is* precisely a status justifying preventive action. To say that you have a right to freedom from violence, but that no one

---

[1] Jan Narveson, "Pacifism: A Philosophical Analysis" in Joe P. White, Editor, *Assent/Dissent* (Dubuque: Kendall/Hunt, 1984), p. 77.

has any justification for preventing people from depriving you of it, is thus (he contends) self-contradictory.[2]

Whitman's basic objection to Narveson's argument is that it fails in light of the fact that pacifists can and do employ priority rules when making moral judgments, including judgments about whether or not political violence is ever morally justified.[3] Precisely what *is* the pacifist's priority rule? Relative to judgments about political violence, Whitman provides the following example of a priority rule used by many pacifists:

> The pacifist strongly disagrees, arguing that the obligations of negative benevolence must *always* be prior; that we should never go to war because the use of physical force is itself a substantive evil and inevitably leads to greater substantive evil than any other immoral act; and that our supreme moral obligation is never to do evil or, if we must choose between evils, never choose the greater. Now given the pacifist's rock-hard priority rule, he can consistently maintain the right to freedom from physical force while denying the right of defense.[4]

Now Whitman's point is not that in employing such a priority rule that the pacifist is in the end correct about the moral unjustifiedness of political violence. Rather, he argues that Narveson is wrong that pacifism is self-contradictory:

> But Narveson holds that he cannot apply it consistently, because having a right (says he) is precisely being in a position which justifies preventive physical action in defense of that right. But this the pacifist may flatly, and rightly, deny. He argues that strict moral obligations confer corresponding rights to have those obligations fulfilled; but he could never agree that all such rights are precisely statuses justifying preventive action of the sort Narveson suggests. In the case of certain contractual obligations   where there is an enforcement clause involved, it may be the case that the violation of a right entails preventive or retributive physical action, if necessary. But it is by no means clear that all strict obligations are of such a contractual, enforcement-clause sort.[5]

Thus it is possible, on logical grounds, for the pacifist to avoid self-contradiction, contrary to Narveson's claim.

Tom Regan points to a different problem latent in Narveson's argument. Regan agrees with Narveson that pacifism is false, but it is not *necessarily* false as Narveson argues when he claims that pacifism is self-contradictory. Regan points out, rather insightfully, that Narveson

---

[2] M. Jay Whitman, "Is Pacifism Self Contradictory?" *Ethics*, 75 (1965), p. 307.
[3] Whitman, "Is Pacifism Self-Contradictory?" p. 307.
[4] Whitman, "Is Pacifism Self-Contradictory?" p. 307.
[5] Whitman, "Is Pacifism Self-Contradictory?" p. 308.

equivocates between "violence" and "force" in his argument that pacifism is self-contradictory:

> Narveson's tendency to treat the concepts of force and violence interchangeably, so that he is led to suppose that anyone who prohibits the use of force must also prohibit the use of violence, and vice versa. In fact, however, these two concepts are logically distinct, and it is both conceivable and has actually been the case that recognized pacifists consistently have spoken out against the use of violence while at the same time sanctioning certain uses of force.[6]

Regan recasts Narveson's argument thusly:

(1) The lesser evil must be preferred to the greater;
(2) A lesser quantity of qualitatively equivalent evils must be preferred to a greater quantity of qualitatively equivalent evils;
(3) The use of force is a substantive evil;
(4) Therefore, a lesser quantity of force must be preferred to a greater quantity of force;
(5) If any given action is necessary to bring about a lesser rather than a greater quantity of qualitatively equivalent evil, then one is obligated to do that action;
(6) Therefore, if any given action is necessary to bring about a lesser rather than a greater quantity of force, then one is obligated to do it;
(7) Therefore, if the use of force is necessary to bring about a lesser rather than a greater quantity of force, then one is obligated to use force.[7]

So, Narveson argues, if the pacifist accepts (1) and (3), then she must concede that there are cases where the use of force is justified in some cases. This is the self-contradiction that Narveson sees in pacifism.

However, in reply to Narveson, Regan argues that (2) is ambiguous. For it assumes that the pacifist must accept (2) because she also accepts (1) and that "a lesser quantity of qualitatively equivalent evils *is a lesser evil than* a greater quantity of qualitatively equivalent evils."[8] And it is this latter point that Regan finds problematic. For when the pacifist considers *how* one brings about force or evil in the future, it makes a difference to the greatness

---

[6] Tom Regan, "A Defense of Pacifism," in Joe P. White, Editor, *Assent/Dissent* (Dubuque: Kendall/Hunt, 1984), p. 99.
[7] Regan, "A Defense of Pacifism," p. 102.
[8] Regan, "A Defense of Pacifism," p. 102.

of the *resultant* evil. Thus the pacifist, Regan argues, can accept the following claim instead of (2):

> (2')   The resultant evil of a given combination, X, is greater than the resultant evil of any other combination, Y, if X is *caused by force*, while Y is not.

As Regan points out, (2') says *that* a given combination of evils was caused by force is enough to make its resultant evil greater than any combination of resultant evil *not* caused by force. In other words, "It is a greater evil to use force than to make additional force possible by refusing to use it . . . no one ought ever to use force."[9] Now this is reminiscent precisely of Martin Luther King, Jr's absolute moral prohibition against the use of political violence. For him, non-violent direct action precludes, on moral grounds, any resort to violence.[10]

How does Regan's objection effect Narveson's argument that pacifism is self-contradictory? Given (1)-(7), the plausibility of (2) in Narveson's argument is weakened by the following consideration. "If *how* future evil is avoided can make a decisive difference to how great is the resultant evil involved in avoiding it, then the greater resultant evil is not always simply a question of how much of what kind of evil is caused or avoided."[11] This means that (2) is problematic, making his argument dubious. Had Narveson not equivocated between "force" and "violence" in his argument about pacifism, he might have seen that pacifism is *not* self-contradictory as Narveson's argument claims. For the pacifist can well accept that as a priority rule *political violence* is never morally justified, while *force* is not only morally justified, it is, as King argues, morally required in some cases. After all, King himself wrote the following words from his jail cell in Birmingham, AL:

> Non-violent direct action seeks to create such a crisis and foster such a tension that a community which has constantly refused to negotiate is forced to confront the issue. It seeks so to dramatize the issue that it can no longer be ignored. . . . Just as Socrates felt that it was necessary to create a tension in the mind so that individuals could rise from the bondage of myths and half-truths to the unfettered realm of creative analysis and objective appraisal, so must

---

[9] Regan, "A Defense of Pacifism," p. 103.

[10] For a philosophical analysis of Martin Luther King, Jr's concept and practice of Non-Violent Direct Action, see J. Angelo Corlett, "Political Integration, Political Separation, and the African-American Experience: Martin Luther King, Jr. and Malcolm X on Social Change," *Humbodlt Journal of Social Relations*, 21 (1995), pp. 191-208, and below in the discussion of civil disobedience.

[11] Regan, "A Defense of Pacifism," p. 104.

> we see the need for non-violent gadflies to create the kind of tension in society that will help men rise from the dark depths of prejudice and racism to the majestic heights of understanding and brotherhood. The purpose of our direct-action program is to create a situation so crisis-packed that it will inevitable open the door to negotiation. . . . We know through painful experience that freedom is never voluntarily given by the oppressor; it must be demanded by the oppressed.[12]

Now where does this leave us? We found that, contrary to Immanuel Kant, there is no absolute moral obligation to obey the law. Arguments for there being such an obligation seem to run counter to the rather strong moral intuition that there are unjust laws that need to be disobeyed, or that not every law enjoys the support of reason that would require our obedience to it. And if Joel Feinberg is right, then there is not even a *prima facie* moral obligation to obey the law. Now it does not follow from these claims, as Feinberg himself cautions, that we are free to disobey the law as we please. Nor does it follow straightaway that political violence is morally justified. It means that we must discover in philosophical earnest and precisely under what sorts of conditions it is morally justified to break a law, and why.

We have found, in studying the Narveson-Whitman-Regan debate on pacifism, not only what pacifism *is*, but whether or not it is necessarily self-contradictory. Narveson has not given us sufficient reason to think that pacifism is self-contradictory. We have, then, good reason to think that pacifism, in at least some cases, is morally justified as a way of disobeying the law. This holds true even if pacifism is wrong about whether or not it is even morally justified to engage in violence of any sort.

However, that pacifism is morally justified hardly entails that there are no other morally justified ways to disobey the law. This is especially true since the only manner in which pacifism can be rescued from Narveson's charge of self-contradiction is to construe pacifism in a less than extreme or absolutist manner, wherein under certain circumstances certain priority rules would permit actions that are not non-violent. This makes conceptual room for other forms of confronting political authority. It is helpful, then, to ask what is civil disobedience, and is it morally justified? What is, non-violent direct action and is it morally justified?

CIVIL DISOBEDIENCE AND NON-VIOLENT DIRECT ACTION

The "orthodox" view of civil disobedience is one that (1) distinguishes between the nature and moral justification of civil disobedience; (2) distinguishes between civil disobedience, on the one hand, and other forms

---

[12] Martin Luther King, Jr., "Letter from Birmingham Jail," in Paul Harris, Editor, *Civil Disobedience* (Lanham: University Press of America, 1989), pp. 59-60.

of political disobedience to the law, on the other hand; (3) distinguishes between civil disobedience and mere criminal activity; (4) holds that civil disobedience may target not only positive law, but social and institutional practices; (5) holds that positive law cannot, on pain of inconsistency, permit civil disobedience; (6) holds that civil disobedience is in theory equally genuine and open to moral justification whether or not the law it violates is the law or policy it protests; (7) holds that the greater the distance between the law protested and the law being broken in civil disobedience, the more unlikely that civil disobedience will be morally justified; (8) holds that, *prima facie*, all civil disobedience is morally *un*justified and in need of defense; and (9) holds that there are no strictly necessary and sufficient conditions for the moral justification of civil disobedience.[13]

Perhaps the most important aspect of the orthodox view is (1). This is a crucial contribution made by the orthodox view. For if we do not carefully separate the questions of definition from those of moral justification, then it is easy to beg crucial questions in favor of some forms of disobedience to the law over others simply on the grounds that we do not favor or appreciate them. But question-begging definitions are not good ones, and we must not sneak into the definition of "civil disobedience" anything that would morally condemn or praise it outright, without independent argument.

Philosophical discussions of obedience to political authority trace at least as far back into Western philosophy as the exchange found between Socrates and Crito in Plato's *Crito*.[14] For many who believe that there is no absolute moral obligation to obey such authority,[15] civil disobedience poses

---

[13] Hugo Adam Bedau, "Review of Carl Cohen, *Civil Disobedience: Conscience, Tactics, and the Law*," *The Journal of Philosophy*, 69 (1972), p. 181.

[14] For discussions of the concept of political authority in Plato's *Crito*, see R. E. Allen, "Law and Justice in Plato's *Crito*," *The Journal of Philosophy*, 69 (1972), pp. 557-67; Eva Brann, "The Offense of Socrates: A Re-reading of Plato's *Apology*," *Interpretation*, 7 (1978), pp. 1-21; Ann Congleton, "Two Kinds of Lawlessness," *Political Theory*, 2 (1974), pp. 432-46; R. D. Dixit, "Socrates on Civil Disobedience," *Indian Philosophical Quarterly*, 8 (1980), pp. 91-8; J. Peter Euben, "Philosophy and Politics in Plato's *Crito*," *Political Theory*, 6 (1978), pp. 149-72; Gene G. James, "Socrates on Civil Disobedience and Rebellion," *The Southern Journal of Philosophy*, 11 (1973), pp. 119-27; Robert J. McLaughlin, "Socrates on Political Disobedience," *Phronesis*, 21 (1976), pp. 185-97; Rex Martin, "Socrates on Disobedience to the Law," *The Review of Metaphysics*, 24 (1970), pp. 21-38; Harry Prosch, "Toward an Ethics of Civil Disobedience," *Ethics*, 77 (1967), pp. 181f.; Gregory Vlastos, "Socrates on Political Obedience and Disobedience," *Yale Review* (1974), pp. 517-34; Francis C. Wade, "In Defense of Socrates," *The Review of Metaphysics*, 25 (1971), pp. 311-25; A. D. Woozley, "Socrates on Disobeying the Law" in Gregory Vlastos, Editor, *The Philosophy of Socrates* (New York: Anchor-Doubleday, 1971), pp. 299-318; Gary Young, "Socrates and Obedience," *Phronesis*, 19 (1974), pp. 1-29.

[15] See Stuart M. Brown, Jr., "Civil Disobedience," *The Journal of Philosophy*, LVIII, (1961), pp. 669-81; Joel Feinberg, "Civil Disobedience in the Modern World," *Humanities in Society*, 2 (1979), pp. 37-60; Michael Walzer, "The Obligation to Disobey," *Ethics*, 77 (1967), pp.

genuine philosophical problems. What *is* civil disobedience, and is it ever morally justified?[16] In his discussion of the content of the principles of natural duty and obligation in a well-ordered society, John Rawls defines the nature, moral justification, and role of civil disobedience.[17] I challenge the plausibility of Rawls' analysis of civil disobedience in a well-ordered society, arguing that a class of actions is a species of civil disobedience even though they employ threats. Such acts not only qualify as civilly disobedient ones, but they can under certain circumstances be morally justified forms of civil disobedience. My discussion is limited to Rawls' notion of civil disobedience, which, I believe, is for the most part indicative of the traditional view.[18]

In this section, I argue for a modification of the Rawlsian model of the nature of civil disobedience by providing what on the Rawlsian analysis is a disputed instance of civil disobedience; this case is a genuine instance of justified civil disobedience which requires relocating the Rawlsian boundaries of the nature of civil disobedience. However, I do not deny the plausibility of the core notions of the traditional view of the nature, justification, and role of civil disobedience.

163-75; Richard Wasserstrom, "The Obligation to Obey the Law," in Joe P. White, Editor, *Assent/Dissent* (Dubuque: Kendall/Hunt, 1984), pp. 29-44.

[16] It has been pointed out, however, that neither absolute legalists nor absolute individualistic moralists construe civil disobedience as a real problem. See Alan Gewirth, "Civil Disobedience, Law, and Morality: An Examination of Justice Fortas' Doctrine," *The Monist*, 54 (1970), pp. 536f.

[17] John Rawls, *A Theory of Justice* (Cambridge: Harvard University Press, 1971), pp. 363-91; see also, John Rawls, "The Justification of Civil Disobedience," in Joe P. White (Editor), *Assent/Dissent* (Dubuque: Kendall/Hunt, 1984), pp. 225-36; John Rawls, "Legal Obligation and the Duty of Fair Play," in Joe P. White (Editor), *Assent/Dissent* (Dubuque: Kendall/Hunt, 1984), pp. 45-56.

[18] Views on the nature and justification of civil disobedience range from Immanuel Kant's denial that there is any legitimate place for it in a social order to Paul Harris' view that certain violent actions can be species of civil disobedience, thereby blurring the distinction between, say, terrorism and civil disobedience. As we saw, Kant writes, "It is the people's duty to endure even the most intolerable abuse of supreme authority" [See Immanuel Kant, *The Metaphysical Elements of Justice* John Ladd, Translator (London: Macmillan Publishing Company, 1965), p. 86]. For a discussion of Kant's view of civil disobedience, see Roger Hancock, "Kant and Civil Disobedience," *Idealistic Studies*, 5 (1975), pp. 164-76. Harris states that "I agree with these arguments as reasons for excluding nonviolence from the definition of civil disobedience" [See Paul Harris, Editor, *Civil Disobedience* (Lanham: University Press of America, 1989), p. 12]. Of course, Berel Lang argues "that acts which meet the criteria of civil disobedience need not be nonviolent" [Berel Lang, "Civil Disobedience and Nonviolence: A Distinction With a Difference," *Ethics*, 80 (1970), p. 156].

RAWLS' VIEW OF CIVIL DISOBEDIENCE

The traditional view of civil disobedience is often associated with such thinkers as Mohandas Gandhi[19] and, within the analytical tradition, Rawls and King.[20] The views of these thinkers have had the most impact on the Western understanding of what constitutes a civilly disobedient act. What follows is both an explication of this traditional view in its Rawlsian form, as well as a challenge to it. The result, I hope, is a clearer understanding of what actions qualify as civilly disobedient, without sacrificing what is essential to the traditional conception of civil disobedience.

THE NATURE OF CIVIL DISOBEDIENCE

Rawls defines "civil disobedience" as "a public, non-violent, conscientious yet political act contrary to law usually done with the aim of bringing about a change in the law or policies of the government."[21] Civil disobedience is *public* in the sense that it is engaged in openly and with fair notice. It is never secretive or covert, showing that the civil disobedient is a member of public life.[22] Civil disobedience is a *non-violent* act that is the final expression of one's case to the majority to whose sense of justice one appeals. This means arrest and reasonable punishment are accepted without incident or resistance.[23] Rawls writes,

---

[19]   M. K. Gandhi, *Non-Violent Resistance*, Bharatan Kumarappa, Editor (New York: Schocken Books, 1961).
[20]   For a discussion of both of these views of civil disobedience, see Vinit Haksar, *Civil Disobedience, Threats and Offers: Gandhi and Rawls* (Delhi: Oxford University Press, 1986); "Coercive Proposals (Rawls and Gandhi)," *Political Theory*, 4 (1976), pp. 65-79; "Rawls and Gandhi on Civil Disobedience," *Inquiry*, 19 (1976), pp. 151-92.
[21] Rawls, *A Theory of Justice*, p. 364; "The Justification of Civil Disobedience," p. 229; H. A. Bedau, "On Civil Disobedience," *The Journal of Philosophy*, 58 (1961), pp. 653f.
[22] Rawls, *A Theory of Justice*, p. 366; "The Justification of Civil Disobedience," p. 230. See also Feinberg, "Civil Disobedience in the Modern World." Hannah Arendt argues that civil disobedience is essentially a species of collective action [Hannah Arendt, *Civil Disobedience* (New York: Penguin Books, 1973). For a critical discussion of Arendt's position, see Kella Sarala, "Hannah Arendt on Civil Disobedience," *Indian Philosophical Quarterly*, 13 (1986), pp. 261-9], Rawls' analysis of civil disobedience does not limit the agents of civil disobedience to groups. Nor does Hugo Adam Bedau, "Civil Disobedience and Personal Responsibility for Injustice," *The Monist*, 54 (1970), pp. 517-35.
[23] Rawls, "The Justification of Civil Disobedience," p. 230. As A. D. Woozley argues, "The civil disobedient claiming a principled right to break the law cannot deny the law enforcer the right to keep it" [See A. D. Woozley, "Civil Disobedience and Punishment," *Ethics*, 86 (1976), p. 331]. However, as Marshall Cohen states, "it does not follow from the fact that the disobedient is willing to pay the penalty that the government ought to exact it" [See Marshall Cohen, "Liberalism and Disobedience," *Philosophy and Public Affairs*, 1 (1972), p. 288].

> To engage in violent acts likely to injure and to hurt is incompatible with civil disobedience as a mode of address . . . any interference with the civil liberties of others tends to obscure the civilly disobedient quality of one's act. Sometimes if the appeal fails in its purpose, forceful resistance may later be entertained. Yet civil disobedience is giving voice to conscientious and deeply held convictions; while it may warn and admonish, *it is not itself a threat.*[24]

Civil disobedience, according to Rawls, is non-violent because it "expresses disobedience to law within the limits of fidelity to law."[25] This quality of civil disobedience distinguishes it from militant action, where the majority's sense of justice is not appealed to in that the militant understands the majority's sense of justice to be plainly wrong. The militant, according to Rawls, also differs from the civilly disobedient because the former is not willing to be arrested and punished for disobeying the law. Thus, militancy, though sometimes justified, is not disobedience to law within the limits of fidelity to law. It advocates a replacement of the standing law instead.

Furthermore, Rawls' reason for excluding (violent or non-violent) threats from the category of civil disobedience is that traditional civil disobedience appeals to the majority's sense of justice, whereas threats intimidate. Threats force the majority to choose, rather than attempting to persuade or convince via the majority's own sense of justice. Rawls is assuming that appeals to the majority's sense of justice and intimidation cannot co-exist.

When Rawls defines "civil disobedience" as a *conscientious* act he means that civil disobedience is a sincere appeal to the sense of justice of those in power, of those whose views and practices need to be altered. Also, civilly disobedient persons do not act merely out of personal or group interest.

That such activity is aimed at those in power and is informed and guided by political principles is what makes civil disobedience *political.*[26] Essentially, civil disobedience is an attempt to sway the views and practices of the ruling majority by appealing to its sense of justice.

Rawls argues "that the right to civil disobedience should, like any other right, be rationally framed to advance one's ends or the ends one wishes to

---

[24] Rawls, *A Theory of Justice*, p. 366, emphasis provided. For a definition of "civil disobedience" which is akin to Rawls' except for the notion of civil disobedience *not* being a threat, see W. T. Blackstone, "The Definition of Civil Disobedience," *Journal of Social Philosophy*, 2 (1971), pp. 3-5.

[25] Rawls, *A Theory of Justice*, p. 366; "The Justification of Civil Disobedience," p. 230. For a discussion of violent and non-violent actions, see R. K. Gupta, "Defining Violent and Non-Violent Acts," *Journal of the Indian Council for Philosophical Research*, 9 (1992), pp. 157-62; "Defining Violent and Non-Violent Acts: A Supplement," *Journal of the Indian Council for Philosophical Research*, 10 (1993), pp. 109-11.

[26] Rawls, *A Theory of Justice*, p. 365.

assist."[27] But Rawls does not describe the nature of the right to civilly
disobey the law. Is it, to use Wesley Hohfeld's terminology, a liberty-right, a
claim-right, a power-right, or an immunity-right?[28] Granted, the question of
the nature of the right to civilly disobey the law is not one which casts doubt
on the overall plausibility of Rawls' view of civil disobedience. However, it
would have been helpful had Rawls clarified the nature of such a right.

One might describe the right to civilly disobey the law in the following
way, making use of Feinberg's notion of a right and argue that the right to
civilly disobey requires that the right-holder be in a (moral) position to claim
his or her own right to do so.[29] This claim imposes a duty on other citizens to
not interfere with one's civilly disobedient action. However, such a claim
does not hold against the state in that the state is likely to either penalize or
punish law-breakers, even civilly disobedient ones. It is just such a right,
though, which affords the right-holder the power to address another as an
equal under the law. It is what gives the right-holder the power to voice her
own concerns and to protect herself under the law. It is that which protects
the right-holder from the adverse effects of another's acting out of her own
interests.

The right to civilly disobey the law is a moral liberty (i.e., absence of a
moral duty not to) but not a legal liberty, since there is a legal duty to obey
the law and hence not to disobey it. A moral claim-right of non-interference
holds against private citizens. But such a right does not hold against police
officers who are "at liberty" to arrest and hence have no duty to refrain.
There do not appear to be any legal immunities or powers involved with the
right to civil disobedience.

Now that we have before us a picture of the orthodox view of the nature
of civil disobedience, let us consider its plausibility. The *condition of
illegality* states that civil disobedience must break a rule of law. This seems
to be an uncontroversial traditional condition of the nature of civil
disobedience.

But what about its related *condition of civility*? This condition states
that the disobedient act out of moral conscience. Some have argued that this
is hardly a condition that defines civil disobedience. Instead, it is a condition
of its moral justification. In fact, it is argued that "the notion of civility, of

---

[27] Rawls, *A Theory of Justice*, p. 376.
[28] Wesley Hohfeld, *Fundamental Legal Conceptions* (New Haven: Yale University Press, 1919).
[29] Joel Feinberg, "The Nature and Value of Rights," *The Journal of Value Inquiry*, 4 (1970), pp. 243-57. Also, see Joel Feinberg, *Freedom and Fulfillment* (Princeton: Princeton University Press, 1992), Chapters 8-10; *Rights, Justice, and the Bounds of Liberty* (Princeton: Princeton University Press, 1980).

what it means to be a participant in the public life of a community, is a vital consideration for the moral justification of civil disobedience."[30]

Rawls argues that civil disobedience is *both* a "conscientious yet political act contrary to law."[31] In favor of Rawls' inclusion of conscientiousness and against the proposal to exclude this as a defining condition of civil disobedience, we might consider the following. What separates, among other things, civil disobedience from mere criminal behavior just is that civil disobedience is done out of a moral conscience, whereas mere criminal acts are not. In fact, it is the civility condition that helps us to make full sense of the condition of protest, below. Thus we have some good reason to agree with Rawls that civil disobedience requires both violation of the law but also that such violation is motivated by moral conscience.

The Rawlsian condition that civil disobedience is *public* means that those engaging in civil disobedience act openly and with fair notice; one's identity is not concealed. Civil disobedience is overt, not covert in nature. For "the public nature of civil disobedience is an indication that the disobedient acts as a member of a civil community, and hence as a participant in public life."[32] There is widespread agreement amongst theorist that this is indeed a defining condition of civil disobedience. I find no reason to challenge its plausibility.

What about the *condition of protest*? It is the communication of a grievance and a desire for change regarding serious matters of society and politics. Rawls and others seem to concur that such protest might be of one of two types. If civil disobedience targets the law it protests, it is engaged in *direct civil disobedience*. But if civil disobedience breaks a law other than the one it protests, then it engages in *indirect civil disobedience*. The orthodox view of civil disobedience holds that direct civil disobedience is more easily morally justifiable than indirect civil disobedience. Recall (7), above, which states that the greater the distance between the law that is broken in civil disobedience and the law that is protested, the more unlikely it is that civil disobedience is morally justified. The moral preference of the orthodox view for direct civil disobedience is based on the fact that civil disobedience is a form of political address to the sense of justice of the majority (or those) in power. The assumption here seems to be that direct civil disobedience communicates more clearly to that majority (or those) in power what injustices require change.

Perhaps the most controversial putative condition of civil disobedience is that of the *condition of non-violence*. Rawls argues that civil disobedience

---

[30] Harris, *Civil Disobedience*, p. 7.
[31] Rawls, *A Theory of Justice*, p. 364.
[32] Harris, *Civil Disobedience*, p. 7.

is *never* violent.[33] One virtue of this orthodox conception of civil disobedience is that it makes it easier to distinguish between civil disobedience and forms of political violence such as terrorism, revolution, etc. It might be argued that there are some other reasons why traditionalists hold to the non-violent condition of civil disobedience. First, the traditions of Gandhi and King, hold to non-violence. But this reason will not do because neither of them was a proponent of civil disobedience as I am discussing it. So an appeal to these traditions in favor of the non-violence condition of civil disobedience is problematic. Secondly, non-violence signals the seriousness of one's cause. But this reason is weak in that seriousness may also be flagged by violent responses to injustice.[34] Thus this is no good reason to require that civil disobedience be non-violent. Thirdly, satisfying the non-violence condition shows that civil disobedience is committed to the system that it seeks to improve. However, why should it be required of civil disobedience that it work within the system instead of trying to replace it? This reason, along with the second one, pertains more to the moral justification of civil disobedience than to its definition.[35] Michael Walzer concurs that civil disobedience need not be non-violent. For to insist that it is non-violent is to beg a crucial question about what sort of political disobedience places one outside of the community's pale.[36] To argue that to write into the definition of civil disobedience that it cannot be violent is to imply that violent acts of political disobedience are not morally justified.[37] But that would be a bad argument. For nothing of the sort is being implied, and it surely is not implied by Rawls, who admits that violent militancy might be morally justified, and the same is true of some other theorists who are not strict pacifists. Thus while orthodox theorists such as Rawls subscribe to the non-violence condition of civil disobedience as being a defining one, others argue that it is not part of what makes something civil disobedience. Rather, it might be a condition of civil disobedience's moral justifiedness.

What about the *condition of conscientiousness*? This seems similar to the condition of civility, above. It means that moral reasons are what motivate ones disobedience to political authority. Rawls thinks that this is a defining condition of civil disobedience, while others prefer to employ it as a justificatory condition of civil disobedience. When Rawls avers that civil disobedience is a conscientious act, he means that it is a sincere appeal to the sense of justice of the political majority.

---

[33] Rawls, *A Theory of Justice*, p. 366.

[34] Harris, *Civil Disobedience*, p. 11.

[35] Harris, *Civil Disobedience*, p. 11.

[36] Harris, *Civil Disobedience pp.* 11-2.

[37] Michael Bayles, "The Justifiability of Civil Disobedience," *The Review of Metaphysics*, 24 (1970), p. 5.

What about *acceptance of the political legitimacy of the state and submission to arrest and reasonable punishment* for civil disobedience? Are these defining conditions of civil disobedience? Noam Chomsky argues that these are *not* defining conditions of civil disobedience.[38] He implies that the orthodox view of the nature of civil disobedience begs the question of what constitutes civil disobedience. For it assumes that civil disobedience must submit itself to arrest and reasonable punishment by the system. Why, they ask, must this be so?

Is the orthodox view of civil disobedience adequate? Rawls' conception of civil disobedience does seem to wreak less havoc with our folk understanding of the nature of civil disobedience as it concerns the matter of civil disobedience's being non-violent, whereas the conception of civil disobedience which does not rule out violence tends to blur the conceptual distinction between civil disobedience and various species of political violence such as terrorism. In common parlance, however, this distinction seems useful in discussions of various modes of political activity. Since this is true, Rawls' conception of civil disobedience, since it preserves the valuable distinction between violent and non-violent political activity, is to be preferred.

The significance of Rawls' theory of civil disobedience is perhaps greater than one might think. For it not only articulates clearly the traditional view, but it provides an admonition for us to separate questions of definition from those of moral justification as we discuss civil disobedience (In a subsequent chapter, I will argue that this distinction also applies to some other concepts as well, namely, those of political violence such as terrorism and secession).

Contrary to Kant, then, there is no absolute moral obligation to obey the law. And if Feinberg is right, we do not have even a *prima facie* moral obligation to obey the law. Pacifism as political action is one form of justified disobedience to the law. Whether or not pacifism is self-contradictory, it does not rule out certain other forms of protest against political authority such as civil disobedience, which, as Rawls argues, is morally justified under certain conditions. This is a sketch of Rawls' notion of the nature of civil disobedience.[39] As he writes, these are the "grounds of civil disobedience . . . in a (more or less) just democratic regime."[40] Given the nature of a genuinely civilly disobedient act, how does this Rawlsian conception of civil disobedience align with the thinking of King on the

---

[38] Noam Chomsky, *For Reasons of State* (New York: Pantheon Books, 1973), p. 295.
[39] For a discussion of varieties of civil disobedience, see Rex Martin, "Civil Disobedience," *Ethics*, 80 (1970), pp. 123-39.
[40] Rawls, *A Theory of Justice*, p. 363.

matter of non-violent social change, and what conditions must obtain if such an act is to be morally justified?

MARTIN LUTHER KING, JR. ON NON-VIOLENT SOCIAL CHANGE[41]

Having explicated Rawls' conception of the nature of civil disobedience, it is helpful to distinguish civil disobedience from King's notion and practice of "non-violent direct action."[42] King argues that non-violent direct action "is a powerful demand for reason and justice."[43] Non-violent direct action is the use of "soul force" which is capable of triumph over the physical force of one's oppressor.[44] Far from its being a form of pacifism, non-violent direct action effectively disarms the opponent, "exposes his moral defenses, weakens his morale and works on his conscience."[45] On a number of occasions, King notes the multifarious features of non-violent direct action. First, it *is* a form of resistance to oppression and injustice.[46] Secondly, non-violent direct action does not seek to defeat or humiliate the opponent, but to win her friendship and understanding.[47] Thirdly, non-violent direct action is aimed, not at persons or personalities, but against the forces of evil themselves.[48] Fourthly, non-violent direct action avoids the employment of any kind of violence, physical or nonphysical, external or internal (i.e., "violence of the spirit").[49]

---

[41] This section is a condensed version of part of what is pointed out in Corlett, "Political Integration, Political Separation, and the African-American Experience: Martin Luther King, Jr. and Malcolm X on Social Change," pp. 191-207.

[42] This distinction is especially helpful given that some philosophers have conflated these rather different modes of political and social change (See Martin, "Civil Disobedience," p. 124).

[43] Martin Luther King, Jr., "Next Stop: The North," in James M. Washington, Editor, *A Testament of Hope: The Essential Writings of Martin Luther King, Jr.* (New York: Harper and Row, 1986), p. 193.

[44] King, "The Rising Tide of Racial Consciousness," in Washington, *A Testament of Hope*, p. 149.

[45] King, "An Address Before the National Press Club," in Washington, *A Testament of Hope*, p. 102.

[46] King, "Nonviolence and Racial Justice, in Washington, *A Testament of Hope*, p. 7; "The Current Crisis in Race Relations," in Washington, *A Testament of Hope*, p. 86; "An Experiment in Love," in Washington, *A Testament of Hope*, p. 17.

[47] King, "Nonviolence and Racial Justice," p. 7; "The Current Crisis in Race Relations," p. 87; "The Most Durable Power," in *A Testament of Hope*, p. 10; "The Power of Nonviolence," in Washington, *A Testament of Hope*, p. 12; "An Experiment in Love," pp. 17-18.

[48] King, "Nonviolence and Racial Justice," p. 8; "The Current Crisis in Race Relations," p. 87; "An Experiment in Love," p. 18. This feature of non-violent direct action is urged as a defining condition of civil disobedience in Prosch, "Towards an Ethics of Civil Disobedience," pp. 176f.

[49] King, "Nonviolence and Racial Justice," p. 8; "The Current Crisis in Race Relations," p. 87; "An Experiment in Love," p. 18.

Finally, non-violent direct action assumes an optimistic view of the triumph of justice in the world, i.e., that the world is on the side of justice.[50] Thus the non-violent resistor accepts suffering without retaliation.[51]

Note the differences between Rawlsian civil disobedience and non-violent direct action. While civil disobedience has no essential spiritual overtones, non-violent direct action does. Moreover, while it is essential that civil disobedience break a rule of law, there is nothing about non-violent direct action which requires the breaking of a law. These differences show that civil disobedience and non-violent direct action are distinct concepts and practices.

Now that I have clarified the differences between Rawlsian civil disobedience and non-violent direct action, it is important to set forth and examine philosophically the Rawlsian justificatory conditions of civil disobedience. Assuming that pacifism and non-violent direct action are morally justified methods of political reform, under what conditions might civil disobedience be a morally justified form of political address?

THE MORAL JUSTIFICATION OF CIVIL DISOBEDIENCE[52]

Rawls provides "presumptive conditions"[53] for morally justified civil disobedience in regard to injustices internal to a given well-ordered society. The first condition is that the focus of civil disobedience be on obvious and substantial forms of injustice, such as violations of either the equal liberties principle or the difference principle (or both).[54] The second requirement is

---

[50] King, "Nonviolence and Racial Justice," p. 9; "The Current Crisis in Race Relations," p. 88; "An Experiment in Love," p. 20.

[51] King, "An Experiment in Love," p. 18.

[52] For alternative discussions of the justificatory status of civil disobedience, see Bayles, "The Justifiability of Civil Disobedience," pp. 3-20; W. T. Blackstone, "Civil Disobedience: Is it Justified?" *The Southern Journal of Philosophy*, 8 (1970), pp. 233-50; Carl Cohen, "Defending Civil Disobedience," *The Monist*, 54 (1970), pp. 469-87; Leslie MacFarlane, "Justifying Political Disobedience," *Ethics*, 75 (1965), pp. 103-11; "More About Civil Disobedience," *Ethics*, 77 (1967), pp. 311-13.

[53] Rawls' wording seems to reflect the following caution concerning our thinking about civil disobedience and its moral justification:

> Any principle that could do the job required, being a principle of conduct, would itself be open to the very kind of demurrers and controversy it was designed to settle. Second, there is no compelling reason for anyone to adopt any principle in advance of knowing exactly what it will require of him. Since the kind of principle at issue here is likely to be formulated in the chronically open-textured moral concepts of justice, rights, . . . one cannot know [Hugo Adam Bedau, "On Civil Disobedience," *The Journal of Philosophy*, 58 (1961), pp. 663-64].

[54] Rawls, *A Theory of Justice*, p. 372; "The Justification of Civil Disobedience," pp. 231-32. This condition is denied as a defining condition of civil disobedience in Bedau, "On Civil Disobedience," p. 660.

that "the normal appeals to the political majority have already been made in good faith and that they have failed."[55] Rawls adds the following caution:

> Note that it has not been said, however, that legal means have been exhausted. . . . free speech is always possible. But if past actions have shown the majority immovable or apathetic, further attempts may reasonably be thought fruitless, and a second condition for justified civil disobedience is met. This condition is, however, a presumption. Some cases may be so extreme that there may be no duty to use first only legal means of political opposition. . . . even civil disobedience might be much too mild, the majority having already convicted itself of wantonly unjust and overtly hostile aims.[56]

Rawls holds that these first two conditions, when satisfied, are often sufficient to justify civil disobedience. Sometimes, however, a third condition for justified civil disobedience is necessary: if a certain person or group is justified in engaging in civil disobedience, then any other person or group in relevantly similar circumstances is likewise justified in civilly disobeying the law.[57]

One might think that this third Rawlsian justificatory condition of civil disobedience creates a difficulty for each group which claims to be justified in engaging in civil disobedience. What if everybody with a cause or grievance is equally justified in engaging in civil disobedience and equally bent on using it? Will this not produce an intolerable affront to the constitutional order and a cacophony of shrill messages getting in each other's way? Would it not follow that, under such circumstances, not all groups are justified in resorting to the use of civil disobedience – perhaps that none are?

Rawls addresses this problem by arguing that such instances place limits on the extent to which civil disobedience can be used without leading to a "breakdown in the respect for law and the constitution."[58] He admits "the effectiveness of civil disobedience as a form of protest declines beyond a certain point" in such cases.[59] Rawls then offers his solution to such a problem, arguing for a "cooperative political alliance of the minorities to regulate the overall level of dissent."[60]

To these three conditions of justified civil disobedience Rawls adds what might be called a practical condition. Those who engage in civil disobedience should do so rationally and such that their actions are carefully

---

[55] Rawls, *A Theory of Justice*, p. 373; "The Justification of Civil Disobedience," p. 231.
[56] Rawls, *A Theory of Justice*, p. 373.
[57] Rawls, *A Theory of Justice*, p. 373; "The Justification of Civil Disobedience," p. 232.
[58] Rawls, *A Theory of Justice*, p. 374.
[59] Rawls, *A Theory of Justice*, p. 374.
[60] Rawls, *A Theory of Justice*, p. 374.

designed to achieve their desired and justified aims. Concerning the right to civilly disobey the law Rawls writes,

> . . . the exercise of the right should be rational and reasonably designed to advance the person's aims, and that weighing tactical questions presupposes that one has already established one's right, since tactical advantages in themselves do not support it.[61]

These are his criteria for morally justified acts of civil disobedience.

THE ROLE OF CIVIL DISOBEDIENCE

But Rawls does not stop at giving an analysis of civil disobedience and its justificatory conditions. He also says something about its role in a nearly just society. For Rawls, the role of civil disobedience is one of stability. It maintains and strengthens just institutions. It "introduces stability into a well-ordered society, or one that is nearly just."[62]

Such is Rawls' notion of civil disobedience, its justificatory conditions, and its role in a well-ordered society. But just how plausible is Rawls' analysis?

A DIFFICULTY FOR THE RAWLSIAN CONCEPTION OF CIVIL DISOBEDIENCE

As intuitively appealing as Rawls' account of civil disobedience is, a class of actions exists which constitute civilly disobedient ones, but which the Rawlsian account of civil disobedience precludes from the category of civil disobedience. For some acts are species of civil disobedience even though they employ threats. Moreover, such acts can be morally justified.

Clearly, given Rawls' understanding of civil disobedience, an act which employs a threat of violence is not a species of civil disobedience. But it does not follow from this that no type of action which employs a threat qualifies as civil disobedience. For non-violent actions which are threats can be carried out in such a way that they meet Rawls' other conditions for justified civil disobedience.

---

[61] Rawls, "The Justification of Civil Disobedience," p. 234. In *A Theory of Justice*, these words are supported by the following claim: "Thus the right to civil disobedience should, like any other right, be rationally framed to advance one's ends or the ends one wishes to assist" (p. 376). However, in *A Theory of Justice* Rawls does not make this a further condition of justified civil disobedience.

[62] Rawls, *A Theory of Justice*, p. 383. As Fred R. Burger writes, "Civil disobedience may contribute to greater order and a more stable legal system by helping to remove . . . causes of disorder" [Fred R. Burger, "'Law and Order' and Civil Disobedience," *Inquiry*, 13 (1970), p. 254].

Consider the following example. Imagine a group of migrant farm workers whose fundamental human rights are continually infringed by a law which prohibits the fair treatment of such workers. Let us assume that such unfairness toward the farm workers is a clear violation of either Rawls' equal liberties principle or his difference principle[63] (let us say that they are citizens of the country but are prohibited from voting in public elections). Furthermore, the farm workers have for years tried to negotiate their case with local, state, and federal politicians, legislators, and other officials without success. It is the sincere belief of the farm workers that any person or group in their situation (or akin to it) is justified in engaging in civil disobedience. So the farm workers carefully study tactics of civil disobedience that might best advance their cause. While they are considering tactics of civil disobedience it becomes evident to them that their protest must be announced to the public so that the majority whom they are trying to persuade will hear their plea for justice. Indeed, the case for the farm workers needs to be heard by both the citizenry and its political leadership. Moreover, such a plea must reflect, they agree, their fidelity to the law (even though their action is likely to break a law).

But the farm workers have a difficulty regarding method. In the past they have tried virtually every known form of non-violent disobedience or protest. A team of respected and politically neutral experimental social cognitive psychologists informs them that the ongoing efforts of the farm workers have produced a "numbing effect" on the society and that such actions have not only failed to produce results in the past, but they have little or no chance of succeeding if utilized again. Thus, the farm workers face a problem: if they are to successfully persuade society of it's case of injustice (or have a good chance in doing so), then how might they proceed in a civilly disobedient manner? By definition, any violent action is out of the question here. On the other hand, sit-ins, marching, and other more traditional methods of civil disobedience are ruled out as unsuccessful on social scientific grounds (i.e., the farm workers have tried them in the past and such methods failed, and they are not likely to be successful in the current situation). How might the farm workers sincerely appeal to the sense of justice of their community?

The farm workers decide on the following plan. They are to publicly inform the rather patriotic and sentimental citizenry and politicians of the injustices farm workers suffer, warning them that if they refuse to negotiate with the farm workers, and if significant social, political, and economic changes do not occur, then certain of the farm workers will take and hide one of the community's most valuable and irreplaceable artifacts and no person

---

[63] For statements of such principles, see Rawls, *A Theory of Justice*, p. 60: *Political Liberalism* (New York: Columbia University Press, 1993), pp. 5-6.

or thing shall be physically harmed by them in the process. The farm workers add that the purpose of such an act is to assure themselves of a "bargaining chip" so that their plea for justice is most likely to be heard and the community's sense of justice addressed. Nothing is said as to precisely when such an event will occur. It might happen the following day, or the next year, whenever security of the premises surrounding a valuable artifact breaks down due to the exorbitant cost of such security over time. Furthermore, the farm workers inform the authorities precisely who will be involved in the operation and where they can be located by authorities. Refusing to deal with those whom they consider "terrorists," the politicians and citizenry decline to negotiate with the farm workers, and the Liberty Bell is taken from a gallery and hidden by the farm workers. At this point the citizens and political leaders become fearful concerning the plight of the bell, thinking that it will likely be destroyed or damaged (intentionally or unintentionally). Several farm workers are arrested and jailed (without incident) on the grounds that they were involved in the operation. But the Liberty Bell is nowhere to be found. Only certain farm workers know the location and condition of the bell, but they remain silent as to its whereabouts (they do, however, inform the public that the bell is undamaged). After time, the political leadership agrees to negotiate with the farm workers. While the negotiations are going on the politicians and many citizens are experiencing fear regarding the fate of the symbol of their freedom which they (the farm workers and the remainder of the citizenry) so highly value. Eventually, the farm workers are promised fair treatment, laws are changed to ensure this, and the Liberty Bell is returned undamaged.

This example illustrates a class of non-violent disobedient activity that is thought by Rawls *not* to be a genuine act of civil disobedience because it involves or constitutes a threat. Yet the farm workers' action satisfies each of the other Rawlsian conditions of civil disobedience. Although the act of taking and restoring the Liberty Bell employed or constituted a threat to persuade society that farm workers were maltreated by the system, it was not violent. No physical harm or damage was inflicted on any person or thing. Nor did the farm workers resist arrest and punishment. In fact, the Liberty Bell was promptly returned after agreements were reached and in the same condition as it was in prior to its being taken! Although the actual taking of the bell was a secretly planned action, the farm workers' action was an act of civil disobedience in that it was public. Prior to taking the Liberty Bell they announced to the public that it would be taken. It was not a covert act, for everyone was warned about the possibility of the event should the plea of the farm workers not be considered. Moreover, the whereabouts of the farm workers was disclosed to the authorities by the farm workers themselves. Their act was also a species of civil disobedience in that it appealed to the sense of justice of the community. It was a conscientious act, addressing the politicians and others in power. Finally, it was an unlawful act in that the taking of the Liberty Bell is prohibited by law. Knowing this, the farm workers believed that such an act is very likely to become a signpost to the remainder of the community and "hit" them where their interests are strong.

Not only is the above act a type of civil disobedience, it is a form of *justified* civil disobedience. The reasons why this is the case are plain. First, every effort was made to use the normal channels of appeal prior to engaging in civil disobedience. Second, what the farm workers were protesting was a significant violation of justice. Third, the farm workers understood that any other person or group in similar circumstances had a right to civil disobedience under relevantly similar circumstances. Finally, the farm workers went so far as to consult experimental social cognitive psychologists regarding the most effective non-violent strategy to advance their cause. Thus, the farm workers' action constitutes, for all Rawls says about the nature and justification of civil disobedience, an act of justified civil disobedience.

OBJECTIONS AND REPLIES

Some objections might be raised against my proposal that acts such as the taking of the Liberty Bell can be species of justified civil disobedience. One such objection is that the securing of the Liberty Bell constitutes a coercive threat and, as such, violates what might be called the "non-violence condition" that civilly disobedient action is never a threat. Another such objection is that what the farm workers did was not a direct, but an indirect, appeal to their community's sense of justice. But a truly civilly disobedient act must be a direct appeal to the sense of justice of the community. This objection argues that what the farm workers did violates what might be referred to as the "political condition" of civil disobedience. I shall consider each of these objections in turn.

THE FIRST OBJECTION: COERCIVE THREATS

It might be argued that what the farm workers did is violent because it constitutes or employs a threat.[64] And as Feinberg points out, "the most obvious cases of coercion . . . involve the making of threats."[65] A threat is "a proposal to inflict an evil, a harm, or at least something unwelcomed or unwanted . . . it is a proposal to inflict on a person something he wants not to

---

[64] For an excellent analysis of coercion and threats, see Joel Feinberg, *Harm to Self* (Oxford: Oxford University Press, 1986), pp. 191f.
[65] Feinberg, *Harm to Self*, p. 216.

have, whose existence he finds unwelcomed, something he would prefer not having to having."[66]

Now the farm workers' public announcement is coercive because it involves the use of the following implied threat: "Negotiate with us" (coercive demand), "or we will deprive you of the Liberty Bell" (coercive threat). Although the members of the community have the option of not meeting the farm workers' demand, such an alternative is far too "expensive" for them given their valuation of the Liberty Bell. The farm workers' threat, then, is a form of coercion. As Feinberg argues,

> What distinguishes the clearest cases of coercion is that they employ *threats*. . . . the use of threats backed up by credible evidence of the power to enforce them applies "pressure" to a person's *will*; they are ways of making *him* choose to do what the coercer wishes. They force him to *act* and not merely to be moved or restricted in his bodily motions. In cases of coercion by threat, there is a sense in which the victim is left with a choice. He can comply, *or* he can suffer the probable consequences.[67]

Thus, the farm workers' action at least implies a threat to their community. And it constitutes a form of coercion. As such, their action cannot qualify as a species of civil disobedience in Rawls' sense of "civil disobedience" because Rawls clearly states that genuine civil disobedience warns and admonishes but is never a threat. Depriving the community of the Liberty Bell cannot constitute a sincere appeal to the majority's sense of justice in that it is or involves a threat and intimidation. Since the taking of the Liberty Bell employs or constitutes a threat, it cannot be a form of civil disobedience in that it violates the non-violence condition. If it is not a form of civil disobedience, then it cannot be a morally justified form of civil disobedience.

A REPLY TO THE FIRST OBJECTION

But by "threat" does Rawls mean a threat of physical or non-physical harm? When Rawls claims that a civilly disobedient act cannot be a threat he says this in the context of the non-violence condition.[68] This implies that what Rawls means by "threat" is a threat of physical harm or evil, not a threat of non-physical harm or evil. Thus, it is hard to understand how the farm workers' taking of the Liberty Bell employs or constitutes a threat in the requisite sense. Although the taking of the bell involves a *risk* of physical harm to the bell, it does not constitute a *threat* of physical harm to it.

---

[66] Feinberg, *Harm to Self*, p. 216.
[67] Feinberg, *Harm to Self*, p. 192.
[68] Rawls, *A Theory of Justice*, p. 366.

There is a difficulty with this view even if Rawls did take the position that civil disobedience cannot constitute or employ a threat or coercion of any kind (physical or non-physical). For Rawls' conception of civil disobedience would exclude the farm workers' taking of the Liberty Bell on the grounds that this act constitutes or employs an implied coercive threat of a non-violent kind. That is, the farm workers force the community to negotiate by "creating a solitary and unappealing alternative"[69] to a course of action which the community as a whole finds intolerably evil.

However, did not even the Rosa Parks incident[70] constitute this kind of a threat (to the European-American segregationist)? When refusing to relinquish her seat on the bus, Ms. Parks says, in effect, "Go ahead, arrest me (or have me arrested) for breaking the law prohibiting persons of color from occupying seats in the front of the bus (reserved for European Americans)" (coercive offer). "But if you do arrest me (or have me arrested), my friends and I will intensely and adversely publicize your action, fundamental laws, and lifestyle, something which will shame you in the eyes of the world" (coercive threat). Indeed, Ms. Parks' act contains such an implied threat to those European segregationists who greatly fear the drastic social change that is likely to ensue from such publicity and outrage. Moreover, Ms. Parks' action is intended to force[71] the community to attend to her plea for justice, just as the farm workers' action implies a coercive threat which appeals to

---

[69] Feinberg, *Harm to Self*, p. 246.

[70] Here I assume that the Rosa Parks incident is a paradigm (for Rawls and other traditionalists) of civil disobedience, though it may have been the case that certain civil rights activists supporting her move deemed her action as a test case for civil disobedience to the law. Recall that Ms. Parks is the African American woman who refused to give up her seat to a European American person seeking her seat on the bus, an incident which resulted in Ms. Parks' being arrested for breaking a city ordinance which was part of segregationism in that day.

[71] Indeed, Martin Luther King, Jr. notes that:

> Nonviolent direct action seeks to create such a crisis and establish such creative tension that a community that has constantly refused to negotiate is *forced* to confront the issue. . . . there is a type of constructive nonviolent tension that is necessary for growth. . . . So the purpose of the direct action is to create a situation so crisis-packed that it will inevitably open the door to negotiation. . . . we have not made a single gain in civil rights without determined legal and nonviolent *pressure*. History is the long and tragic story of the fact that privileged groups seldom give up their privileges voluntarily. . . . freedom is never voluntarily given by the oppressor; it must be *demanded* by the oppressed. [See Martin Luther King, Jr., "Letter From Birmingham Jail," in Joe P. White, Editor, *Assent/Dissent* (Dubuque: Kendall/Hunt, 1984), pp. 167-168. My emphasis].

It is obvious that the paradigm cases of civil disobedience involve a certain amount or type of force which either implies or directs a threat. In fact, the civil rights movement succeeded in delimiting racial segregation largely because the European American business class became convinced that further turmoil and publicity would spell trouble for their businesses, not because they suddenly became convinced of the righteousness of the demands of the oppressed.

their community's sense of justice. Neither action is *itself* a form of addressing the community's sense of justice. But each act is a way of getting the community's attention so that the protester can then address that community's sense of justice. Moreover, each of the actions in question involve or employ an implied threat.

What the farm workers did was neither *physically* harmful, nor a coercive threat in the relevant sense. If by "threat" Rawls means a threat of physical or non-physical harm, then Rawls' analysis of civil disobedience is problematic because an action's being coercive and employing a threat rules out, in principle, the Rosa Parks incident as a genuinely civilly disobedient act. Any analysis of civil disobedience that has this result is tenuous.

The objection that the farm workers' action does not qualify as a candidate for civil disobedience (and, therefore, is not a form of justified civil disobedience) because it is a coercive threat is not telling. For it results in the collapsing of the notion of a coercive threat into a threat of non-physical harm, which implies that some paradigm cases of civil disobedience (such as the Rosa Parks incident) are precluded as genuine cases of civil disobedience. The extent to which this objection fails is the extent to which Rawls' non-violence condition is problematic. In order to retain this condition he must either recant his statement that civil disobedience "is not itself a threat" or provide an informative and plausible account of threats which clearly and non-arbitrarily distinguishes between types of civil disobedience which legitimately employ threats as opposed to forms of civil disobedience which do not.

A REBUTTAL TO THE REPLY TO THE FIRST OBJECTION

In defense of Rawls' view of civil disobedience, one might argue that, though the farm workers' and Rosa Parks respective incidents each constitute or employ coercive threats, there is a crucial difference between the two cases, a difference which demarcates the latter (but not the former) incident as a true case of civil disobedience. One might argue that an answer to the question, "To what is X a threat?" is important to distinguish truly civilly disobedient actions from actions which are not civilly disobedient. The Rosa Parks incident was a threat to the stability of the institution of ethnic discrimination, while the farm workers' taking of the Liberty Bell is a threat to the public's interest in possessing property. When Rawls stipulates that civil disobedience must not employ or constitute a threat he means, one might argue, that such an act cannot pose a physical threat to private or public property in the sense that one's interests in possessing such property are set back. Certainly the Rosa Parks incident fails to violate this construal of a civilly disobedient act's neither being nor employing a threat. But since the taking of the Liberty Bell does violate this condition of civil disobedience, what the farm workers did was not truly civilly disobedient. Thus it cannot be a justified form of civil disobedience.

A REPLY TO THE REBUTTAL

Although this construal of the non-violence condition is not inconsistent with what Rawls says about civil disobedience, it is hardly non-arbitrary. Why is it that non-violent threats to property are not candidates for civil disobedience while non-violent threats to institutions, ideas or lifestyles are? It is difficult to understand how such a distinction is warranted, especially when certain items of property (such as the Liberty Bell) just *are* symbols of institutions, ideas or lifestyles. Assuming that the Rawlsian condition of civil disobedience (excluding his point about threats) are met, would not a slave's taking and hiding of the original draft of either the Fugitive Slave Laws, the United States Constitution or the Declaration of Independence constitute an act of civil disobedience?[72] This is a symbolically rich act which, when publicized and backed by community support in the way that the Rosa Parks incident was, poses a threat to the institution, idea and lifestyle of slavery in the Old South. Yet it is also a deprivation of public property, just as with the farm workers' securing of the Liberty Bell. Moreover, the state of affairs of the farm workers taking the bell is such that it includes threats to institutions, ideas and lifestyles that support the oppression of the farm workers. For unless things that need to be changed are in fact changed, the community is forever deprived of one of the greatest symbols of that which it prizes: freedom, justice and democracy.

The distinction between threats to institutions, ideas or lifestyles and threats to property is not an adequate basis on which to make a distinction between civilly disobedient acts and non-civilly disobedient ones. For if it is not an arbitrary distinction, it is unsuccessful in doing much more than showing a difference between acts which directly threaten an institution, idea or lifestyle versus those which do so indirectly. But such a distinction requires an argument in support of the claim that actions which directly threaten (non-violently) institutions, ideas, or lifestyles can be civilly disobedient ones while those that do so only indirectly cannot.

Rawls himself states that one difference between militancy and civil disobedience is that the latter appeals to the majority's sense of justice, while

---

[72] This claim is consistent with Paul Harris' observation that civil disobedience to the Fugitive Slave Laws was an important part of the abolitionist movement [See Harris, *Civil Disobedience*, p. 1]. For more on the enforcement and interpretation of the Fugitive Slave Laws by the judiciary, see Robert M. Cover, *Justice Accused* (New Haven: Yale University Press, 1975); Ronald Dworkin, "Review of Robert M. Cover, *Justice Accused*," *Times Literary Supplement*, 5 December 1975.

the former does not.[73] But Rawls also argues that the use of force can be part of a civilly disobedient act:

> By engaging in civil disobedience a minority *forces* the majority to consider whether it wishes to have its actions construed in this way, or whether, its view of the common sense of justice, it wishes to acknowledge the legitimate claims of the minority.[74]

Thus the use of force does not disqualify an act from being a civilly disobedient one, on Rawls' view. In fact, force can be a part of one's civilly disobedient mode of address, a part of a minority's sincere appeal to the majority's sense of justice.

Now one might argue that, though the use of force can be rightly construed as part of civil disobedience, it does not follow that the use of a threat can be part of a truly civilly disobedient act. For all Rawls says, one might argue, warnings and force may be used in civil disobedience, but not threats.

This point assumes that the farm workers' act cannot constitute an appeal to the majority's sense of justice because it involves a threat. But, as I have argued, the Rosa Parks case involves a threat. Furthermore, it appeals to the majority's sense of justice at the same time. Thus it is arbitrary for one to argue that one case constitutes genuine civil disobedience while the other does not. For both the Rosa Parks incident and the case of the farmworkers involve threats and appeal to the senses of justice of their respective communities. Rawlsian traditionalism faces the following dilemma: either it must deny that the Rosa Parks incident is a genuine instance of civil disobedience (thereby denying what most traditionalists themselves consider to be a paradigmatic case of civil disobedience), or it must arbitrarily distinguish the two cases in question insofar as their civilly disobedient status is concerned.

Thus what the farm workers did satisfies the non-violence condition and does not constitute a threat of either violent or non-violent harm which would at the same time preclude it as being an act of genuine civil disobedience. Again, it is suggested that Rawls recant his claim that civil disobedience is not itself a threat in order to make sense of the Rosa Parks incident as a truly civilly disobedient act. In so doing, he can, as a traditionalist, maintain that the non-violence condition must be satisfied for an act to be a civilly disobedient one. But non-violence must now be understood to include the use of threats (at least in some cases). Thus Rawls' non-violence condition is not rejected, it is modified, and the traditional conception of the nature and justification of civil disobedience is clarified

---

[73] Rawls, *A Theory of Justice*, p. 367.
[74] Rawls, *A Theory of Justice*, p. 366. Emphasis provided.

and made more plausible. This first objection, then, provides insufficient reason to preclude what the farm workers did as a genuinely civilly disobedient act. Since it is also a morally justified act (as I argue above) their securing of the Liberty Bell is a justified form of civil disobedience.

A SECOND OBJECTION: DIRECT VERSUS INDIRECT APPEALS

Furthermore, one might object that what the farm workers did is not an appropriate way by which a person or group appeals to the sense of justice of those in the targeted community. What civil disobedience requires is one's *direct* appeal to the community's sense of justice, such as when Ms. Parks refused to give up her seat on the bus. By arresting her the state is showing precisely how unjustly Ms. Parks and others like her are treated! The very act of failing to relinquish her seat on the bus "speaks" directly to the problem that is at issue. And this is essential, it is argued, to civil disobedience. But the farm workers make no such direct appeal to the community's sense of justice. Their taking of the Liberty Bell in no way "speaks" directly to the problem of their rights being infringed (except, perhaps, symbolically). The taking of the bell is an *indirect* manner by which to address the community's sense of justice. As such, it does not qualify as an act of civil disobedience. The difference between this objection and the previous one is that, while the previous objection focuses on the farm workers' action being or employing a threat of some kind or other, the second objection asks whether or not (regardless of the threat status of the act) their act is a proper form of address.

A REPLY TO THE SECOND OBJECTION

In response to this criticism, it must be conceded that Ms. Parks' refusal to relinquish her seat on the bus *in itself* does serve as an act that speaks directly to the problem of ethnic discrimination. Surely one can discern by her act alone (the alleged civilly disobedient act in itself) that people of color are being maltreated because of their ethnicity.

What this objection points to is a constructive distinction between two ways of appealing to a community's sense of justice: directly or indirectly. Civil disobedients appeal directly to a community's sense of justice when the very law they are protesting is the one they violate, such as in the Rosa Parks case. Civil disobedients appeal indirectly to the community's sense of justice when the law they protest is not the law they break in protest.[75] This is a useful distinction for better understanding civil disobedience. And it is, I think, what Rawls has in mind when he argues that it is not necessary "that

---

[75] Harris, *Civil Disobedience*, p. 27.

the civilly disobedient act breach the same law that is being protested."[76] But it does not show that either of these methods of appealing to the community's sense of justice (namely, the indirect way) is not an act of civil disobedience. "It may be easier to justify civil disobedience when it is done according to requirements of the tradition, but that ought not to color the definition of civil disobedience itself."[77]

In fact there are good reasons why indirect appeals to a community's sense of justice, such as the taking of the Liberty Bell by the farm workers, should count as civilly disobedient actions. First, it ensures that each individual can, in principle, civilly disobey a law. Otherwise, those ineligible for the draft would not be able to civilly disobey the draft laws if they wish to disobey them. Secondly, there can be civil disobedience where what is protested is the lack of a certain law. So it is vital to acknowledge that civil disobedience can be either direct or indirect. But if this is true, then what can be objectionable about what the farm workers did? Why cannot it qualify as a justified civilly disobedient act?

An argument might be marshaled against the farm workers' taking of the Liberty Bell as an indirect act of civil disobedience. It is that such an act is more difficult to justify (as an act of civil disobedience) than a direct act of civil disobedience (such as the Rosa Parks case) in that it is less effective. But against this point it might be asked, "Why is either the difficulty of justification or a mode of protest's effectiveness relevant to either the civilly disobedient status of an act or its justification?" The issue is whether or not the taking of the bell can be a civilly disobedient act, not whether it is easy or difficult to justify it. Moreover, the farm workers' circumstance was such that they had no genuine choice between a variety of actions to protest their maltreatment. They tried various other methods of non-violent protest in the past, and were informed by leading social scientists that none of those methods were likely to work given current social conditions. Furthermore, it should not be overlooked that the securing of the Liberty Bell by the farm workers had some relationship to what was being protested. As such, the bell served as a symbol of the lack of liberty the farm workers believed they had in that society. In taking the bell they say to their community, "You have deprived us of our freedom, now we shall deprive you of the symbol of your freedom."

Thus the objection that the farm workers' securing of the Liberty Bell is not an instance of civil disobedience because it is an indirect appeal to the community's sense of justice is not telling. For civil disobedience can be either direct or indirect in its appeal to the community's sense of justice. So even though there is a difference in the directness of address between Ms.

[76] Rawls, *A Theory of Justice*, p. 364.
[77] Harris, *Civil Disobedience*, p. 4.

Parks' act and that of the farm workers, that fact does not preclude either of these actions as being genuine instances of civil disobedience. And since such an act meets the Rawlsian conditions requisite and sufficient for morally justified civil disobedience (as I argue above) what the farm workers did constitutes a justified civilly disobedient act.

These two objections fail to disqualify what the farm workers did as a justified act of civil disobedience. It seems that there are no reasons that might suffice to justifiably preclude the civil disobedient status of their form of protest.

In conclusion, I have argued that certain cases such as the farm workers securing the Liberty Bell constitute genuine forms of justified civil disobedience because they satisfy the basic Rawlsian conditions of both the nature of civil disobedience and morally justified civil disobedience. What the farm workers did, even if it did employ a coercive threat of a non-violent kind, not only qualifies as civilly disobedient, but (under the circumstances imagined) it also qualifies as a morally justified act. This broadens the scope of civil disobedience, urging us to rethink the scope of what is normally understood as civil disobedience (and justified civil disobedience as well).

Rawls' notion of civil disobedience cannot preclude the farm workers case as an instance of justified civil disobedience without excluding certain clear cases of genuinely justified civil disobedience. This provides a rationale for the claim that the farm workers' action is a plausible candidate for justified civil disobedience. And this holds even if what the farm workers did was or employed a coercive threat to property. However, Rawls' non-violence condition is not rejected, but modified, eventuating in a more promising theory of civil disobedience. The consequence is that the traditional conception of the nature and justification of civil disobedience is clarified and made more plausible. Unlike certain other analyses of civil disobedience that allow for violent acts to be properly categorized as civilly disobedient ones,[78] this new proposal upholds the necessity of the non-violence condition.

Given that there is no absolute or even *prima facie* moral obligation to obey political authority, and given that pacifism, non-violent direct action, and civil disobedience are morally justified modes of disobedience to the law, it is important to ask whether or not political violence is ever morally justified. In so doing, it is crucial to understand the nature of political violence, conceptually speaking. Subsequently, I shall explore the question of whether or not there are specific modes of political violence that are morally justified, including terrorism.

---

[78] Harris, *Civil Disobedience*, p. 12.

CHAPTER 3

POLITICAL VIOLENCE

Political violence in its various forms seems to have been with us throughout much of human history. In recent times, however, it has become a primary mode of political address in an increasing number of global contexts. Whether it is the two World Wars, the assassination attempt on Adolf Hitler, or numerous assassination attempts made on the life of Cuban president Fidel Castro by the United States Central Intelligence Agency, the assassinations of former U.S. president John F. Kennedy, Malcolm X, Martin Luther King, Jr., former U.S. presidential candidate Robert Kennedy, the terrorism of the 1972 Olympic Games in Munich, Germany, the 1983 suicide car bombing of the U.S. embassy in Beruit, the 1983 suicide car bombing on the headquarters of the U.S. military in Lebanon, the 1984 bombing of the U.S. embassy in Bogata, Colombia, the 1985 hijacking of a TWA jet in the Mediterranean, the 1985 car bombing of a U.S. military base in Frankfurt, Germany, the 1985 hijacking of the "Achille Lauro," the 1985 attacks on the U.S. and Isreali check-in desks at the airports in Rome and Vienna, the 1986 bombing of a TWA jet landing in Athens, Greece, the 1986 bombing of a disco in West Berlin, the 1988 bombing of a Pan American jet over Lockerbie, Scotland, the 1993 bombing of the U.S. World Trade Center, the 1995 truck bombing of the U.S. Federal Building in Oklahoma City, the 1996 fuel truck bombing of U.S. Military in Khobar, Saudi, Arabia, the 1997 taking of hostages at the Japanese embassy in Lima, Peru, by the Tupac Amuru Revolutionary Movement, the 1998 bombings of the U.S. embassies in Nairobi and Tanzania, or the 2001 terrorist attacks on the World Trade Center and the U.S. Pentagon building, one thing is clear. Political violence varies in motive and method.

But why do some employ political violence? Terrorism, for example, is often performed in retaliation to governments that are, relative to the country(ies) or group(s) the general interests of which the terrorists are claiming to represent, far too powerful to challenge at conventional warfare. Perhaps the terrorists are responding to perceived unjustified economic sanctions imposed on their country by a more powerful country. In other cases, terrorism might be a response to perceived injustice concerning the possibility of regaining territory that the terrorists believe belongs to them. In still other instances, terrorism might be a method of attempting to achieve political autonomy and self-determination. In these and other cases, terrorists seem to have given up on more conventional means of social change, believing that the political and economic systems of the governments they attack violently are beyond reform and in need of revolutionary change.

"Terrorism" is used by most people in a rather unfortunately hypocritical manner. It appears that politicians of various countries condemn as "terrorism" acts of political violence (of whatever variety) against their own countries, or those of their allies, while they fail to admit that their own governments sponsor actual terrorism. The U.S. is a clear instance of this. While many of its politicians condemn any political violence against U.S. targets as being "terrorist" and "criminal" actions, not worthy of moral respect, the U.S. has sponsored, through its CIA, various terrorist activities, including attempted assassinations, covert wars, etc. Furthermore, the U.S. was in part founded on terrorism. For the Boston Tea Party, and some other non-conventional techniques of warfare against the British military by the Colonists amounted to terrorism. So for a U.S. citizen or representative to condemn terrorism outright would be for her to condemn part of the very foundation of the "American Revolution"! If terrorism is never morally justified, then no form of it is. And this would include forms of terrorism that are sponsored by any and every government, no matter which ones. What is needed is an understanding of political violence that permits persons to think rationally about it, see it for what it is, and assess it in a fair and honest fashion, untainted by personal prejudice, and pseudo-patriotism.

One form of political violence, terrorism, has evolved over the years. Although it still seems to be a primary method of political address rather than engaging in conventional warfare with a political opponent, terrorism has changed part of its method of operation. During the 1970s, for example, terrorist bombings were followed by a claim of responsibility by the terrorists. No doubt this was an attempt to make clear the aim of the violence, whether economic reform, political reform, and so forth. But in recent times, and with the emergence of rather sophisticated counter-terrorist measures and organizations financed by the U.S., the former Soviet Union, Israel, and some other countries, terrorist organizations have become reticent about publicizing their responsibility for their actions for fear of retaliation.

But prior to asking questions of the nature and moral status of terrorism, it is important to delve into questions of the nature and justification of political violence. For if political violence is never morally justified, how could terrorism, being a species of political violence, be justified? Furthermore, before the nature and possible justification of political violence is explored, it is helpful to analyze philosophically the nature of violence more generally. Whatever political violence amounts to, it is surely a form of violence *simpliciter*.

VIOLENCE

C. A. J. Coady avers that, as Hannah Arendt recognized, a variety of conflicting purposes in linguistic contexts often make the task of defining "violence" a rather untidy and indeterminate one.[1] What we can hope for, however, is a degree to which our understanding of the nature of violence might be sharpened such that the consideration of borderline cases of violence leads us to refine our ordinary use of the concept.

Coady considers three different kinds of definitions of "violence:" wide, restricted and legitimate definitions. *Wide definitions* of "violence" serve the interests of the political left by including within the extension of the term "violence" a great variety of social injustices. For example, Newton Garver argues that "The institutional form of quiet violence operates when people are deprived of choices in a systematic way by the very manner in which transactions normally take place."[2] Note how this definition broadens the understanding of the nature of violence to include a wide range of things that serve leftist political views. For if violence is a bad thing, as most think that it is, and if social injustices that are not usually considered to be violent are indeed violent, then those social injustices must be corrected. This is implied by the definition articulated by Garver.

Legitimate definitions of "violence" are based in politically right-wing ideology and hold that violence is necessarily a form of lawlessness in the use of force. An example of this kind of definition is that of Sidney Hook, who defines violence as "the illegal employment of methods of physical coercion for personal or group ends."[3] Note how this kind of definition writes into the concept of "violence" that which is in the minds of most persons morally deplorable, namely, the use of coercion and illegality. This is what makes the definition essentially question-begging.

Coady's own preference is the *restricted definition* of "violence" because, he argues, it is the least question-begging and neutral. On this sort of definition, violence is primarily seen as being the infliction of physical harm on another.[4]

Subsequent to a discussion of the distinction between personal and structural violence is Coady's discussion of negative and positive violence.[5] A key notion in the distinction between positive and negative violence pertains to the ideas of, on the one hand, our positive actions to cause harm to others or to self, and on the other hand, our omissions which would have prevented harm to others or to self. The former constitute positive acts of

---

[1] C. A. J. Coady, "The Idea of Violence," *Journal of Applied Philosophy*, 3 (1986), p. 3.
[2] Cited in Coady, "The Idea of Violence," p. 4.
[3] Cited in Coady, "The Idea of Violence," p. 4.
[4] Coady, "The Idea of Violence," p. 4.
[5] Coady, "The Idea of Violence," p. 10.

violence, while the latter constitute negative acts of violence. But note that the key to Coady's view of the nature of violence entails the notion of intentional action. Where actions are intentional on behalf of the agent, the harms which result therein are positive acts of violence. Where actions are unintentional, and where they are omissions to act, the harms that result are negative acts of violence. Coady believes that this restricted definition of "violence" evades the ideological question-begging of both the wide and legitimate definitions.[6]

POLITICAL VIOLENCE

With a general conception of violence in mind, we may now move forward in analyzing the notion of *political violence*. Since some historically prominent philosophers have devoted some time and energy to the nature and justification of political violence, I shall articulate critically their respective views, however concisely. Let us take a look at what John Stuart Mill thinks about political violence. Then we will continue our historical query by examining Kantian and Marxian conceptions of political violence. In so doing, we will have appropriate background information with which to address the nature and moral statuses of terrorism, secession, and other kinds of political violence.

Theorists have often posed an alleged "puzzle" for political liberals concerning political violence. Such liberals are devoted to the prominence of reason in human affairs, and the idea is that the use of reason prevails in all matters, including those of social change. Where there is injustice, reason ought to be the means by which social problems are to be resolved. The difficulty arises when one considers cases where reason does not seem to suffice for contexts of injustice and where violence seems necessary for positive social change. This implies that the political liberal might need to adopt a strategy for social change that permits the use of violence, which is construed as a means of problem-solving that conflicts with reason.

MILL ON POLITICAL VIOLENCE

Mill concurs with the use of political violence in some circumstances.[7] So Mill, a paradigmatic political liberal, argues that there *are* instances where political violence *is* justified. Does this really pose a puzzle for

---

[6] For an alternative philosophical analysis of the concept of violence, see R. K. Gupta, "Defining Violent and Non-Violent Acts," *Journal of the Indian Council of Philosophical Research*, 9 (1992), pp. 157-61; "Defining Violent and Non-Violent Acts: A Supplement," *Journal of the Indian Council of Philosophical Research*, 10 (1993), pp. 109-11.
[7] John Stuart Mill, "The Contest in America," in John M. Robson, Editor, *Essays on Equality, Law, and Education* (Toronto: University of Toronto Press, 1984), pp. xxi, 137.

political liberalism? By implication, it does not for John Rawls, for whom, as we saw in Chapter 2, there are instances where "militancy" is morally justified. So should we be surprised that Mill would hold a similar view? *Perhaps, I will argue, it is because some theorists have unwarrantedly assumed that reason and violence conflict necessarily that they pose such a "puzzle" for liberalism.* Perhaps, then, what we have is a tradition of interpreters of these and other prominent political liberals essentially conservative concerning political violence, ones who assume at the outset that violence is wrong at least in part because it is "against" reason (Surely, they aver, reason is contrary to the use of force and violence).

But we can look at what Mill says about violence to see that the morally proper use of violence in political contexts *just is* based on reason. For an act to be morally justified means that it is based on what the balance of reason says is morally right, all things considered. So for theorists to argue that reason and violence are contraries begs the question as to the moral justification of political violence. In essence, it disallows that violence can ever be inspired by reason or justified by it. But this conservative view of reason and violence cries out for an independent argument in its favor.

If we consider what Mill himself says about political violence, we see that it can be justified when certain things are taken into account. "If good is to come of evil [where violence is an evil, on Mill's view] it must be practiced with an awareness of the need to curtail its general tendency to produce even more evil."[8] This is a reasonable thing to say about the use of violence in political contexts. Thus *political violence is morally justified to the extent that its employment minimizes the amount of evil in the world, all things considered.*

Mill goes on to aver that most folk in society are not the types who think critically about social change and who are likely to challenge the status quo. And they should not be held to high political awareness standards. Revolutionary violence, Mill states, should consider this fact. *Thus political violence, by implication, ought not to demand too much of the citizenry of a society.* For the citizenry is often misled, for instance, by propaganda by the state and private industries such that it is asking too much of folk to think critically about it and to have a revolutionary mindset.

So thus far Mill argues by implication that political violence is morally justified to the extent that it does not increase the overall evil in society. This is a bit vague, but he seems to mean that the evil of violence should not lead to more evil than there would have been had violence not been used to resolve a severe social problem. Moreover, Mill states that *those resorting to political violence should be sensitive to the fact that the political majority are not typically of a revolutionary mindset.* Perhaps what he has in mind

---

[8] Geraint Williams, "J. S. Mill and Political Violence," *Utilitas*, 1 (1989), p. 103.

here is that a certain level of patience needs to be exercised with the public prior to and during the use of violence when trying to resolve social problems of injustice.

But Mill also argues that when the government restricts or bans freedom of the press or of speech, that it has thereby taken away the principle means by which protesters can and ought to attempt to address issues of injustice. Therefore, such protesters are released from the normal duty to change society by non-violent means. As Mill argues,

> A government cannot be blamed for defending itself against insurrection. But it deserves the severest blame if to prevent insurrection it prevents the promulgation of opinion. If it does so, it actually justifies insurrection in those to whom it denies the use of peaceful means to make their opinions prevail. . . . Who can blame persons who are deeply convinced of the truth and importance of their opinions, for asserting them by force, when that is the only means left them of obtaining even a hearing? When their mouths are gagged, can they be reproached for using their arms?[9]

This much of what Mill avers is held in common with Karl Marx, who argues both for freedom of expression and revolutionary violence over capitalist forces.[10] Mill goes on to argue that there are two *criteria of morally*

---

[9] John Stuart Mill, "The French Law Against the Press," John M. Robson, Editor, *Collected Works of John Stuart Mill* Volume 25 (Toronto: University of Toronto Press, 1982), p. 1238.

[10] That Karl Marx advocates revolutionary violence is well-known. But that he even pre-dates Mill's writings on freedom of expression is perhaps less known. In 1842, Marx argued that

> As soon as one facet of freedom is repudiated, freedom itself is repudiated, and it can lead only a mere semblance of life, since afterwards it is pure chance which object unfreedom takes over as the dominant power. Unfreedom is the rule and freedom the exception of chance and caprice [Karl Marx, *On Freedom of the Press and Censorship*, Saul K. Padover, Editor and Translator (New York: McGraw-Hill, 1974), p. 46].

Of freedom of the press in particular, Marx writes: "The essence of a free press is the characterful, reasonable, ethical essence of freedom. The character of a censored press is the characterless ogre of unfreedom; it is a civilized monster, a perfumed abortion" (Marx, *On Freedom of the Press and Censorship*, p. 26). Not only, then, does Marx express his unambiguous support of freedom of expression in publication, he condemns any attempt of a government to suppress it or to limit it in any way. And Marx's words are not the rantings of an opinionist with merely emotive content. For as a philosopher, he wants to consider rationally the putative justifications for censorship: "we must above all examine whether censorship is in its essence a *good* means" (Marx, *On Freedom of the Press and Censorship*, p. 28). His conclusion is that censorship of the press is but a police measure that does not even achieve what it wants to achieve: "The censorship is thus no law but a police measure, but it is itself a *bad police measure*, because it does not achieve what it wants and it does not want what it achieves" (Marx, *On Freedom of the Press and Censorship*, p. 31). This is because "censorship is a constant attack on the rights of private persons and even more so on ideas" (Marx, *On Freedom of the Press and Censorship*, p. 34). Marx derives this inference from the premise that freedom in general is a good thing, and a good thing to protect: "If freedom in general is justified, it goes without saying that a facet of freedom is the more justified the greater the splendor and the development of essence that freedom has won in it"

justified political violence: the justice of the cause and its likelihood of success.[11] These appear to constitute the moral and the political dimensions of assessment of the use of political violence, according to Mill. Now the condition that the cause underlying political violence must itself be morally justified seems quite appropriate, especially given that, as was noted in Chapter 2, Rawls cites such a condition for civil disobedience. If the justice of the cause underlying political action is a condition of civil disobedience, we can surely expect it to be a condition of the use of political violence as well! For political violence being grounded in a just cause would ensure against indiscriminate violence, say, against innocent parties.

However, Mill seems also to add to the analysis of morally justified political violence the condition that it has a certain likelihood of success. This seems, though, to confuse moral justification with its political expediency. Why should the moral justification of political action of any kind be contingent on its likelihood of success? Should a greatly oppressed people in a highly organized and militarily powerful regime wait until the regime is about to weaken and fall in order to finally attempt to gain its independence from brutal oppression? Again, this is an essentially conservative argument (that is, it is an argument biased in favor of the status quo) that begs the question against revolutionary and/or retaliatory violence, especially in contexts of severe political oppression. I have in mind here the case of U.S. slavery of Africans, or of U.S. genocide against Native Americans, or of the South African oppression of Blacks, of the Nazi oppression of Jews, or even of Israeli oppression of Palestinians.[12] In no sense were the oppressed peoples in question likely to succeed in a revolt against their respective oppressors due to the powerful nature of their oppressors' military might. So on Mill's view, they would not have been justified in revolting under those circumstances. But does Mill mean to imply that only in circumstances where (the success of a) revolution is likely, namely, where the oppressive regime is, say, sufficiently weak to be defeated or otherwise changed, that those in bondage are morally justified in revolting by way of political violence? If so, then Mill has articulated a rather conservative view, one which is not entirely in line with the moral intuitions that many have about when political violence may be justified. It would seem that the consequences of the likelihood of "success" in the

---

(Marx, *On Freedom of the Press and Censorship*, p. 39). Although Mill's defense of freedom of expression differs from Marx's in certain respects, it would be incorrect to suppose that it is Mill who first argued in favor of the right to freedom of expression.

[11] John Stuart Mill, "Radical Party in Canada," John M. Robson, Editor, *Collected Works of John Stuart Mill*, Volume 6 (Toronto: University of Toronto Press, 1982), p. 414.

[12] For a philosophical discussion of the Israeli-Palestinian conflict, see Haig Khatchadourian, *The Quest for Peace Between Israel and the Palestinians* (New York: Peter Lang Publishers, 2000).

employment of political violence ought to be tempered with moral principles that provide for the protection of basic human (moral) rights the violation of which justifies on moral grounds (in some cases) the use of political violence.

Perhaps the Millian might reply to my objection by arguing that it does not require victory to have success. Drawing significant attention to one's just cause may suffice for the moral justification of political violence here. However, this reply will not do. For what if extreme oppression and a just cause for political violence obtain, yet the propaganda machine of the oppressing regime makes it virtually impossible for the oppressed group to communicate successfully its message to the citizenry? Is the likelihood of communicative success, then, a condition for morally justified political violence?

Moreover, the Millian might argue that those who seek to use violence in order to achieve positive social change must be sure that their actions will eliminate or destroy the injustice to which the violence is meant to be a response. But in what way can one *know*, except in some precarious inductive sense, what the outcome of violence would be in any circumstance? Although the path of violence demands moral understanding and political judgment, it surely does not follow logically from the fact that success at using violence to achieve a just political end is *desired* that it is thereby *morally required.*

Nonetheless, Mill argues that although there are some instances where peaceful and reasonable means can achieve positive social change, he admits that there are other contexts where violence is a necessary evil. This seems to be a reasonable view. Mill's analysis of morally justified political violence is based on a carefully *reasoned* position. This implies, if I am right, that reason and violence are not necessarily at odds with one another. Indeed, violence might in some cases be the reasonable, the rational, thing to do, all things considered.

Thus we have a Millian account of what would morally justify political violence. Political violence is morally justified to the extent that it: (1) does not increase overall evil in the world; (2) is sensitive to the fact that most citizens are not of a revolutionary mindset; (3) is based on a just cause; and (4) has a likelihood of success. Whether or not these conditions are meant by Mill to constitute necessary, sufficient, or necessary and sufficient conditions of what would morally justify political violence is unclear. But what we do know is that these are on Mill's view important moral considerations for anyone contemplating the use of political violence in order to achieve positive social change. My arguments supported as necessary conditions (1)-(3), and rejected (4). Now that we have considered a Millian view of political violence, let us take a look at what might be said about political violence from the perspective of Kant.

A KANTIAN CONCEPTION OF POLITICAL VIOLENCE

Barbara Herman argues that "In Kantian ethics it cannot be what happens to an agent as a result of what is done that makes an action morally wrong. . . . killing is not wrong because it brings about death. . . Moral wrongness is not a function of consequences but of willings."[13] By implication, then, political violence is either morally justified or not based, not on the probable or foreseeable consequences of the action, but rather on the basis of whether or not the political violence follows a rule that demands that the value of rational agents be respected. As Herman points out, it is the ultimate reliance on the content of the Categorical Imperative procedure for value judgments that makes Kantian ethics deontological.[14]

Of course, the *Categorical Imperative*, at least in two of its many formulations in Kant's ethical writings, reads that *we must never treat anyone as a mere means to an end, but as an end only, and that we ought to perform that action that would be consonant with a rule that we would will to be a universal maxim*. Coupled with the Categorical Imperative is, Herman notes, the passage from Kant's *Groundwork* where Kant describes the value of a rational being. *Autonomy*, Kant argues, is the capacity to will what is intrinsically or unconditionally good, and that it is this property that gives humanity a value, and that this value is what Kant refers to as "dignity."[15] For Kant, *dignity* places humanity "beyond all price, with which it cannot in the least be brought into competition or comparison without, as it were, violating its sanctity."[16]

Now all of this is meant to address, Herman believes, what a Kantian would have to say, on pain of logical consistency, about the morality of political violence. In light of the version of the Categorical Imperative that says that we must act according to a rule that we will to be a universal law, we must, Herman argues, ask if performing a politically violent act could ever qualify as such a universal maxim. As Herman argues, "A universal law involving the dispersal of agency cannot be conceived as a law for rational agents."[17] Why is this so, according to a Kantian ethic?

Herman answers this question by considering self-defense as a test case for cases of conscience on a Kantian ethic. Self-defense is particularly difficult for the Kantian. How could violence ever be justified in self-defense even when one is defending against an aggressor? Simply that one is an

---

[13] Barbara Herman, "Murder and Mayhem: Violence and Kantian Casuistry," *The Monist*, 72 (1989), p. 422.
[14] Herman, "Murder and Mayhem: Violence and Kantian Casuistry," p. 423.
[15] Herman, "Murder and Mayhem: Violence and Kantian Casuistry," p. 422.
[16] Herman, "Murder and Mayhem: Violence and Kantian Casuistry," p. 422.
[17] Herman, "Murder and Mayhem: Violence and Kantian Casuistry," p. 423.

aggressor does not thereby render her without rational agency. Indeed, a rational agent just might be an aggressor. That is, rational agency may at times call for aggression. Thus self-defense against aggression seems to be no justification to commit violent acts against another. And Herman argues that this seems to leave us at each other's mercy, morally speaking.[18]

Now one might object to such a Kantian view against the use of political violence that under some circumstances if I do not use violence in self-defense that I would lose my life, thereby losing my dignity since my living is a necessary condition of my dignity.[19] But Kant might reply to this objection by arguing that if I am justified in doing whatever I must – even engaging in violence – to preserve my life, then it looks as though the self-defense argument would permit an act consequentialism that would in turn permit the taking of another's life to preserve my life. After all, on this objection to Kant, it is the preservation of my own life that justifies the action, whether political violence in self-defense, or whatever. So what would, by parity or reasoning, prohibit my taking the life of another to preserve my own life? Is self-preservation by way of self-defense a moral trump card here? If the critic of Kant denies that she can do whatever she wants to preserve or defend her own life, then it seems that it is self-defense against aggression that is the real issue, not the preservation of her life come what may. That is, self-defense is justified against aggression, but not to preserve my life no matter what. But then this reasoning takes us right back to the previous point, that on a Kantian view violence against aggression cannot be justified because the aggressor too is a rational agent.

At this point, Herman states that a Kantian account of self-defense must answer three related questions: (1) What gives moral importance to loss of life through aggression when death itself is not morally bad and in itself does not morally justify violence? (2) Why cannot the original aggressor accuse the self-defender of aggression? and (3) If I can save my life without taking the life of an aggressor, must I?

In answer to (1), there seems to be a moral presumption against the use of political violence, or against violence moral generally. So what arguments might be marshaled in support of the use of such violence? As we saw, it cannot be that I may kill in order to save myself from death. For whatever

---

[18] Herman, "Murder and Mayhem: Violence and Kantian Casuistry," p. 426. Perhaps this is what Martin Luther King, Jr. faced when he argued incessantly that violence was *never* morally justified. Even when questioned about cases of self-defense, he never admitted that violence was morally right. He was in this sense a Kantian: he believed that all humans possessed dignity and intrinsic worth and are to always be treated as such. See Chapter 2 wherein the concept of non-violent direct action is discussed. See also, James M. Washington, Editor, *A Testament of Hope: The Essential Writings of Martin Luther King, Jr.* (New York: Harper and Row, 1986).
[19] Herman, "Murder and Mayhem: Violence and Kantian Casuistry," p. 426.

moral status I have is not compromised by death, according to Kant. Instead, on a Kantian account, I may justify killing for self-defense against aggression because the aggressor is seeking to use me as a mere means to his end. *This* is what I resist, on Kantian grounds. His act of aggression against me violates Kant's Categorical Imperative: For no one should ever use another as a mere means to an end, but as an end only. I cannot assent to become the victim of aggression, according to Kantianism. To do so would be to renounce what is necessary to me, namely, my humanity, dignity, and rational agency.

Now this imposes, not just a moral permission, but a Kantian moral *requirement* to resist aggression on the stated grounds. For just as it is, according to the Categorical Imperative, a *requirement* that we never treat another as a mere means to an end, this implies a *requirement* that we resist all efforts to disrespect our dignity by treating us as being less than rational agents. Even though I may fail in my defense against the aggressor, this in no way minimizes my duty of not being passive in defending my dignity against his aggression. This does not imply that I must respond violently to aggression against me. But it does mean that I must not, morally speaking, *not* respond at all. The upshot of this Kantian answer to the first question Herman raises about self-defense is that "the circumstances of aggression rebut the presumption against violence" on a Kantian view.[20]

As to the second question Herman raises, the Kantian can argue consistent with Kant's moral philosophy that self-defense against aggression amounts to an assertion of my status as a rational agent; it is an act of self-respect: "I am not acting to save my life (as such), but to resist the use of my agency (self) by another. . . . I am not acting to preserve myself through violent means. In stopping aggression with force I am asserting my status as a rational agent. It is an act of self-respect."[21] This is essentially the position, by the way, of many terrorists when they assert the (sometimes) need for political violence against the forces that oppress them or those in whose name they act.

In reply to Herman's third question, not just any response to aggression will do, even in self-defense. For as Herman points out, a Kantian view respects human agency wherever it is found, as it were. And aggressors are still rational agents on Kant's view. Thus any politically violent response to aggression, it would follow, must take into account this fact and never violate the Categorical Imperative. One is reminded here of Kant's own words about degrees of proportional punishment in the *Metaphysical Elements of Justice*, where he states that "any undeserved evil that you inflict

---

[20] Herman, "Murder and Mayhem: Violence and Kantian Casuistry," p. 427.
[21] Herman, "Murder and Mayhem: Violence and Kantian Casuistry," p. 427.

on someone else among the people is one that you do to yourself. If you vilify him, you vilify yourself."[22] Or, as Herman states in a Kantian tone,

> The justification of a *maxim* of resistance does not justify every action that would stop the aggressing agent. The action of resistance needs to be guided by what is necessary to defuse the actual or perceived threat, constrained by *other* regulative maxims or concerns. If violence in self-defense is justified as an act of resistance to aggression, it would seem to be justified as an act of last resort.[23]

The problem with what Herman says here is that it hardly follows logically from the Kantian point that responses of self-defense to aggression must be made proportional to the level of aggression and that the rational agency of the aggressor must always be considered in using political violence against even aggressors, that political violence is justified "as an act of last resort." We have already seen that civil disobedience was said by some to be justified as a last resort. But arguing that political action was justified as a last resort is essentially conservative of the socio-political status quo because it seems that no political action like disobedience to the law (violent or non-violent) would ever occur in that there are always other means to try to effect social change. recall Rawl's point (noted in the previous chapter) that freedom of expression is often, if not always, an option.

Nonetheless, a Kantian view of political violence begins to emerge from Herman's analysis. On Kant's view, *political violence is morally justified in cases where either my own or another's rational agency is threatened in a serious way. In such cases, I am defending myself or another from a fundamental violation of Kant's Categorical Imperative. Secondly, political violence may be justified as an act of self-respect and assertion of my human dignity and as a rational agent. Thirdly, whatever violence I use must take into consideration the rational agency of the aggressor. Not just any violent action will do.* The common rule governing our law enforcement officers comes to mind here: "Use only that force which is necessary to control the situation."

Thomas Hill, Jr. rejects Kant's absolute moral prohibitions against breaking the law and revolution on the way toward devising a Kantian perspective on political violence. He points out that Kant deplored war, but that Kant endorsed killing in a "just" war.[24] Yet, as Hill further points out, Kant insisted that participation in revolutionary violence is always wrong.[25]

---

[22] Immanuel Kant, *Metaphysical Elements of Justice*, John Ladd, Translator (Indianapolis: Bobbs-Merrill, 1965), p. 101.
[23] Herman, "Murder and Mayhem: Violence and Kantian Casuistry," pp. 427-28.
[24] Thomas Hill, Jr., "A Kantian Perspective on Political Violence," *The Journal of Ethics*, 1 (1997), p. 105.
[25] Hill, "A Kantian Perspective on Political Violence," p. 106.

He notes that there are some contradictions in Kant's philosophy, especially pertaining to his views on morality and the law. A careful study of Kant's *Metaphysical Elements of Justice* shows us that he thought that breaking a rule of law was always wrong, and this included any form of revolutionary violence. Kant's is an essentially conservative view of the law in that it invokes an absolute standard of legal obedience. But we have just seen from Herman how a Kantian case might be made for the employment of political violence. So it appears that Hill is right in stating that there are some important tensions in Kant's thoughts on morality and the law.

Hill defines "political violence" as having the primary aim of not merely profit, revenge, personal grudge or the like, "but at least in part to gain or retain control of legal and political institutions, to express ideology, to gain or assert a perceived right, etc."[26] This seems to be a good definition of political violence, except that it does not include the idea that such violence can be either physical or non-physical, actual or threatened. Terrorist threats, for instance, constitute a form of political violence in the minds of most people.

After defining the concept of political violence, Hill contrasts Kant's extreme prohibition against it with a "best case scenario for political violence:"

> It would be politically motivated against property, without resulting in death, mayhem, or loss of vital resources. It would be directed against a government (or other political institution) that was deeply, persistently, and grossly unjust and oppressive, guilty of heinous past crimes against humanity and increasing in its power and resolve to continue on the same path. All non-violent avenues of reform would have been exhausted, all reasonable appeals and compromises rejected. There would be strong convincing evidence that the proposed violence is both necessary and likely to be successful in producing favorable change. The protesters would be well intentioned, cautious in guarding against causing more damage than necessary. The property owners, the only ones liable to suffer significantly from the damage, would be corrupt, undeserving tyrants and their cohorts. A more just, less oppressive regime would very likely result from the change, and political stability based on respect for just laws would then become possible. Finally, the proposed violence may be easier to justify if the ruling regime's initial claim to authority was dubious on historical or moral grounds, though (for simplicity) let us assume the political violence is illegal.[27]

Hill restates these conditions in a more exact form. Consistent with Herman's Kantian analysis of political violence, Hill argues that *there is room in Kant's moral philosophy to see political violence as being*

---

[26] Hill, "A Kantian Perspective on Political Violence," p. 108.
[27] Hill, "A Kantian Perspective on Political Violence," p. 109.

sometimes morally justified, subject to certain constraints:[28] *First, "killing and maiming human beings is worse, other things being equal, than damaging property. And doing irreparable damage to vital resources is worse than damaging replaceable property inessential to human needs." Second, "political violence targeted specifically against the grossly unjust is better than random political violence." Third, "political violence directed selectively to force specific reforms from a government that resists all peaceful appeals is preferable, other things being equal, to revolutionary violence that aims to bring down the whole governing structure." Fourth, "political violence used as a 'last resort' is presumably preferable from a Kantian perspective to violence as a general strategy to be employed whenever deemed likely to be effective." Fifth, one's motive for using political violence is relevant: one has to determine first that one has a right to be violent, and that determination must not be consequentialist in nature. Sixth, those seeking to employ political violence must take into account the probability of harm [to innocents?] caused by the violence over against the harm of the prevailing injustice.* This is an important consequentialist consideration, not unlike Kant's consequentialist considerations of utility concerning the justification of punishment that we find in his *Metaphysical Elements of Justice.*[29] In any case, Hill points out, "No one, then, is treated as a mere means; no thought that 'ten are *worth* ten times as much as one' is invoked." *Finally, a Kantian perspective on political violence would be, as I myself have already noted, conservative.* By this it is meant only that it would be a view that promotes as many and often peaceful measures of reform prior to engaging in violence as a means of positive social change.

These are Hill's Kantian principles of political violence. There is good reason to think that it is plausible to attribute these views to Kant, based on Kant's writings. But there are questions here. First, How plausible are these principles on their own, whether or not Kant held them? Also, how does Hill's analysis of the Kantian perspective on political violence compare to and contrast with that of Herman's? Taking the second question first, it would appear that Herman's and Hill's respective Kantian analyses compliment each other. They are, it seems, logically consistent with one another, meaning that no one Kantian principle of Herman's is logically incompatible with any one Kantian principle of Hill's.

However Kantian this account of the justification of political violence might be, it is dubious, and for a number of reasons. First, that "all non-violent avenues of reform would have been exhausted" has already been rejected by Rawls in that there is, he argues concerning the justification of

---

[28] Hill, "A Kantian Perspective on Political Violence," p. 137-39.
[29] J. Angelo Corlett, *Responsibility and Punishment* (Dordrecht, Kluwer Academic Publishers, 2001), pp. 30, 60.

civil disobedience, always another attempt at non-violence to make, thereby postponing forever less conservative modes of social and political change.[30] And what Rawls argues about civil disobedience seems to apply as well to political violence. It simply begs the moral question against the use of political violence to require that all non-violent modes of social and political reform be attempted. This is tantamount to requiring that political violence be construed as a method of "last resort," which in turn would almost always mean that it is a road never taken. For there would always appear to exist means of attempted (not necessarily successful or morally justified) political change other than violent ones. Moreover, why ought there to be "strong and convincing evidence" that political violence is "necessary and likely to be successful in producing favorable change?" Like Thomas Hobbes, Kant held that the only acceptable alternative to a Hobbesian state of nature is a political state in which questions of external liberty are answered by a duly recognized political/legal system of government. Like Jean-Jacques Rousseau, Kant held that we must always act under the idea that a social contract in fact exists, a contract that binds the respective wills of the citizenry to the authority of the general will of the people. But also like Hobbes, Kant believes that there must be a head of state that is presumed to speak definitively for the will of the people. It would seem to follow, then, that on Kant's view there can be no lawful resistance to the head of state because lawfulness requires the backing of the will of the people and breaking the law means breaking the will of the people. Thus it follows, on Kant's view, that resistance to political authority is not justified. Yet Hill argues quite correctly that "it should have remained an open question for Kant whether it is ever *morally right*, and just . . . to rebel violently against a tyrant."[31] For, I would add, might not political violence be justified on grounds that it simply punishes oppressors who deserve it, or because it overthrows an evil regime without which the world would be a better place? Even if no replacement regime is in order, might not political violence be justified nonetheless? This seems especially true if the leaders of oppression are corrupted tyrants and their cohorts. Why must some anti-anarchist position be assumed here? Is not no government at all better than a severely oppressive one, at least in some cases? Would not our moral intuitions tell us that if our only alternative to a Nazi regime is no political structure at all that having no such structure, while not preferable to a democratic one, is nonetheless preferable to Nazism? If so, then the requirement that political violence succeed in leading to a more just regime seems philosophically presumptuous against political anarchism. Furthermore, since for Kant, "ought" implies "can," the moral fact is that we ought to seek justice, peace

[30] John Rawls, *A Theory of Justice* (Cambridge: Harvard University Press, 1971), p. 373.
[31] Hill, "A Kantian Perspective on Political Violence," p. 115.

and happiness and that this implies that we can actually achieve these ends. But Hill argues that "ought" implies "can," in some contexts means that we must rebel – even violently–against political forces that would hinder seriously our efforts and abilities to achieve the Kantian ends of justice, peace, and happiness.[32] The point here is not that anarchism is to become the goal of morally justified political violence. Rather, it is simply that the reasonable chance of success in establishing a replacement regime is not a necessary condition for justified political violence. For there are times when injustice is so severe and context and circumstance simply will not permit the time that it takes to employ any other means of social change in order, say, to protect endangered lives of innocent people.

A MARXIST CONCEPTION OF POLITICAL VIOLENCE

Having assessed Millian and Kantian conceptions of political violence, we will now consider a Marxian position on it. A Marxian view of political violence is especially important in that, unlike the respective moral philosophies of Mill and Kant, Marx's political philosophy is almost identified with that of his revolutionary ethic. So it behooves us to devote considerable attention to it. Marx and other revolutionary philosophers use "revolution" in two senses: narrow and broad. In the *narrow sense*, Marx uses the term to refer to a violent overthrow of a regime that was fundamentally unjust. But he also used the term in a *broad sense* to refer to a social and peaceful social change.[33] And it is, of course, the narrow sense of "revolution" that concerns us in this chapter on political violence. John Harris sets forth and defends what he considers to be a distinctively Marxian view of political violence. First, he argues that we are causally responsible for whatever harm we could have prevented from happening. Secondly, such harm may rightly be construed as violence. This, he argues, is a Marxist conception of violence.[34]

Harris bases the first of his Marxian claims on Plutarch's famous dictum that a person who fails to protect another from death when that person could have prevented the death from occurring is just as guilty of the death as the one who directly caused it.[35] That this point is Marxist is seen from a study of Frederich Engels' *The Condition of the Working Class in England*:

---

[32] Hill, "A Kantian Perspective on Political Violence," p. 112.

[33] Adam Schaff, "Marxist Theory on Revolution and Violence," *Journal of the History of Ideas*, 34 (1973), p. 264.

[34] John Harris, "The Marxist Conception of Violence," *Philosophy and Public Affairs*, 3 (1974), pp. 192-93.

[35] Harris, "The Marxist Conception of Violence," p. 193.

...Murder has also been committed if society places hundreds of workers in such a position that they inevitably come to premature and unnatural ends. The death is as violent as if they had been stabbed or shot. Murder has been committed if thousands of workers have been deprived of the necessities of life or if they had been forced into a situation in which it is impossible for them to survive. Murder has been committed if the workers have been forced into a situation in which it is impossible for them to survive. Murder has been committed if the workers have been forced by the strong arm of the law to go on living under such conditions until death inevitably releases them. Murder has been committed if society knows perfectly well that thousands of workers cannot avoid being sacrificed so long as these conditions are allowed to continue. . . . If a worker dies no one places the responsibility for his death on society, though some would realize that society has failed to take steps to prevent the victim from dying. But it is murder all the same.[36]

The difficulty with this passage from Engels is, however, that strictly speaking it is incorrect to say of working conditions, no matter how harsh, that they constitute "murder." For (in the U.S., at least) murder is a distinctly legal category, and typically involves malicious intent. Since it is highly unlikely that employers, no matter how ruthless yesteryear or today, would intend that their employees die, it is misleading to categorize working conditions and their results – even when deadly – as constituting *murder*. What Engels argues here is just as misleading as the anti-abortionist who declares with all of the certitude she can muster that "abortion is murder," when it is nothing of the sort unless we are speaking of a case where the woman or physicians involved in the abortion are motivated by genuine malicious intent toward the fetus! But since that is hardly, if ever, the case, it is incorrect (or, at least, misleading) to term abortion murder, and the same holds by analogy with workers in even the harshest working conditions. But let us set aside the minor matter of what Engels *calls* the wrong doing, and focus on the wrong doing itself.

What I think Engels is trying to do is make a deeper point about social being. And his argument, (substituting "murder" and its cognates for "killing" and its cognates) is straightforward (Let us refer to this as Engels' "Argument for Collective Responsibility"):

(1) Whatever results in death from force and knowledge that the circumstances in which people are living make it impossible for workers to survive is the illicit killing of persons;

(2) Workers sometimes die and are sometimes forced to sell their labor power under conditions where it is impossible for them to survive;

[36] Frederick Engels, *The Condition of the Working Class in England*, Henderson and Chaloner, Translators and Editors (Oxford: Oxford University Press, 1958), p. 108.

(3) Society "knows perfectly well that thousands of workers cannot avoid being sacrificed so long as these conditions are allowed to continue;"[37]

(4) Therefore, sometimes workers are wrongfully killed.

I believe Engels is making the point that the conditions of several working class people are such that they are wrongfully killed as the result of harsh working conditions that end their lives prematurely. Engels argues that "If a worker dies no one places the responsibility for his death on society, though some would realise that society has failed to take steps to prevent the victim from dying. But it is murder all the same."[38] Perhaps what Engels has in mind here is the contemporary notion that where knowledge and force are conditions that obtain in society, murder can occur whether it is a direct act of killing, or whether it is an omission to let someone die. It would follow that malice aforethought is really not necessary for murder in Engels' sense of the term.

Thus, for Engels, letting someone die as the result of conditions that you know could have been prevented at little cost to yourself or others constitutes a harm (e.g., illicit death) to another. Indeed, Marx argues that where human intervention could have prevented a harm, then failure to prevent that harm is a cause of it:

> Wherever there is a working day without restriction as to length, wherever there is night work and unrestricted waste of human life, there is the slightest obstacle presented by the nature of the work to a change for the better is soon looked upon as an everlasting barrier erected by Nature.[39]

Thus Marx's and Engels' view of the causal efficacy of omissions. Whether or not this view really is Marx's is of historical importance to philosophy. But let us assume that it is Marx's view. Its significance for our purposes is that it implies something about collective responsibility for wrong doing. For if a society allows or fails to prevent what it well could have prevented without much cost to itself, then if that circumstance eventuates in a wrong doing, then society becomes, morally speaking, an accomplice in or cause of the wrong doing. Society becomes collectively responsible for the wrong doing. This seems to be the Marxist view.

The conception of collective responsibility is a crucial one for our study of political violence.[40] For it helps us, if it is plausible at all, to identity

---

[37] Harris, "The Marxist Conception of Violence," p. 194.

[38] Harris, "The Marxist Conception of Violence," p. 195.

[39] Quoted in Harris, "The Marxist Conception of Violence," p. 197.

[40] For discussions of collective responsibility, see J. Angelo Corlett, *Responsibility and Punishment* (Dordrecht: Kluwer Academic Publishers, 2001), Chapter 7; Joel Feinberg, *Doing and Deserving* (Princeton: Princeton University Press, 1970), Chapter 8; Larry May,

collectives such as governments guilty of perpetrating unjustified political violence for purposes of our dealing with them appropriately. But it also enables us to identify collectives (say, a citizenry) who are guilty of complicity in wrong doing to an extent that members of the collective might qualify as legitimate targets of political violence. Thus it is important to analyze the concept of collective responsibility because it is closely related to the concepts of political violence.

Marx was not the only philosopher who thought that omissions or negative actions could constitute harm and have moral consequences that deserve our attention. Jeremy Bentham, like Mill, agreed that negative actions often had moral importance. The difficulty, however, is to provide an account of when a failure to act has moral importance and when it does not.[41]

But what we do not want to confuse are causes with mere conditions of harm: "Wherever there is a possibility of preventing harm, its non-prevention is a necessary condition of the harm's occurring, but is something more required for a necessary condition to become a cause?"[42] It is one thing to not act such that the conditions of harm persist; it is quite another to be the "primary cause", to use Aristotle's category, of that harm.

Moreover, there are various ways in which I might omit to act. I might omit to act knowing that my not acting is causing another harm, but not myself believing that I could have saved the person from harm without undue cost to myself. Or, I might omit to act knowing that my not acting is causing another harm, while simultaneously believing that I could have saved the person from harm. Thirdly, I might omit to act, without knowing one way or another as to whether my not acting would or could cause another harm. What seems intuitively clear is that my not acting seems to entail an epistemic condition if I am to be held accountable for my omission, just as in the case of positive actions. Thus it is only in the case where I omitted to act with the requisite knowledge that I could have prevented the harm that I should be held blameworthy and accountable for what I failed to do without undue cost to myself. And this is what many states (in the U.S.) and their "Bad Samaritan" laws tell us.[43]

The Morality of Groups (Notre Dame: University of Notre Dame Press, 1987); Larry May and Stacey Hoffman, Editors, Collective Responsibility (Savage: Rowman and Littlefield Publishers, 1991); Burleigh Wilkins, Terrorism and Collective Responsibility (London: Routledge, 1992); The Journal of Ethics (special issue on collective responsibility), 6 (2002), pp. 111-98.

[41] Harris, "The Marxist Conception of Violence," p. 198.

[42] Harris, "The Marxist Conception of Violence," p. 205.

[43] For discussions of bad Samaritan laws, see Joel Feinberg, "The Moral and Legal Responsibility of the Bad Samaritan," in Joel Feinberg, Freedom and Fulfillment (Princeton: Princeton University Press, 1992), pp. 175-96; John Kleinig, "Good Samaritanism," in Joel

The important point for us to see here is the Marxist distinction between *mere causal responsibility* and blame or *moral responsibility*. Even if it is true that I, in omitting to act, fail to prevent a harm that I might have been able to prevent, I am not morally responsible for the harm unless I knew that my not acting would likely prevent the harm from occurring. In other words, what separates mere causal responsibility from moral responsibility for harm by omission is nothing less than an agent's being epistemically aware that she could have prevented a harm by acting instead of by not acting.

When an individual is morally responsible for a harm as regards positive actions, she must at least act intentionally and voluntarily, not just knowingly. So even if the epistemic condition is necessary for moral responsibility for negative actions or omissions, the two conditions of intentionality and voluntariness must also be satisfied by the negative actor. This means that in being morally responsible for a negative act that causes a harm, I must also intend to not act, whether or not I intend that my not acting causes the harm in question. Also, I must have been able, in not acting, to act positively (e.g., been able to do otherwise) to prevent the harm.

Thus one's not acting knowingly is insufficient for one's being morally responsible for an inaction. For I can act knowingly, but not do the wrong thing accidentally. Even in knowing that I am not acting, I can accidentally have not prevented harm from occurring. Yet the only action or inaction that brings with it *moral* responsibility is that which is done or not done *intentionally*. Recall that it is our acting or not acting *with intention* that separates, in large measure, merely causal from moral responsibility. Moral responsibility, in other words, is never a matter of pure moral luck or accident. For one is morally responsible to the extent that (among other things) she will or desires to act, not act, or attempt to act (as the case of harming may be). Thus acting or not acting knowingly and intentionally are necessary for moral responsibility.[44]

Moreover, the fact that I can *not* act, but not have a reasonable alternative action available to me (in other words, I could not have committed a positive act to prevent a harm), means that voluntary agency or non-agency is also necessary for morally responsible inaction. So simply because I omit to act and that a harm results is not enough to make me morally responsible for a harm. I must also have intended to not act, and I must also have been able to act positively to prevent the harm. If I acted to cause a harm, even if I acted intentionally in doing what I did, but lacked the ability to act freely, then I am, on most accounts, *not* morally responsible for

---

Feinberg and Hyman Gross, Editors, *Philosophy of Law*, Fifth Edition (Belmont: Wadsworth Publishing Company, 1995), pp. 529-32.

[44] For excellent discussions of the concepts of harm and responsibility, see Joel Feinberg, *Harm to Others* (Oxford: Oxford University Press, 1984); *Harm to Self* (Oxford: Oxford University Press, 1986).

the harm that ensues from my action. Why? Because we must have been able to act freely in order to be held morally responsible for what we do. This makes voluntariness a necessary condition of moral responsibility. And if this is so with positive actions, then we can expect it to hold for negative actions as well.

Thus morally responsible negative actions require, at the very least, intentional, voluntary and epistemic inaction. Although it is right to draw an important distinction between my causing harm by failing to act and my bringing about that harm by failing to do so, or between negative causation and negative action, negative action also requires intentionality and voluntariness. I am arguing that the distinction between mere causal responsibility and moral liability responsibility cannot fully be made out unless we work into the analysis intentional and voluntary action. Would we really say that a society is morally responsible for the plight of the working poor if all that was true was that society failed to act to prevent the harm experienced by the working poor? Even if society "knew" the plight of the working poor, as Engels stated, would this knowledge suffice to make society morally and collectively responsible for the plight of the working poor? Would we not also expect that if society is so responsible, that it also not act *intentionally* to prevent the harm to the working poor? And would we not also require that if society is so responsible, that it have the capability of *voluntarily* acting to prevent the harm to the working poor? For "I do not see how we can escape the conclusion that in whatever sense we are morally responsible for our positive actions, in that same sense we are morally responsible for our negative actions."[45]

Now that we have a reasonably accurate and generous interpretation of the Marxist conception of political violence, is it plausible? Recall that it states that we can be morally responsible for harm that we could have prevented, and that such harm is sometimes a form of violence. Nothing about what I have argued works against what is most essential to this Marxist conception of political violence.

We know that violence is experienced by the working poor and in a variety of ways, by positive and negative *causation*. One question is whether or not there is moral responsibility, collective or otherwise, for such harm. And for that it must be the case that, negative or positive actions must be performed knowingly, as well as intentionally and voluntarily. The question is this: Does society omit to act knowingly, intentionally and voluntarily such that it is in some significant measure morally responsible for the harms to the working poor? If the answer to this question is negative, then society is not collectively responsible for the plight of the working poor as I have articulated it. But if the answer to the question is positive, then there is, on

---

[45] Harris, "The Marxist Conception of Violence," p. 211.

the Marxian account, reason to hold society morally accountable for the plight of the working poor, and to such an extent that sometimes political violence directed against society would be morally justified. Whether we refer to such harms as "violence" or not, if they are deserving of the response of political violence, that is all the Marxist needs to establish the main point of the moral justification of political violence against society, at least in some cases (Recall that the Marxist does not hold that political violence is always morally justified, but that it is sometimes justified). When Marx and Engels write of revolutionary violence as a response to injustices that the proletarian class experiences, they are arguing that such revolutionary violence is justified as a response to injustices wrought on the working class by the ruling classes, whether by positive or negative actions.

SOME CONTEMPORARY CONCEPTIONS OF POLITICAL VIOLENCE

Moving from historic conceptions of political violence, let us consider what some contemporary philosophers have noted about it. An analysis of morally justified political violence must, Robert Audi argues, *recognize considerations of justice or injustice,*[46] *considerations of freedom,*[47] and *the importance of considerations of welfare.*[48] Thus Audi proposes that we consider the moral status of political violence in light of considerations of justice, freedom and welfare.

What about the plausibility of the claim that political violence "cannot be justified unless all channels of non-violent protest have been exhausted?"[49] This view wrongly assumes that there *is* a definite number of channels of non-violent protest, or that we can ever know what it takes to exhaust a particular channel of protest. Yet even if these problems could be overcome, Audi argues that these factors could take so long that in some circumstances of severe injustice "much moral wrong" could occur in the meantime that some degree of political violence might reasonably been seen as rectifying injustice or significantly solving a major moral wrong.[50] Thus we can reject the claim that political violence is justified only as a last resort, that is, when all other avenues of non-violent reform have been exhausted. Again, Rawls rejected such a view concerning the moral justification of civil disobedience.

---

[46] Robert Audi, "On the Meaning and Justification of Violence," in Jerome Schaffer, Editor, *Violence* (New York: McKay, 1971), p. 75.
[47] Audi, "On the Meaning and Justification of Violence," p. 75.
[48] Audi, "On the Meaning and Justification of Violence," p. 80.
[49] Audi, "On the Meaning and Justification of Violence," p. 87.
[50] Audi, "On the Meaning and Justification of Violence," pp. 88-9.

What about the claim that political violence is never morally justified in a democratic society? The answer to this query is contingent on what is meant by "democratic." If "democratic" means that the power of government lies with "the people," then it is false that political violence is never morally justified in a democratic society. For the majority of society sometimes do or support policies that are eradicable only by violent means.[51] But if "democratic" refers to a society that takes seriously Audi's three principles of injustice, freedom and welfare, then it is unclear that political violence is morally justified.

As an answer to this latter problem of the moral status of political violence in a reasonably just democracy, Audi makes the following proposal:

> What I propose is that in deciding whether violence would be justified in a given case in which it is being considered as a means of correcting certain grave moral wrongs, we should ascertain its probable consequences for justice, freedom, and human welfare, and compare these with the probable consequences of the most promising non-violent alternative(s) we can think of on careful reflection, choosing the course of action which satisfies, or comes closest to satisfying, the requirements of the principles of justice, maximization of freedom, and maximization of welfare.[52]

Now I should note that Audi's analysis is a consequentialist one. It says that whatever the truth is about the moral status of political violence, it must consider justice, freedom and welfare, but that considerations of justice and freedom have moral priority over those of welfare:

> ...considerations of justice and freedom have priority over considerations of welfare. In comparing violent and non-violent strategies of reform, our first concern should be to determine what would establish, or come closest to establishing, justice and maximum freedom possible within the limits of justice. Secondarily, we should consider the consequences for welfare of adopting a violent as opposed to a non-violent strategy.[53]

This analysis is congruent with that of Rawls' principles of justice insofar as Rawls ranks the Equal Liberties Principle above the Difference Principle, and the Difference Principle over that of the Fair Equality of Opportunities Principle.[54]

But as an analysis of the moral justifiedness of political violence, Audi's position is problematic in at least the following respects. First, on his view violence seems to be justified without concern for nonhuman animals,

---

[51] Audi, "On the Meaning and Justification of Violence," pp. 88-9.

[52] Audi, "On the Meaning and Justification of Violence," p. 89.

[53] Audi, "On the Meaning and Justification of Violence," p. 90.

[54] Rawls, *A Theory of Justice, p. 60*; *Political Liberalism* (New York: Columbia University Press, 1993, pp. 5-6).

or for the environment. The chief concern of the analysis is human welfare, as if the only "grave moral wrongs" were those that pertain to humans. But might not political violence be morally justified because of grave moral dangers to nonhuman animals, or to the environment? Short of a speciesist reply, what might be said in defense of the analysis along these lines is unclear. Secondly, even if human welfare and grave wrongs against humans were our only legitimate concern in matters of political violence and its possible moral justification, precisely *which* group of humans is to be considered here? Is welfare maximization to be indexed to the majority? If so, what about the rights of minority groups? What if an oppressed minority group finds that the employment of political violence simply cannot maximize justice, freedom or welfare for the majority oppressor group? Would not considerations of freedom, justice and welfare dictate that at least in some circumstances that the rights of minority groups which are oppressed by majority groups take precedence over the majority's interests such that political violence is morally justified? Whatever else a full-blown theory of morally justified political violence must do, it must at least answer plausibly the question of how the moral gains of justice, freedom and welfare are to be rightly weighed against those of human lives lost in the process of inflicting political violence. There are problems in measuring how much injustice, unfreedom or suffering serve as the legitimate basis of morally justified political violence. At what point is it morally justified to rebel violently against oppression? How does one know when to stop practicing civil disobedience, pacifism or non-violent direct action and when political violence is morally required or justified?

Yet another contemporary perspective on political violence is that articulated by Kai Nielsen. Nielsen's basic argument is that, though political violence is *prima facie* morally wrong, there are circumstances in which it is morally justified. Assuming that pacifism is incorrect, Nielsen discusses two kinds of cases where political violence might be justified, morally speaking: revolutionary violence where the goal is to overthrow the existing state, and political violence that is meant to change a serious problem within a state but to leave the basic social and political structure of the state intact.[55] This is a helpful distinction Nielsen makes. For we have been discussing cases of revolutionary violence. Yet an interesting question is whether or not political violence is justifiable in a reasonably just society, one where the basic structure is just. It would appear that the use of political violence in such a society is harder to justify than it would be under a grossly unjust regime.

In cases where political violence is morally defensible, namely, where it enhances the sum total of human freedom, Nielsen argues, we must distinguish between degrees of violence, and between violence to persons

---

[55] Kai Nielsen, "On Justifying Violence," *Inquiry*, 24 (1981), p. 27.

and violence to property.[56] Moreover, assuming that we want life to continue in some optimal way, Nielsen argues that the evil being prevented by the violence must be greater than the evil caused by the violence. Now we remember this kind of language from Mill, who referred to violence as "evil," and couched the justification of it in the same basic terms. However, Nielsen reminds us that real life circumstances are usually such that non-violence is not always just as feasible, all things considered, as violence. And this is especially the case in that, as Nielsen writes, "The ruling class is not likely to relinquish its privileges and control of society without a fight."[57] Similar words were used earlier by Martin Luther King, Jr. in arguing for the moral justification of non-violent direct action.[58]

Nielsen argues that our consequentialist calculation for using political violence must include the following:

> In defending engaging in revolutionary violence, reasonable and humane persons will require, for the situation in question, specific good reasons for believing that in that situation more evil will be prevented by violence than by refraining from such revolutionary acts. As Marcuse stresses, a revolutionary movement, in advocating the use of violence, must "be able to give rational grounds for its chances to grasp real possibilities of human freedom and happiness and it must be able to demonstrate the adequacy of its means for obtaining this end."[59] If there are equally adequate alternative non-violent means, it must use them. ...
>
> In sum, when it is the case – as sometimes it has been the case with revolutions – that, everything considered, the sum total of human misery and injustice has been lessened by a violent revolution more than it could have been in any other achievable way, then that revolution and at least some (though very unlikely all) of its violence was justified, if not, not.[60]

Note that the interpretive use of "when" by Nielsen of Herbert Marcuse's words construe the content of Marcuse's words about justified violence as being a *sufficient condition*, not a necessary one, for justified political violence. Yet in studying the passages cited in their context in Marcuse, it is not at all evident that Marcuse intends these consequentialist considerations to be merely sufficient. Perhaps Marcuse means them to also be necessary conditions of morally justified political violence. This is especially plausible given that consequentialist considerations hardly serve as a sufficient

---

[56] Nielsen, "On Justifying Violence," p. 35.
[57] Nielsen, "On Justifying Violence," p. 36.
[58] See Chapter 2.
[59] Nielsen also cites the following words from Herbert Marcuse: "...these revolutions attained progress in the sense defined, namely, a demonstrable enlargement of the range of human freedom; they thus established, in spite of the terrible sacrifices exacted by them, an ethical right over and above all political justification" (Nielsen, "On Justifying Violence," p. 37).
[60] Nielsen, "On Justifying Violence," p. 36-7.

condition of morally justified political violence. For considerations of desert, for example, are necessary for morally justified political violence. And if this were not true, then it would hold that the use of political violence against one person who is innocent, for example, would be morally justified as long as such violence eventuated in the betterment of society as a whole. Yet this kind of view, consistent with Nielsen's position, runs roughshod over that innocent individual's *moral rights* to protection from such unwarranted intrusions! Thus Nielsen's characterization of Marcuse's position on morally justified political violence is questionable in that it is uncharitable, as no reasonable person could hold such a view.

However, Nielsen's analysis seems to suffer from the error just mentioned, namely, that it is purely consequentialist in nature. Nielsen argues,

> Like all acts of violence in a political context, terrorist acts, if they are to be justified at all, are to be justified by their political effects and their moral consequences. They are justified (a) when they are politically effective weapons in the revolutionary struggle, and (b) when everything considered, we have sound reasons for believing that, by the use of that type of violence, there will be less injustice, suffering, and degradation in the world than if violence were not used or some other form of violence was used.[61]

But there are some difficulties here. Are (a) and (b) sufficient conditions for morally justified political violence, as Nielsen avers? Does not the counter-example I just provided render implausible Nielsen's analysis insofar as individual justice and rights, especially of the innocent, are concerned? Does not Nielsen need as a way out of this problem a concept of moral desert as a guard against my counter-example? For surely it is *implausible to think that a majority's benefiting from political violence can ever outweigh violence perpetrated against even one innocent person or animal*! The problem is not in his holding that the likely consequences of political violence are "relevant"[62] to whether or not political violence is ever morally justified. Rather, it is that *such considerations are never in themselves sufficient. What are also needed are non-consequentialist considerations.*

In the end, Nielsen's political violence consequentialism sees violence as a "tactic" that is sometimes "useful" in the workers' struggle against oppression, agreeing with Rosa Luxemburg.[63] But might political violence be morally justified even if it does *not* or is not likely to eventuate in the liberation of oppression? Does not the concept of *desert* figure into the analysis? Why cannot political violence be in part or wholly a matter of *retribution* (or even revenge) aimed at oppressors by the oppressed or their

---

[61] Nielsen, "On Justifying Violence," p. 39.
[62] Nielsen, "On Justifying Violence," p. 40.
[63] Nielsen, "On Justifying Violence," p. 42.

allies? Or, might Locke's notion be correct, namely, that political revolution is justified in cases where the ruling government fails significantly to protect citizens' rights? Or, further, that politically violent revolution is both a right and a duty against tyranical government, as the United States' Declaration of Independence boldly proclaims?

Thus two objections to Nielsen's consequentialism are (1) that it fails to account for the morally innocent as victims of putatively morally justified political violence; and (2) that it fails to see that political violence might be morally justified in that it is what is deserved for those who are truly responsible for the harms committed that would indeed justify such violence in the first place. I argue that any analysis of morally justified political violence must plausibly account for at least these two points: Either it must argue effectively that such non-consequentialist considerations are irrelevant or inappropriate, morally speaking, to the analysis, or it must argue that they are relevant in a particular way. My suggestion is that the latter course be taken.

Furthermore, Nielsen makes a rather curious point when he argues, that political violence and terrorism have different moral statuses.[64] But how could political violence have one moral status, namely, that it is sometimes morally justified on Nielsen's own purely consequentialist grounds, and yet terrorism, *as a species of political violence*, have a different justificatory status? Nielsen's position here is that in cases of extreme injustice in non-democratic regimes that terrorism is sometimes morally justified as a tactic in fighting oppression. However, he adds, terrorism hurts the cause of socialism when it is employed in contexts of reasonably democratic regimes. Nielsen's argument for this claim is not found, however. So one is left wondering what might ground it. This wonderment increases when one considers that his claim seems to commit a version of the "is-ought fallacy" in that the question at hand is whether or not political violence is morally justified, *not* whether or not it "hurts the cause of socialism." After all, one must *not* assume that political violence (or terrorism, more specifically) cannot be morally justified aside from the goals of socialism.

Although the contents of this chapter are historical and somewhat exploratory, some points become clear. First, an idea of the nature of political violence emerges. Secondly, though there are a number of difficulties with various proposed moral justifications of political violence, the problems noted hardly suggest that political violence is always morally unjustified. What is needed is an analysis of the conditions under which political violence *per se* is morally justified. Such an analysis would provide philosophical substance to the respective views of Kant, Bentham, Mill,

---

[64] Nielsen, "On Justifying Violence," p. 43.

Marx and certain contemporary philosophers on the nature and justification of political violence.

Now that we have defined the concept of political violence and have explored some of the putative conditions under which it might be morally justified, we are in a good position to answer questions of the nature and justification of secession and terrorism as species of political violence. What is secession, and is it ever morally justified? What is terrorism, and can it ever be morally justified? If either secession or terrorism is morally justified, then there are instances of political violence that are justified. If this is true, then the respective analyses of morally justified secession and terrorism would serve as analyses of specific kinds of acts of justified political violence. It is to these matters that I now turn.

CHAPTER 4

SECESSION

In light of various historical and contemporary secessionist movements worldwide (in Canada and in Spain, just to name two contemporary movements; the former is a peaceful attempt, while the latter is not), there is a dearth of philosophical discussion about secession. Only recently have even relatively few philosophers devoted their attention to this vital problem.[1] More noticeable still is the paucity of work in political philosophy devoted to the Native American experience as it relates to the problems of

---

[1] Some examples of philosophical works on secession include: Allen Buchanan, *Secession* (Boulder: Westview, 1991); "Toward a Theory of Secession," *Ethics*, 101 (1991), pp. 322-42; "Quebec, Secession and Aboriginal Territorial Rights," *The Network* (March, 1992), pp. 2-4; "A Reply to Grand Chief Coon Come and Mr. David Cliché," *The Network* (May, 1992), p. 13; "The Right to Self-Determination: Analytical and Moral Foundations," *Arizona Journal of International and Comparative Law*, 8 (1990), pp. 41-50; "Self-Determination and the Right to Secede," *Journal of International Affairs*, 45 (1992), pp. 347-65; "Federalism, Secession, and the Morality of Inclusion," *Arizona Law Review*, 37 (1995), pp. 53-63; "Self-Determination, Secession, and the Rule of Law," in Robert McKim and Jeff McMahan, Editors, *The Morality of Nationalism* (Oxford: Oxford University Press, 1997), pp. 301-23; "Theories of Secession," *Philosophy and Public Affairs*, 26 (1997), pp. 31-61; "What's So Special About Nations?" *Canadian Journal of Philosophy* (Supplementary Volume), 22 (1996), pp. 283-309; Thomas Christiano, "Secession, Democracy, and Distributive Justice," *Arizona Law Review*, 37 (1995), pp. 65-72; David Copp, "Democracy and Communal Self-Determination," in Robert McKim and Jeff McMahon, Editors, *The Morality of Nationalism* (Oxford: Oxford University Press, 1997), pp. 277-300; "International Law and Morality in the Theory of Secession," *The Journal of Ethics*, 2 (1998), pp. 219-45; J. Angelo Corlett, "The Right to Civil Disobedience and the Right to Secede," *The Southern Journal of Philosophy*, 30 (1992), pp. 19-28; "The Morality and Constitutionality of Secession," *Journal of Social Philosophy*, 29 (1998), pp. 120-28; "Secession and Native Americans," *Peace Review*, 12 (2000), pp. pp. 5-14; R. E. Ewin, "Peoples and Secession," *Journal of Applied Philosophy*, 11 (1994) pp. 225-31; David Gauthier, "Breaking Up: An Essay on Secession," *Canadian Journal of Philosophy*, 24 (1994), pp. 357-71; Avishai Margalit and Joseph Raz, "National Self-Determination," *The Journal of Philosophy*, LXXXVII (1990), pp. 439-61; David Miller, "Secession and the Principle of Nationality," *Canadian Journal of Philosophy* (Supplementary Volume), 22 (1996), pp. 261-82; Darrel Moellendorf, "Liberalism, Nationalism and the Right to Secede," *The Philosophical Forum*, 28 (1996-97), pp. 87-99; Kai Nielsen, "Secession: the Case of Quebec," *Journal of Applied Philosophy*, 10 (1993), pp. 29-43; Daniel Philpott, "In Defense of Self-Determination," *Ethics*, 105 (1995), pp. 352-85; Thomas W. Pogge, "Cosmopolitanism and Sovereignty," *Ethics*, 103 (1992), pp. 48-75; Christopher Wellman, "A Defense of Secession and Political Self-Determination," *Philosophy and Public Affairs*, 24 (1995), pp. 142-71; Burleigh Wilkins, "Secession," *Peace Review*, 12 (2000), pp. 15-22.

injustice.[2] Yet it would seem that a state that respects the rights of its citizenry must face the question of whether or not a group of its constituents ought to be granted rights, and in particular, the right to secede.[3]

Allen Buchanan distinguishes between *"Remedial Right Only"* and *"Primary Right"* theories of secession. These are positive theories of secession, that is, theories that, unlike skeptical ones denying the possible justification of secession, affirm that there are instances n which secession is justified. A Remedial Right Only theorist himself, Buchanan argues for a fault model according to which secession is a right that accrues to groups within a state which experience significant violations of human rights by the state and to a certain degree of harshness: "Remedial Right Only Theories assert that a group has a general right to secede if and only if it has suffered certain injustices, for which secession is the appropriate remedy of last resort."[4] Furthermore, he denies that "there is a *general* right to secede that is not a remedial right,"[5] and argues that "there is no (general) right to secede from a just state."[6] Indeed, "a group has a right to secede only if: 1. The physical survival of its members is threatened by actions of the state . . . or it suffers violations of other basic human rights . . . *or* 2. Its previously sovereign territory was unjustly taken by the state . . ."[7]

---

[2] Some examples of philosophical works on the Native American experience include: Allen Buchanan, "The Role of Collective Land Rights in a Theory of Indigenous Peoples' Rights," *Transnational Law and Contemporary Problems*, 3 (1993), pp. 90-108; J. Angelo Corlett, "Reparations to Native Americans?" in Alexandar Jokic, Editor, *War Crimes and Collective Wrongdoing* (London: Blackwell Publishers, 2000), pp. 236-69 *Race, Racism and Reparations* (Ithaca: Cornell University Press, 2003), Chapter 9; John R. Danley, "Liberalism, Aboriginal Rights, and Cultural Minorities," *Philosophy and Public Affairs*, 20 (1991), pp. 168-85; David Lyons, "The New Indian Claims and Original Rights to Land," *Social Theory and Practice*, 4 (1977), pp. 249-72. James W. Nickel, "Ethnocide and Indigenous Peoples," *Journal of Social Philosophy*, 24 (1994), pp. 84-98; James Tully, "Aboriginal Property and Western Theory: Recovering a Middle Ground," *Social Philosophy and Policy*, 11 (1994), pp. 153-80. For discussions of moral and political issues related to aborigines in Australia, see John Bigelow, Robert Pergetter and Robert Young, "Land, Well-Being and Compensation," *Australasian Journal of Philosophy*, 68 (1990), pp. 330-46; Ross Poole, "National Identity, Multiculturalism, and Aboriginal Rights: An Australian Perspective," *Canadian Journal of Philosophy* (Supplementary Volume), 22 (1996), pp. 407-38; Janna Thompson, "Land Rights and Aboriginal Sovereignty," *Australasian Journal of Philosophy*, 68 (1990), pp. 313-29, *Taking Responsibility for the Past* (Cambridge Polity, 2002).

[3] Indeed, this claim might be derived from the first of John Rawls' principles of the Law of Peoples: "Peoples are free and independent, and their freedom and independence are to be respected by other peoples" [John Rawls, *The Law of Peoples* (Cambridge: Harvard University Press, 1999), p. 37]. An argument for the claim itself is provided below.

[4] Buchanan, "Theories of Secession," p. 34-5.

[5] Buchanan, "Theories of Secession," p. 36.

[6] Buchanan, "Theories of Secession," p. 37.

[7] Buchanan, "Theories of Secession," p. 37; "Self-Determination, Secession, and the Rule of Law," p. 310.

In contrast, Primary Right Theories of secession aver that "a group can have a (general) right to secede even if it suffers no injustices, and hence it may have a (general) right to secede from a perfectly just state."[8] Buchanan differentiates between two kinds of Primary Right Theories. *Ascriptive Group Theories* of secession hold that "it is groups whose memberships are defined by what are sometimes called ascriptive characteristics that have the right to secede (even in the absence of injustices)."[9] And "it is first and foremost certain *nonpolitical* characteristics of groups that ground the group's right to an independent political association."[10] Such theories typically subscribe to the nationalist principle according to which every nation or people is entitled to its own state.[11]

Another kind of Primary Right Theory of secession is what is called *Associative Group Theories*. Buchanan describes such theories in the following way:

> . . . Associative Group versions of the Primary Right Theories do not require that a group have any ascriptive characteristics in common such as ethnicity or an encompassing culture, even as a necessary condition for having a right to secede. The members of the group need not even believe that they share any characteristics other than the desire to have their own state. Instead, Associative Group Theorists focus on the *voluntary political choice* of the members of a group (or the majority of them), their decision to form their own independent political unit. Any group, no matter how heterogeneous, can qualify for the right to secede. Nor need the secessionist have any common connection, historical or imagined, to the territory they wish to make their own state. All that matters is that the members of the group voluntarily choose to associate together in an independent political unit of their own. Associative Group Theories, then, assert that there is a right to secede that is, or is an instance of, *the right of political association.*[12]

A version of this kind of Primary Right Theory is a "plebiscite theory," according to which "any group that can constitute some sort of majority . . . in favor of secession within a portion of the state has the right to secede."[13]

I shall proffer a normative theory of secession that concurs with Buchanan to the extent that he argues that experienced injustice is a sufficient condition of the moral right to secede. Yet it disagrees with Buchanan's Remedial Right Only Theory insofar as my theory holds that experienced injustice is *not* a necessary condition of the right to secede. This

---

[8] Buchanan, "Theories of Secession," p. 41.

[9] Buchanan, "Theories of Secession," p. 38.

[10] Buchanan, "Theories of Secession," p. 38.

[11] Avishai Margalit and Joseph Raz speak of "encompassing groups" along these lines, in Margalit and Raz, "National Self-Determination," pp. 445-47.

[12] Buchanan, "Theories of Secession," pp. 38-9.

[13] Buchanan, "Theories of Secession," p. 39. An example of this theory is found in Wellman, "A Defense of Secession and Political Self-Determination," pp. 160-64.

makes my theory a Primary Right one. However, it differs from Associative Group Theories in that not just a simple majority group can decide its way "into" a right to secede. Democratic consensus, on my view, is a necessary but insufficient condition of the right to secede. Mine is something like an Ascriptive Group Theory of the right to secede. However, unlike an existing Ascriptive Group Theory,[14] mine makes territorial rights (along with the satisfying of two other conditions, discussed below) both necessary and sufficient for the right to secede.

In proceeding, I shall first delineate some desiderata for an adequate theory of secession. Following this I shall analyze the nature of groups which qualify for possession of a right to secede. Next I shall analyze the nature of the moral right to secede, articulating and answering some important objections that might be raised to my theory. Finally, I shall explain what my theory would aver or imply about certain historical and current movements to secede. All the while, I shall remain respectful of the admonition "that unless institutional considerations are taken into account from the beginning in developing a normative theory of secession, the result is unlikely to be of much value for the task of providing moral guidance for institutional reform."[15] The theory of secession I set forth and defend herein is a critique of putatively democratic societies in that the analysis of the moral right to secede is claimed to be capable of being successfully constitutionalized. If this claim is plausible, then lacking telling objections not considered herein, no credible democracy can neglect guaranteeing a constitutional right to secede. As Buchanan puts it,

> . . . Surely a political philosophy that places a preeminent value on liberty and self-determination, highly values diversity, and holds that legitimate political authority in some sense rests on the consent of the governed must either acknowledge a right to secede or supply weighty arguments to show why a presumption in favor of such a right is rebutted.[16]

Like David Copp, I assume that justice requires, among other things, that states be governed (to some meaningful extent) democratically.[17] Democracy involves, among other things, respecting persons as political beings. Respect for persons demands respect for basic human liberties and essential collectives to which persons belong. Respect for basic human liberties and collectives requires, among other things, that democratic states guarantee rights of freedom of individuals and collectives to associate or not to

---

[14] Copp, "Democracy and Communal Self-Determination;" "International Law and Morality in the Theory of Secession."

[15] Buchanan, "Theories of Secession," p. 32.

[16] Buchanan, *Secession*, p. 4. A similar statement is found in Buchanan, "Self-Determination and the Right to Secede," p. 350.

[17] Copp, "Democracy and Communal Self-Determination," p. 277.

associate, freedom to live under the authority of the state or *freedom to leave it*. Hence respect for persons and the groups to which they belong implies respect for their *freedom to leave the state*.[18] In other words, democracy requires the autonomy of both individuals and collectives that rights to self-determination are needed to protect.[19] Since the right to secede is a collective right to self-determination, then under specified conditions the right to secede is owed to members of democracies out of respect for them by the state (or by each other, if one prefers). As Daniel Philpott argues, " . . . self-determination is a unique kind of democratic institution, a legal arrangement that promotes participation and representation, the political activities of an autonomous person."[20] Insofar as the right to secede is a right of self-determination, then, a right to secede seeks to promote the exercise of self-determination, at least when secession is justified on moral grounds.

SOME DESIDERATA OF A THEORY OF SECESSION

Desiderata of a theory of secession include, first, a definition of "secession." This definition might be non-stipulative, stipulative, or an admixture of both kinds of definition. But there must be a definition of "secession" for there to be a theory of secession. Otherwise, equivocation and other kinds of confusions result. This is the *Definitional Desideratum of a Theory of Secession*.

A second desideratum of a theory of secession is that such a theory seek to influence constructively international and various national laws, and that the theory is applicable to what is morally valid in bodies of law, both internationally and nationally. This is the *Legal Desideratum of a Theory of Secession*.[21] It assumes a kind of positive relationship between law and

---

[18] See also Corlett, "The Morality and Constitutionality of Secession," p. 122. Note that I have not argued that ethnic groups ought to be treated differently than non-ethnic groups. My arguments and analyses assume nothing special about ethnic groups that would be incongruent with the claim that "in deciding what group rights we, as a society, may or should grant to various groups, we ought not to favor groups of one type, as such, over groups of another" [Thomas W. Pogge, "Group Rights and Ethnicity," *NOMOS*, 39 (1997), p. 187].

[19] Similarly put, " . . . it is democratic institutions that imply self-determination" (Philpott, "In Defense of Self-Determination," p. 358).

[20] Philpott, "In Defense of Self-Determination," p. 358.

[21] This point is similar to Buchanan's criterion of 'minimal realism:' "A theory is morally progressive and minimally realistic if and only if its implementation would better serve basic values than the *status quo* and if it has some significant prospect of eventually being implemented through the actual processes by which international law is made and applied" (Buchanan, "Theories of Secession," p. 42). However, if the processes of international law are corrupted, then it might be that no arguments or proposals for a right to secede would be approved and implemented. Yet one would not think, as Buchanan's criterion seems to imply, that such corruption would or ought to count against the plausibility or practicality of a certain (rational and reasonable) theory of secession. One must be ever mindful to not allow whatever

morality, namely, at least, that for the most part it is desirable for the law to rest on an adequate moral foundation.[22]

A third desideratum of a theory of secession is that it take seriously all relevant moral considerations,[23] and that bodies of law are to track true morality as much as wisdom and practicality permit when such laws pertain to secession. This is the *Moral Desideratum of a Theory of Secession*. It requires a secession theory's taking seriously possible risks of secession to democratic regimes,[24] considerations of "perverse incentives," such as policies of "discriminatory redistribution,"[25] rights to land and natural resources, etc. Also assumed is the idea that the question of whether or not there is a moral right to secede is prior to the legality of secession as a right.[26]

A fourth desideratum of a theory of secession is that it recognize the importance of the distinction between legal and moral questions of secession. Failure to keep in mind this distinction might well result in the committing of some variant of the "is-ought fallacy," assuming without independent argument that what the law says or fails to say about secession is the way the putative right of secession ought to be construed. Moreover, such a theory should distinguish the question of defining secession from the question of under what conditions secession is morally justified. This is the *Desideratum of Clarification of a Theory of Secession*. Satisfaction of this criterion guards against the conflation of these questions that might result in, say, the infiltrating into the very definition of "secession" a feature (for example, the *illegitimate* dissolution of the relationship between a collective and the state having authority over it, or for instance, the use of *violence* against *innocent* parties to gain freedom from the state) that might condemn it on moral grounds. This kind of move would constitute question-begging in regards to whether or not secession could ever be justified, or whether or not it ought ever to become a right. Yet the problems of secession cannot be settled by defining away its possible legitimacy. Argument must be employed in attempt to settle questions related to this complex phenomenon.

---

is the case in a political or legal context dictate the parameters of what ought to become the case.

[22] I do not assume, however, any kind of foundationalist theory of moral knowledge or justification. For some recent discussions of moral epistemology, see Walter Sinnott-Armstrong and Mark Timmons, Editors, *Moral Knowledge?* (Oxford: Oxford University Press, 1996); Mark Timmons, *Morality Without Foundations* (Oxford: Oxford University Press, 1998).

[23] This includes taking into account Buchanan's "absence of perverse incentives" criterion (Buchanan, "Theories of Secession," p. 43).

[24] Buchanan, "Self-Determination, Secession, and the Rule of Law," pp. 301-03.

[25] Buchanan, *Secession*, pp. 38-45; "Self-Determination, Secession, and the Rule of Law," p. 310.

[26] Copp, "International Law and Morality in the Theory of Secession," p. 222.

A fifth desideratum of a theory of secession is that the analysis it offers of morally justified secession is generalizeable. This means that no double standard of when the conditions of justified secession are satisfied is legitimate. If secession is justified for a certain collective under the prescribed analysis, then all other collectives facing relevantly similar circumstances are also justified in seceding from their respective countries. Nor is it appropriate to introduce principles or arguments that lack rational support, or that are self-serving or question-begging. This is the *Desideratum of Fairness and Rationality of a Theory of Secession.*

Having articulated some desiderata of an adequate theory of secession, I shall set forth and defend a new theory that satisfies to a significant degree each of the above desideratum. What *is* secession, and under what conditions, if any, is it morally justified?

A TERRITORIALIST RIGHTS-BASED THEORY OF SECESSION

I proffer a *"Territorialist Rights-Based Theory of Secession,"* one which, in satisfying each of the above desiderata for a theory of secession, holds that (among other things) fault is a sufficient but not a necessary condition of justified secession. As a Primary Right Theory, this Territorialist Rights-Based Theory of Secession is not an Associative Group Theory in that not just a simple majority collective within a state can vote and thereby make real its right to secede.[27] For "the consent argument for a right to secede fails because it neglects a vital component of any sound justification for secession: a valid territorial claim on the part of the secessionists."[28] Unlike an Ascriptive Group Theory, furthermore, the Territorialist Rights-Based Theory of Secession takes territorial rights (along with the satisfying of the two other conditions, discussed below) as both necessary and jointly sufficient for the right to secede. It holds to the "Territoriality Thesis," according to which "every sound justification for secession must include a valid claim to the territory on the part of the secessionists."[29] But the Territorialist Rights-Based Theory of Secession demands more. For the Territoriality Thesis does nothing to answer the question of what counts as a collective's having a valid claim to territory. In providing an answer to this question, I distinguish between *ownership rights to territory* and *occupation rights to territory*. Because of various difficulties raised against theories of rights to ownership of land and to private property

---

[27] This also distinguishes the Territorialist Rights-Based Theory of Secession from a simple plebiscite theory.
[28] Buchanan, "Toward a Theory of Secession," p. 328.
[29] Buchanan, "Toward a Theory of Secession," pp. 330, 340.

more generally (such as, for example, the theory of John Locke),[30] I couch
the substance of the Territoriality Thesis in terms of occupation rights to
land. For a collective might have a valid claim (based on a valid
interest/choice) to occupy a territory without having a valid claim to
ownership of it.[31] The question of what exactly *is* a valid claim to territory is
answered below.

Secession is the exercise of the right to self-determination by a political
collective. It involves, among other things, the collective's claiming of
territory as its own.[32] Secession does not oppose or seek to overthrow the
government. Instead, it attempts to break away from its authority. Secession
need not (as in the case of the peaceful secession of Brasil from Portugal in
1822) become physically violent, though it often leads to violence where
severe conflicts arise concerning territorial boundaries, alleged human rights
violations, etc.

Not all movements of secession involve the desire of a collective to
become an independent state.[33] For in some cases, a collective simply seeks
to opt out of the authority of one state and become subject to another state's
authority. An example of this would most likely occur should Quebec
succeed in seceding from Canada. The Cree nation has made it clear that it
would under such circumstances secede from Quebec and remain under
Canada's authority.[34] Moreover, instead of either forming an independent
state or integrating into an existing one, a seceding conglomerate might
choose a relationship of free association with an independent state.[35] Nor
must secession be justified only in cases where it leads to the formation of a
political democracy. For as a right to self-determination, the right to secede
is a right that can be exercised in whole or in part, as the secessionists see fit,

---

[30] Stephen Buckle, *Natural Law and the Theory of Property* (Oxford: Oxford University
Press, 1991); Matthew H. Kramer, *John Locke and the Origins of Private Property*
(Cambridge: Cambridge University Press, 1997); A. John Simmons, *A Lockean Theory of
Rights* (Princeton: Princeton University Press, 1992); "Makers' Rights," *The Journal of
Ethics*, 2 (1998), pp. 197-218; Gopal Sreenivasan, *The Limits of Lockean Rights in Property*
(New York: Oxford University Press, 1995); James Tully, *An Approach to Political
Philosophy: Locke in Contexts* (Cambridge: Cambridge University Press, 1993).
[31] This idea is consistent with what Buchanan refers to as "territorial sovereignty" (Buchanan,
Secession, pp. 108-09).
[32] For a definition of "secession" that does *not* construe it as the claiming of territory by a
secessionist collective, see Moellendorf, "Liberalism, Nationalism, and the Right to Secede,"
p. 88-91.
[33] As Buchanan argues, "It would be an error to define secession as separation from an
existing state in order to become a sovereign state" (Buchanan, *Secession*, p. 10).
[34] Grand Council of the Crees, *Sovereign Injustice: Forcible Inclusion of the James Bay Crees
and Cree Territory into a Sovereign Quebec* (Nemaska: Grand Council of the Crees, 1995).
[35] Glenn T. Morris, "International Law and Politics: Toward a Right to Self-Determination for
Indigenous Peoples," in M. Annette Jaimes, Editor, *The State of Native America* (Boston:
South End Press, 1992), p. 79.

in accordance with their own customs and traditions and their own appreciation of their needs. The secessionists decide for themselves what degree of political autonomy they want to enjoy. Moreover, they themselves decide what sorts of political relationships, if any, they desire to have with other political units.[36]

But under what conditions, if any, should a collective have a right to secede? The normative question of whether or not there ought to be a legal right to secede depends on the answer to the question of whether or not there is a moral right to secede. This is because it is desirous that the law have a sound moral foundation.

COLLECTIVE MORAL RIGHTS

In order to provide a plausible answer to the question of whether or not there is a moral right to secede and whether or not there ought to be a legal right to secede, it is necessary to define the concept of the nature of a collective.[37] A *collective* is a collection of individuals who are members of the same collective type. A collective type is a category to which collections of individuals belong. Stipulatively speaking, collectives are of various kinds. One kind of collective is an *aggregate*, which is a collection of persons loosely associated with each other. Implied by "loosely associated" is the idea that there are no recognized or formal membership conditions required of aggregates. Examples of aggregates include mobs and random collectives. A *conglomerate*, on the other hand, is a collection of persons into a diversified whole. The constituent members of conglomerates share common interests typically related to common goals or interests. Such interests are shared by members of the collective to the extent that each member of the collective holds them *qua* member of the collective. Because persons may and often do have different goals and interests as individuals than they do in their various capacities as members of conglomerates, it is not necessary that constituent members of the collective believe (i.e.,

---

[36] This point is consistent with what is argued in Ward Churchill, *From a Native Son* (Boston: South End Press, 1996), p. 531; Rebecca L. Robbins, "Self-Determination and Subordination: The Past, Present, and Future of American Indian Governance," in M. Annette Jaimes, Editor, *The State of Native America* (Boston: South End Press, 1992), pp. 110-11.

[37] Similarly, "without an account of what constitutes a people, there can be no satisfactory theory of secession" (Ewin, "Peoples and Secession," p. 226).

sincerely assent to) such goals or interests *qua* individuals.[38] Throughout this book, I use "collective" and "conglomerate" synonymously.[39]

It would seem that a necessary condition of a collective's having either a legal or moral right to secede is that it not be a mere aggregate. It must at least *have the capacity to have shared interests and goals among its members*. Its having goals implies that it has the capacity for "effective agency," which means that it deliberates, chooses, intends, acts and self-evaluates[40] as conglomerates typically do to one degree or another. This much appears to be transparent. And it is even more commonsensical that a collection of individuals' constituting a conglomerate is insufficient for its having the right to secede. For the goals and interests of a collective must be valid ones (legally valid in cases of legal rights, morally valid in cases of moral rights).[41] Moreover, such interests or goals must be such that they imply that others have duties to refrain from interfering with the exercise of the collective's interest in or goal of secession. Thus while being a conglomerate is a necessary condition of the collective legal or moral right to secede, it is hardly a sufficient condition. However, it does appear that a conglomerate's having a valid legal or moral interest or goal that holds others to a duty of noninterference does suffice for the conglomerate's having a legal or moral right simpliciter.[42] A few examples of conglomerates

---

[38] A similar concept of a collective is found in J. Angelo Corlett, "The Problem of Collective Moral Rights," *Canadian Journal of Law and Jurisprudence*, 7 (1994), pp. 237-38. For alternative analyses of collective rights, see Michael Hartney, "Some Confusions Concerning Collective Rights," *Canadian Journal of Law and Jurisprudence*, 4 (1991), pp. 293-314; Will Kymlicka, *Multicultural Citizenship* (Oxford: Oxford University Press, 1995), Chapter 3.

[39] It should be noted that there are other collectives that do not fall neatly into either the aggregate or conglomerate categories. Ethnic groups, it might be argued, are neither mere loose associations of people. Nor are they necessarily organized as are conglomerates. An analysis of ethnicity in terms of *un*acquirable memberships is found in J. Angelo Corlett, "Latino Identity," *Public Affairs Quarterly*, 13 (1999), pp. 273-95; "Latino Identity and Affirmative Action," in Jorge J. E. Gracia and Pablo DeGrieff, Editors, *Ethnic Identity, Culture, and Group Rights* (London: Routledge, 1999), pp. 223-34; *Race, Racism, and Reparations* (Ithaca: Cornell University Press, 2003). Alternative philosophical accounts (in terms of acquirable memberships) include those found in Raymond Belliotti, *Seeking Identity* (Lawrence: University Press of Kansas, 1995); Jorge J. E. Gracia, *Hispanic/Latino Identity* (London: Blackwell Publishers, 2000); and Pogge, "Group Rights and Ethnicity," pp. 187-221.

[40] James W. Nickel, "Group Agency and Group Rights," *NOMOS*, 29 (1997), p. 235.

[41] In saying that a right is a *valid* claim, I mean that the interests/choices of the right bearer at a certain time outweigh, all things considered, competing interests/choices of others at that time. For more on this analysis of collective rights, see Buchanan, *Secession*, p. 85; Corlett, "The Problem of Collective Moral Rights;" Carol C. Gould, "Group Rights and Social Ontology," *The Philosophical Forum*, 28 (1996-97), pp. 73-86; Pogge, "Group Rights and Ethnicity," pp. 191-92.

[42] Corlett, "The Problem of Collective Moral Rights," pp. 242-43. As Copp states, " . . . a right to secede would entail a duty on the part of the state not to interfere" (Copp, "International Law and Morality in the Theory of Secession," p. 221).

that have moral and legal rights include the following: the Kumeyaay nation, the Diné nation, Six nations, and the Cree nation.[43] For each has and ought to have, at least in some cases, uncontroversial rights to freedoms of the press, speech, and expression, not to mention various due-process rights. This is partly because ethnic group membership is a primary good, and it involves an important degree of cultural membership. As Will Kymlicka argues, "Once we recognize cultural membership as an important primary good which underlies our choices, then special political rights and status for minority cultures may be required."[44]

Indeed, one might argue that a sufficient condition of a conglomerate's possessing a right is the out-group recognition of the collective as being a political conglomerate that qualifies as having a right. However, this line of reasoning seems to confuse political rights with moral rights. A conglomerate can have a moral right even though no one (not even itself!) knows or even believes that it possesses it. So out-group recognition is not a necessary condition of collective moral rights. But it is not sufficient either in that an out-group can mistakenly identify a collective as a moral rights-bearing party. Thus out-group recognition is neither necessary nor sufficient for a conglomerate's having a moral right.

ANALYZING THE RIGHT TO SECEDE

A question, then, poses itself: "What are the conditions of a collective's having a valid moral claim to secede which would ground a valid legal claim to secede?" Ironically, the United States (a country itself founded on the colonist's secession from England), a self-proclaimed democracy and defender of human rights, grants no right to secede to its member states (indeed, it fought the bloodiest war in its history to *prevent* it!). Nor does it grant the right to secede to any constituent group of its citizenry.[45] Although international law recognizes a right of all peoples to self-determination, this right does not clearly include the right of secession, except under

---

[43] Indeed, each such nation enjoys the legal recognition of its standing as a nation by the U.S. and Canada, respectively. However, lest it is argued that this recognition of the nationhood of each of the Native American nations imply that Native American secession would become nonsense, one must consider that the U.S. has always had *de facto* power over such nations, and has exercised such power, often to the detriment of them. When the U.S. Internal Revenue Service is used to collect taxes from such nations, those nations can hardly be said to be independent in the sense of their being autonomously independent or self-ruling entities.

[44] Will Kymlicka, *Liberalism, Community, and Culture* (Oxford: Oxford University Press, 1989), p. 199.

[45] Even more ironically (from a typical U.S. anti-communist standpoint), the former Soviet Union guaranteed its citizens the constitutional right to secede.

"exceptional circumstances" of "decolonialization."[46] So the answer to the
question of existing legal rights to secede is unclear. The interesting
question, then, becomes a moral one of whether or not there ought to be a
legal right to secede. For "the moral right to secede provides a strong case
for establishing a constitutional right to secede, under certain conditions."[47]

What, according to the Territorialist Rights-Based Theory of Secession,
are the considerations in favor of there being a moral right to secede? What,
might it argue, would ground a moral right to secede? *A conglomerate has a
moral and ought to have a constitutional right to secede to the extent that:
(1) it is under the authority of a state to which it does not, determined by
significant and informed majority vote of the seceding conglomerate, want to
remain a constituent member; (2) it has a valid moral claim (based on a
valid moral interest/choice)[48] to a certain territory within the putative
boundaries of the state of which it is a member; and (3) it is capable of and
willing to pay in full all exit costs of secession (if any) that the conglomerate
might owe to the state.[49]* Such exit costs might include the cost of the state

[46] Buchanan, "Theories of Secession," p. 33, note 2; Grand Council of the Crees, *Sovereign
Injustice*, p. 103.
[47] Buchanan, *Secession*, p. 28.
[48] My notion of the grounding of the moral right to secede is not contingent on a particular
theory of the grounding of rights. Although my account is a Feinbergian one which grounds
rights in valid claims (in turn grounded in valid moral choices/interests), my account of the
grounding of the moral right to secede may be based on whichever theory of rights is in the
end most plausible. For more on rights theory, see Ronald Dworkin, *Taking Rights Seriously*
(Cambridge: Harvard University Press, 1978); Joel Feinberg, *Social Philosophy* (Englewood
Cliffs: Prentice-Hall, 1973), Chapters 4-6; *Rights, Justice, and the Bounds of Liberty*
(Princeton: Princeton University Press, 1980); *Freedom and Fulfillment* (Princeton: Princeton
University Press, 1992), Chapter 8-10; James Griffin, "Welfare Rights," *The Journal of
Ethics*, 4 (2000), pp. 27-43; Loren Lomasky, "Liberty and Welfare Goods: Reflections on
Clashing Liberalisms," *The Journal of Ethics*, 4 (2000), pp. 99-113; *Persons, Rights, and the
Moral Community* (Oxford: Oxford University Press, 1987); David Lyons, *Rights, Welfare,
and Mill's Moral Theory* (Oxford: Oxford University Press, 1994); Eric Mack, "In Defense of
the Jurisdiction Theory of Rights," *The Journal of Ethics*, 4 (2000), pp. 71-98; Thomas
Pogge, "The International Significance of Human Rights," *The Journal of Ethics*, 4 (2000),
pp. 45-69; Joseph Raz, *The Morality of Freedom* (Oxford: Oxford University Press, 1986);
Henry Shue, *Basic Rights* (Princeton: Princeton University Press, 1980); L. W. Sumner, *The
Moral Foundations of Rights* (Oxford: Clarendon, 1987); Judith J. Thomson, *The Realm of
Rights* (Cambridge: Harvard University Press, 1990); Jeremy Waldron, Editor, *Theories of
Rights* (Oxford: Oxford University Press, 1984); *Liberal Rights* (Cambridge: Cambridge
University Press, 1993); "The Role of Rights in Practical Reasoning: 'Rights' Versus
'Needs,'" *The Journal of Ethics*, 4 (2000), pp. 115-35; Carl Wellman, *A Theory of Rights*
(Totowa: Rowman and Littlefield, 1985); *Real Rights* (Oxford: Oxford University Press,
1995); *The Proliferation of Rights* (Boulder: Westview, 1999).
[49] As Copp argues, "A seceding society may have to compensate the remainder of the original
state for investments that the original state made in the society's territory" (Copp,
"Democracy and Communal Self-Determination," p. 280. Exit costs of secession are also
discussed in Buchanan, "Toward a Theory of Secession," pp. 339-42; also in Corlett, "The

for protection (police, military) of those who seek to secede from it during the time that the members of the state were under state protection. Or, it might include other goods and/or services provided the conglomerate by the state that are not outweighed, all things considered, by the benefits the seceding conglomerate brought to the state itself. Or still, exit costs might be paid *by the state* to the seceding conglomerate due to, say, uncompensated and significant injustices against it by the state. These exit costs amount to what might be termed a *"secession settlement."* There seems to be no good reason to think that an international tribunal is in principle or even in practice incapable of adequately arbitrating such matters of a secession settlement, as courts make decisions similar in kind regularly, albeit with fewer complications. The point here is that the complex nature of most secession settlements hardly counts as a good reason to infer that significant compensatory justice cannot be realized between a state and its secessionists. This is especially plausible where a secession settlement is paid over time instead of its being paid in full prior to secession.

If the exit costs owed by a seceding conglomerate are too high for it to pay (even over time, given its reasonably projected fiscal status), then that conglomerate has not satisfied condition (3) which is requisite for it to have a right of secession. On the other hand, the conglomerate can relatively easily satisfy condition (1) as long as a substantial and informed majority of its constituent members concur with the desire to remove itself from the government under which it currently lives.

Note that in order for a conglomerate to satisfy condition (1) it need not be the case that it be willing or able to establish a government of its own. Copp argues that "a society has no right to secede from an existing state, and to create a new state for itself, unless there is a stable and widespread desire for statehood among its members."[50] But it would be overly paternalistic to insist that a seceding group have the ability or desire to form its own government. Moreover, it would require a defeater for political anarchism.[51] Although it might be argued with plausibility that a seceding state must not seek to establish an evil regime which violates basic human rights on a

---

Morality and Constitutionality of Secession," p. 125). It is important to note, however, that neither philosopher discusses the possibility of a *state's* owing and paying exit costs to a secessionist collective for harms done to it by the state. This point, raised above, will be discussed more fully in the context of Native American secession from the U.S., below.

[50] Copp, "Democracy and Communal Self-Determination," pp. 292-93. Also see Copp, "International Law and Morality in the Theory of Secession," p. 227; Wellman, "A Defense of Secession and Political Self-Determination," pp. 161-62.

[51] If this point is plausible, then it would appear that the requirement that secessionist groups seek to establish their own governments begs the question against political anarchism, thereby violating the Criterion of Clarification of a Theory of Secession. For an articulation and defense of political anarchism, see Robert Paul Wolff, *In Defense of Anarchism* (New York: Harper and Row, 1970).

regular basis (e.g., a slaveholding state such as the former U.S. confederacy, or one that obtains land by way of crimes, torts and contract violations of immense proportions), it would hardly follow that a seceding state must form a democracy intent on establishing a government distinct from that of the state from which it secedes.[52] For instance, indigenous Hawai'ians might vote by a substantial majority to secede from the U.S. in order to return to their pre-colonial era of monarchy. Nor would it follow that the seceding conglomerate must not willingly put itself to an end (if only by not propagating itself). For sometimes it is better to bring oneself to an end in that the state in which a conglomerate currently resides is so evil that continuing to exist under its pervasive rule or dominion, locally or globally, is intolerable on, say, social psychological or spiritual grounds. As in cases where the individual's right to die is warranted on the grounds of incurable and painful disease, there are instances where a conglomerate plausibly construes self-genocide as a favorable escape from the harsh realities of oppressive tyranny.[53]

To this line of reasoning it might be argued that the view that a conglomerate seeking political divorce from the state to which it belongs under the conditions just stated provides a fault model of secession, not the no-fault model promised as part of the core of the Territorialist Rights-Based Theory of Secession. So while the argument just provided serves as a justification for such collective action, it is not without contradiction open to the Territorialist Rights-Based Theory of Secession.

However, a conglomerate seeking secession from its reasonably just state might do so instead because it finds that its fundamental aims and values are incongruent with those of the state. Imagine a conglomerate in the U.S. which has the same aims and values of the "typical" Native American nation: respect for nature and its own various rich Native American traditions, is against developments of land and exploitation of natural resources as often found in the U.S. But imagine that the conglomerate itself had experienced no injustice at the hands of the U.S. (the U.S. had not acquired land from the conglomerate illegally or immorally, had not stolen or misacquired from it resources of any kind, etc.).[54] Yet the divergence of worldviews between the two conglomerates is obvious. Indeed, *it might well be impossible or highly unlikely that the conglomerate in question would be*

---

[52] Note that requiring, as condition (1) does, a democratic vote of a seceding conglomerate in favor of secession is not the same as requiring that it form a democracy. For democratic voting procedures are insufficient for democracy in a more robust sense.

[53] Witness the U'was of Colombia who, in protest of U.S.-based Occidental Petroleum's usurpation of U'wa land to build and sustain an oil refinery and pipeline, have threatened to commit mass suicide, a threat that hundreds of U'was carried out in the past.

[54] For a philosophical discussion of this point, see J. Angelo Corlett, *Race, Racism, and Reparations* (Ithaca: Cornell University Press, 2003), Chapter 8.

able to flourish under the rule of a reasonably just state which has quite different aims and values than it. The conglomerate might well survive while satisfying Buchanan's condition (1) (namely, that the physical survival of its members is threatened by actions of the state . . . or it suffers violations of other basic human rights). Yet it would not likely flourish. The extensive power supportive of the aims and values of the state is prohibitive of the conglomerate's flourishing. Thus it would appear *that a morally legitimate[55] conglomerate's being able to not only survive, but flourish, is a right of every such conglomerate.* However, that a conglomerate cannot likely flourish under the state to which it belongs is not straightaway reason enough to think that the state is unjust toward that conglomerate. But since a morally legitimate conglomerate has a right to flourish, and if seceding from a state the authority under which it cannot flourish will increase its likelihood of flourishing, then it would appear that that conglomerate has, subject to other conditions obtaining, a moral right to secede. Perhaps, just as in some marriages, it is not a good match between partners who are in various important respects good persons. An assumption here is that not all legitimate cultures or worldviews are able to flourish together, under the same rule of government. If these points are plausible, then fault models[56] of secession are rendered problematic.

Finally, in regard to condition (1), it is clear that a secessionist collective need *not* consult for approval the state from which it is justifiably seeking to secede. For "a right to decide whether another self can enjoy self-determination would make a mockery of the concept. I am entitled to govern myself with others who govern themselves according to principles of justice: I may not decide who will and who will not be included in my state, or how another group governs its own affairs."[57] Thus condition (1) is satisfiable by a conglomerate by strong and informed majority vote in cases where the conglomerate's ability to flourish is not likely under the authority of the ruling state. Condition (3) is satisfied when all exit costs of secession are able and willing to be paid to the state by the seceding group, should such costs be owed.

But condition (2) requires that a seceding conglomerate have a valid moral claim to the territory it seeks to have as its own, quite apart from state authority. As Copp writes, "Unless there is a territory the society has a special moral right to occupy, a society that does not have a territory does not have a right to self-determination, . . ."[58] Copp confirms that satisfying

---

[55] Assumed here is the idea that not every conglomerate enjoys sufficient moral justification to exist. Putative instances of such conglomerates include those which have perpetrated exceeding levels of injustice, especially without apology and adequate rectification.
[56] See Buchanan, "Theories of Secession;" and Wilkins, "Secession."
[57] Philpott, "In Defense of Self-Determination," p. 363.
[58] Copp, "Democracy and Communal Self-Determination," p. 295.

the terms of the Territoriality Thesis is a necessary condition for the right to secede when he claims that "a group with the right to secede must therefore have some right to the relevant part of the state's territory, . . ."[59] Assuming that the right to secede is an instance of the more general right to self-determination, then this is perhaps the most fundamental condition of the right to secede. For if a conglomerate has no valid moral claim to territory, then it simply cannot have a moral right to secede and claim territory as its own. It is not, as Philpott thinks, that the right to secede is somehow supplemented by an "additional territorial claim,"[60] but rather that the satisfying of the Territoriality Thesis (a collective's having a valid moral claim to and/or moral interest in a given territory) *just is* the basis of the right to secede. Indeed, it might be argued that conditions (1) and (3) are subsidiary conditions of (2). For each presupposes the satisfying of condition (2). I shall not push this point here, though, as it is inessential to my main arguments.

It is important to note that condition (2) does *not* entail the fault model of the right to secede,[61] or the "historical grievance version" of the Territoriality Thesis according to which "the valid claim to territory that every sound justification for secession includes must be grounded in a historical grievance concerning the violation of a preexisting property right."[62] It claims, rather, that a seceding conglomerate must have, above all else, a valid claim to the territory which it seeks as its own over against the state. There need be no injustice at work in such a scenario, though injustice may serve as *a* sufficient condition of morally justified secession[63] as long as condition (2) is satisfied. And it is the Territoriality Thesis (to which Buchanan refers) that is "unproblematic."[64] The mistake that some political philosophers make is to assume that satisfying the Territoriality Thesis requires injustice. Since the Territoriality Thesis itself (aside from the historical grievance version of it) unproblematically does *not* entail injustice, then it is open for the Territorialist Rights-Based Theory of Secession to argue that there is a moral right to secede for conglomerates even where there is no injustice in the state from which the conglomerate seeks to secede, yet simultaneously argue for condition (2) which amounts to the Territoriality Thesis.

One crucial implication of condition (2) of the Territorialist Rights-Based Theory of Secession is that since, as Buchanan argues, " . . . the

---

[59] Copp, "International Law and Morality in the Theory of Secession," pp. 227 and 229.

[60] Philpott, "In Defense of Self-Determination," p. 370.

[61] David Gauthier argues that "Just as there is a moral case for no-fault divorce, so there is a moral case for no-fault secession" (Gauthier, "Breaking Up: An Essay on Secession." p. 357).

[62] Buchanan, *Secession*, p. 68; "Toward a Theory of Secession," p. 330.

[63] Corlett, "The Morality and Constitutionality of Secession," p. 122.

[64] Buchanan, "Toward a Theory of Secession," p. 330.

history of most existing states is so replete with immoral, coercive, and fraudulent takings that it may be hard for most of them to establish the legitimacy of their current borders. . . .,"[65] most, if not all, existing *de facto* independent states are unqualified to possess and exercise the right to secede. For example, given the realities of U.S. history of unjust acquisitions and transfers of lands from Native American nations to various European parties, the confederate south had no right to secede, not simply because, as John Rawls might argue, it sought to establish an unjust (slavery-based) state,[66] but because the territory which it sought to claim as its own was not genuinely its own to claim. From the supposition that the confederacy had certain claims against the union states that might ground its becoming a separate nation from the union states, it hardly follows that the confederate states had a valid moral claim to the lands on which they resided. Moreover, the union states had no right to stop the confederacy's move to secede, as neither of them were in a moral position to be on the land in the first place! Furthermore, the union states were in violation of the Desideratum of Fairness and Rationality of a Theory of Secession in that, while the colonists seceded from the British empire, the colonists hardly made constitutional provisions for a right to secede for the citizens of its newly formed republic. Ironically, the Native American nations themselves are the only parties in the Americas that can possibly satisfy condition (2), except in the few cases where Native American nations ceded land to others voluntarily, knowingly and intentionally (or in the relatively few cases of some such nations conquering others). Their respective claims to territories of the Americas were valid centuries ago, and they are valid (all things considered) today. U.S. or other governmental or juridical denials of justice to Native American nations throughout the generations fail to negate this fact. Nor do morally arbitrary statutes of limitations[67] succeed in legitimizing the justice denied to Native American nations by any government. Let us become and remain cognizant of the fact that the burden of argument here lies squarely on the shoulders of proponents of such moral statutes of limitations, not with the detractors. For this reason, the Territorialist Right-Based Theory of Secession seems to collapse into what might be called an "Indigenous Theory of Secession," at least where secession by indigenous groups is a

---

[65] Buchanan, "Toward a Theory of Secession," p. 330. Also see Buchanan, "Self-Determination and the Right to Secede," p. 353.

[66] Rawls argues that ". . . no people has the right to self-determination, or a right to secession, at the expense of subjugating another people" (Rawls, *The Law of Peoples*, p. 38).

[67] That defenders of a moral statute of limitations on injustice bear the unmet burden of argument is argued in Corlett, *Race, Racism, and Reparations*, Chapters 8-9. For a philosophical analysis of leading arguments in favor of a moral statute of limitations on injustice, see Rodney C. Roberts, "The Morality of a Moral Statute of Limitations on Injustice," *The Journal of Ethics*, 7 (2003), pp. 115-38.

matter of, among other things, reclaiming their lands not ceded to others absent force or fraud.

Perhaps there is some plausibility in the view that rights to territories can be acquired over time, even though a ruling group does not have a claim to the lands as an indigenous group would. Once again, as Buchanan argues concerning the application of rectificatory justice groundings for a moral right to secede, "The chief difficulty . . . is that the history of most existing states is so replete with immoral, coercive, and fraudulent takings that it may be hard for most of them to establish the legitimacy of their current borders."[68] And he goes on to state that "Perhaps the least bad alternative would be for international law to include a convention that accords a presumption of legitimacy to existing borders, subject to the proviso that this presumptive entitlement can be rebutted by strong evidence of unjust taking within some specified time period, say, three generations."[69] However, there are problems with this proposal. First, in the cases of the Native American experiences with the U.S., the "unjust takings" included *genocide*,[70] and there is no U.S. statute of limitations on murder. Since there is no U.S. statute of limitations on murder, what could possibly be the plausible rationale for there being a statute of limitations in either U.S. or international law concerning the attainment of justice concerning the U.S. genocide of Native Americans? It would appear that a negative answer to this question betrays an inability of the statute of limitations proposal to satisfy the Criterion of Fairness and Rationality of a Theory of Secession.

In light of the foregoing, then, *secession rights do not accrue to states that took territories unjustly or that violated human rights in acquiring territories to which they lay claim.* Which existing country is able to lay a valid claim to its own territory? The possible acquisition of rights to territory that are not indigenous rights to it seems only to accrue in cases where conglomerates or persons reside on land *not* having themselves acquired the land unjustly, and where those who have had it taken from them unjustly (by a third party) are deceased and have no living descendants who might be able to claim rights to the land in question. But this hardly applies to the case of the U.S., where the *U.S. itself as a matter of domestic policy* intentionally committed genocide against Native Americans in the name of manifest destiny. Moreover, several Native American nations still exist today and are in positions to continue to claim their moral rights to all of their native lands. Of course, even if no Native Americans existed today, it would not follow

---

[68] Buchanan, "Toward a Theory of Secession," p. 330.

[69] Buchanan, "Toward a Theory of Secession," p. 330, note 13; *Secession*, p. 88.

[70] For a discussion of the nature of genocide in terms of Native America, see Ward Churchill, *Since Predator Came* (Littleton: Aigis, 1995), pp. 75-106. That genocide was effected on various Native American nations by many U.S. citizens as well as by the U.S. Government is argued in Churchill, *Since Predator Came*, p. 30.

logically that the U.S. with its severe and unrectified injustices toward them and others would somehow have a valid moral claim to and/or a valid moral interest in the territory in question in that its severe, persistent and unrectified human rights violations negate, on moral grounds, any such territorial claims. Whether or not Native Americans exist to claim their moral or legal rights to what is deemed by some as U.S. territory, it hardly follows that the U.S. has a valid moral claim to it. So there appears to be no sense in which the U.S. or its citizenry have any moral rights to the lands on which they reside as putative "owners" of them.

A constitutional right to secede would grant Native American nations such as the Diné nation an institutional means by which to leverage the reparations that the U.S. and its citizens deem unjustified even in the least. Yet it is easy to see that if the right to secede from the U.S. was claimed by every Native American nation, then it would spell the end of the U.S. as we know it. Apparently, *genuine democracy* (insofar as this amounts to, at the very least, respect for persons, their rights, and their autonomy) would prove too costly for the U.S. government and its citizenry. For if my previous claim is plausible, then a genuine democracy must guarantee its citizen collectives the right to secede. And simply because a state faces possible, even probable, dissolution in the face of respecting freedom and corrective justice in no way counts against the fact that true democracy demands the right to secede be guaranteed under certain circumstances, namely, the ones set forth in the analysis of the moral right to secede, conditions (1)-(3) above. To argue that such a "drastic" or "radical" proposal is unrealistic and falls short of satisfying Buchanan's criterion of "moral realism" is simply to fail to satisfy the Criterion of Fairness and Rationality of a Theory of Secession. It begs the moral question by presuming a certain kind of self-serving and double standard-based utilitarianism in arguing that the U.S. need not guarantee a right to secede if the exercise of that right would spell the end of the U.S., especially when the demise of the U.S. might well be deserved in light of the morally unjust foundations on which it was built.

Surely it is plausible to think that Native American nations have not and are unlikely to flourish while under U.S. dominion, thus satisfying condition (1). This would make reasonable their desire to not remain under U.S. rule. Certainly it is plausible to believe that Native Americans have valid claims to and/or valid moral interests in most or all of the territories of all fifty states,[71] especially, moreover, after having incessantly sought justice for the unjust takings of their lands in the halls of justice, Congress and the White

---

[71] Including Hawai'i, which might be claimed validly by indigenous peoples other than the Native American nations that qualify as legitimate claimants to the other 49 states in question. Native Hawai'ians had their lands unjustly taken from them by U.S. military force, as detailed in Michael Dougherty, *To Steal a Kingdom: Probing Hawai'ian History* (Waimanalo: Island Style Press, 1992).

House (surely secession would be a "last resort" in their cases), thus satisfying condition (2).[72] As for the capability and willingness of Native American nations to pay their own exit costs for secession, it would be implausible to think that Native American nations owe secession settlement costs to the U.S., especially in light of the genocide perpetrated on them by the U.S. Not even the meager amounts of periodic assistance to a relative few Native Americans over the generations can begin to rectify the unjust takings of land, lives and culture from them by the U.S. If there are exit costs to be paid should Native American nations decide to secede from the U.S., it would be the *U.S.*, not Native American nations, which ought to pay them.[73]

Additional features of the Territorialist Rights-Based (Indigenous) Theory of Secession include its denial that secession must be a "last resort."[74] For something is not an empowering right (that is, not one with meaningful exercise of power for the right holder) if it is *only* justified to exercise it as a last resort. This point further deepens the no-fault character of the right to secede under the Territorialist Rights-Based Theory of Secession. Moreover, if secession is a "right" of "last resort," then it would likely never be a right that is justifiably exercised in that there are almost, if not always, various alternative political strategies that might be employed instead of secession. Recall Rawls' caution in considering the right of civil

---

[72] Thus the *Laches* defense is not open to the U.S. to block Native American secession.

[73] This would not be an example of central or peripheral secessions, but of secession of a worst-off minority group because of wrongful takings and felony murders, and not because of distributive justice concerns, but because of retributive justice.

It is noteworthy that Native American nations not only clearly satisfy the conditions (1)-(3) above, but they also satisfy Buchanan's set of necessary conditions "that would have to be satisfied if the argument from cultural preservation is to succeed in justifying secession as a matter of right:"

> (1) The culture in question must in fact be imperiled. (2) Less disruptive ways of preserving the culture . . . must be unavailable or inadequate. (3) The culture in question must meet minimal standards of justice . . . . (4) The seceding cultural group must not be seeking independence in order to establish an illiberal state, that is, one which fails to uphold basic individual civil and political rights, *and* from which free exit is denied. (5) Neither the state nor any third party can have a valid claim to the seceding territory (Buchanan, *Secession*, p. 61).

I assume that no explanation is needed to show how Native American nations satisfy these conditions. But this analysis of a right to secede is problematic in that it imposes a fault condition on the right to secede and because *there need be no* "less disruptive ways of preserving the culture" available to seceding groups to justify secession. To deny this argument's credibility seems to provide for existing states an unnecessarily conservative protection from their having to live up to democratic standards of guaranteeing, on no-fault standards, a right to secede in terms of the Territorialist Rights-Based Theory of Secession.

[74] That secession is a "remedy of last resort" is argued in Buchanan, "Theories of Secession," p. 36; Philpott, "In Defense of Self-Determination," p. 382.

disobedience as justifiably exercised as a last resort.[75] The doctrine of secession as a final resort tends to impose an overly conservative restriction on secessionists in much the same way that many Anglo segregationists in the U.S., fearful of losing power over African-Americans, sought to hinder freedom's progress for everyone in a then burgeoning democracy. Not unlike civil disobedience and political violence more generally, secession need not be a "last resort" in order for its employment to be morally justified.

APPLICATION OF THE TERRITORIALIST RIGHTS-BASED THEORY OF SECESSION TO THE CASES OF THE U.S. AND CANADA

Considering the moral and legal issues of secession from a Native American perspective sheds a significantly new light on the problem of secession. It exposes, perhaps as never before, the extent to which Native American experiences and rights have been under-appreciated by philosophical accounts of the right of secession. But taking Native American nations seriously casts doubt on claims of existing states to the territories they claim as their own. Furthermore, the fact that no existing state offers its own citizens a constitutional right to secede implies something about the limited seriousness in which they take genuine democracy, construed, among other things, as a regime which respects its citizen individuals and conglomerates in terms of their moral rights to freedom of association and non-association, freedom to remain in or to leave the state.

THE U.S. COLONISTS' SECESSION FROM THE BRITISH EMPIRE AND THE CONFEDERATE ATTEMPT TO SECEDE FROM THE UNION

Once again, in light of the previous considerations, U.S. colonists had no right to secede from the British empire, as neither party had a right to even reside in, much less claim ownership of, any of the territories of the Americas. Only Native American nations did! In turn, the U.S. confederacy did not have a right to secede from the U.S., even if the former were not a slave system. But even if it did have a right to secede, then by parity of reasoning, Native Americans also had a right to secede from both the union and confederacy, and could, moreover, claim as a "trump" *all* (or at least most) of the territory of the Americas as their own, even in light of the Lockean proviso! This would imply that at most confederate states had but a *prima facie* right to secede, one that was clearly overridden by the Native American nations' rights to secede from the U.S. (union and confederate states), claiming (or *re*claiming) their lands in the name of rectificatory

---

[75] See Chapter 2.

justice.[76] Implied here is the claim that the U.S. did not even have a moral right to interfere in the attempted secession of the confederacy, as neither party had a valid moral claim to and/or interest in the lands on which each resided.

It would amount to a self-serving bias to presume that the Lockean proviso was not satisfied in the case of Native American nations, especially in light of the fact that dozens of the hundreds of such nations were nomadic by nature, requiring vast amounts of land on which to reside. To deny that nomadic Native Americans are not entitled to such vast parcels of land requires some ingenious argumentative support (rather than the typical presumptuousness that is pervasive in some philosophical assessments of rights to lands and their resources), as it appears to be yet another self-serving bias in favor of a distinctly Eurocentric manner in which to live. But such presumptuous Eurocentric reasoning must be rejected because it violates the Desideratum of Fairness and Rationality of a Theory of Secession.

QUEBEC, SECESSION, AND THE CREES

Similar conclusions might be reached in the case of Quebec. Quebec has no moral right to secede because it too has no moral right (valid moral claim) to the territory on which it resides – the CREES[77] do! Even if Quebec did have a (*prima facie*) moral right to secede, the Crees would possess a trumping right to claim all of Quebec as their own, or the Crees could simply remain a part of Canada as they have expressed. Like Native American nations under U.S. rule, the Crees, Six Nations, and other Native American nations within Canada would have the right to secede from Canada itself, resulting in a similar sort of dissolution of Canada as we know it.[78] Indeed, the Parti Quebecois' very notion and assertion of Quebec's alleged right to secede from Canada is an arrogant denial of Native American rights to self-determination, ones that trump any interests/claims that the Quebecois might have as the descendants of those living in territory that has never been theirs by valid moral claim. As the French philosopher Jean-Jacques Rousseau

---

[76] Contrast this construal of the events under discussion with that found in Wellman, "A Defense of Secession and Political Self-Determination," pp. 164f.

[77] "The James Bay Crees (Eeyouch) are presently comprised of the Nemaska, Mistissini, Ouje-Bougoumou, Waswanipi, Waskaganish, Whapmagoostui, Chisabi, Wemindji, and Eastman communities of James Bay, Cananda.

The Cree Nation is an organized society and includes approximately 12,000 indigenous people of Cree ancestry. The Grand Council of the Crees is a corporation of the Cree Nation and enjoys consultative status (roster) with the United Nations Economic and Social Council" (Grand Council of the Crees, *Sovereign Injustice*, p. 1).

[78] For a roughly similar view, see Copp, "Democracy and Communal Self-Determination," p. 285.

argues, "It is making fools of people to tell them seriously that one can at one's pleasure transfer people from master to master, like herds of cattle, without consulting their interests or their wishes."[79] Furthermore, the French Declaration of Rights of 1795 states that "Each people is independent and sovereign, whatever the number of individuals who comprise it and the extent of the territory it occupies. This sovereignty is inalienable." These considerations tend to make the Parti Quebecois' assertion of Quebec's right to secede like mere dust in the wind of increasing implausibility as they seek to impose a morally groundless double standard concerning the question of secession in Canada. It appears that the Quebecois' attempt to protect the French language and culture in Quebec by way of seceding from Canada overlooks what French political and legal heritage affirms in the words of one of its most influential political philosophers and France's own 1795 Declaration of Human Rights!

This assessment of the putative right of the Quebecois to secede from Canada differs markedly from Buchanan's.[80] Although he concurs that "the claim of French-speaking Canadians to all of Quebec is also quite problematic because part of that area was similarly gained by conquest from Indians, some of whose descendants are living and can be identified,"[81] Buchanan goes on to support limited secession for Quebec when he asserts that "[t]he Canadian Federation's lack of clear title to Quebec would support secession on grounds of cultural preservation only for those parts of Quebec that are not subject to whatever valid territorial claims existing Indian[sic] groups may have and were not part of the territory ceded to Quebec by the English."[82] However, this assessment of the Parti Quebecois' alleged right to secede runs afoul of condition (2) of the Territorialist Rights-Based Theory of Secession and consequently does not take seriously the rights of the Crees (and certain other indigenous peoples) to the entire territories of Quebec, and even Canada! What Buchanan seems to assume is something at least akin to a moral statute of limitations for Crees' rights to such territories. But as was already argued, such a statute of limitations needs independent argumentative support lest it not satisfy the Desideratum of Fairness and Rationality of a Theory of Secession. As Buchanan himself writes, "Once

---

[79] Quoted in the Grand Council of the Crees, *Sovereign Injustice*, p. 32.

[80] Contrast it also with Wellman, "In Defense of Secession and Self-Determination," pp.165f.

[81] Buchanan, *Secession*, pp. 63-4.

[82] Buchanan, *Secession*, p. 64. A similar view is found in Buchanan, "Self-Determination and the Right to Secede," p. 357. Elsewhere, Buchanan argues that "It is not my aim to argue against Quebec secession . . . the terms of secession must be just, that just terms of secession require a full recognition of the rights of self-determination of native peoples, and that an important element of the exercise of those rights is the equal participation of native peoples in the process by which the terms of secession are negotiated" [Buchanan, "A Reply to Grand Chief Matthew Coon Come and Mr. David Cliché," p. 13].

these complexities are appreciated, one cannot but be struck by the extreme oversimplification with which the issues of Quebec secession are often debated."[83]

OBJECTIONS TO THE TERRITORIALIST RIGHTS-BASED THEORY OF SECESSION, AND REPLIES

Now that there is a new theory of secession before us, it is important to assess its plausibility in light of various and important objections that might be raised against it. There are at least five such objections to the Territorialist Rights-Based (Indiginous) Theory of Secession: the Moral Realism Objection, the Identification of Indigenously Occupied Lands Objection, the Native American Identity Objection, the Proliferation of Indigenous Secession Objection and the Impossibility of Secession Objection. Let us consider each of these concerns in turn.

THE MORAL REALISM OBJECTION

One objection to the Territorialist Rights-Based Theory of Secession might be that it fails to satisfy the Legal Desideratum of a Theory of Secession in that it is not realistic to think that a no-fault model of secession can be dealt with effectively by international law in terms of the no-fault model's posing extreme threats to the territorial sovereignty of states. Buchanan insists that the territorial integrity of existing states be respected. However, this consideration has at best only *prima facie* weight, and then only in circumstances where the existing states have valid moral claims to their territories. Yet recall that Buchanan himself admitted that few, if any, existing states had valid moral claims to their territories due to morally unjust takings, etc. To then insist on the territorial integrity of existing states is excessively conservative, and runs counter to Buchanan's own claims about the fundamental importance of a secessionist group's having a valid moral claim to territory to justify its seceding from the state to which it belongs (i.e., the Territoriality Thesis). For if seceding groups need valid moral claims to and/or valid moral interests in territory, then by parity of reasoning so must states themselves need valid moral claims to and/or valid moral interests in their territorial borders! Thus to the extent that existing states, on Buchanan's own admission, rarely if ever have valid moral claims to and/or valid moral interests in territory, then the objection that the

---

[83] Buchanan, *Secession*, 64. For descriptions of, among other things, the Quebec case of secession which is insensitive to even the existence of the Crees, see Miller, "Secession and the Principle of Nationality;" Paul Piccone, "Secession and Reform in Canada," *Telos*, 106 (1996), pp. 15-63.

Territorialist Rights-Based Theory of Secession, in being a no-fault model, threatens the territorial integrity of existing states seems to fade into implausibility.

However, it might be objected that the Territorialist Rights-Based Theory of Secession, even if sound, is incongruent with Buchanan's criterion of "moral realism" as it pertains to secession and international law. Suppose, it might say, that either the recently formed International War Crimes Tribunal or the International Criminal Court decides that the various Native American nations within U.S. borders are to be granted the right to secede from the U.S., and suppose that each surviving Native American nation decides to claim and exercise its right to secede. The result is that the law passed and decision made by the international community would become inefficacious. What is the point of the tribunal's decreeing it the case that Native American nations have a right to secede from the U.S. if the U.S., presently being the most militarily powerful country in the world, would in all likelihood resist with military force the movements to secede? After all, the U.S. would see its demise if Native American secessionists sought independent statehoods for reasons of securing their respective land regulatory rights or property rights of all of the original land of what is now the U.S.[84] Additionally, secessionist units might well receive from the U.S. (by international tribunal or court order) billions of dollars annually for the thousands of murders committed by the U.S. against Native American nations in the former's genocidal attacks against Native Americans. In order to protect what it construes as its own "right to life," then, the U.S. would in all likelihood resist without defeat the secession attempts supported by the tribunal. Thus the tribunal's decision would be unenforceable.[85]

But to this objection it might be replied, first, that the inefficacy of law fails to demonstrate its ability to serve an expressive function of authoritative disavowal, symbolic non-acquiescence, etc., much as punishment[86] and reparations[87] do. Moreover, the currently combined forces of countries

---

[84] For a distinction between and discussion of various rights that Native American secession might imply, see Buchanan, "The Role of Collective Land Rights in a Theory of Indigenous Peoples' Rights." Moreover, that full recovery of all unjustly taken lands is an "unrealistic goal" is averred in Buchanan, "The Right to Self-Determination: Analytical and Moral Foundations," p. 50.

[85] There is also the concern that an unrestricted right of self-determination might be said to ground an unrestricted right to secede of all ethnic and cultural groups in the U.S. (Buchanan, "The Right to Self-Determination: Analytical and Moral Foundations," pp. 47-8). However, this worry is misplaced since only Native American nations have valid claims to U.S. territories, being the only collectives that can satisfy condition (2).

[86] Joel Feinberg, *Doing and Deserving* (Princeton: Princeton University Press, 1970), Chapter 5.

[87] Corlett, "Reparations to Native Americans?" and *Race, Racism, and Reparations*, Chapter 8.

supportive of the tribunal's or court's decision might include an alliance of countries having sufficient power and willingness to pose a realistic political, military and economic threat to the possible U.S. posture of noncompliance.[88] This would be true, for example, should the tribunal's or court's decision in favor of Native American secession be supported by something like the former Soviet states, China, Japan, Israel, England, Canada, Mexico, and Cuba, for example. Such combined political, military and economic powers could very well force the U.S. to comply with the tribunal's decision to some meaningful extent.[89] Without such conglomerate military and economic support of international law in this case, the U.S. is likely to flaunt the decisions of the international community as it has often done in the past.

Assume, then, that the tribunal's original decision against the U.S. does not receive the necessary support to ensure U.S. compliance. A more realistic decision of the tribunal, or a measure of rectificatory justice that would be more acceptable to the U.S., might be, not the all-out complete claiming of territories of the U.S. by Native American nations (granting Native American nations full property rights to all U.S. territory), but a much more modest claiming of *existing Native American reserves, along with complete sovereignty of Native American nations within their reserves.* This measure, along with billions of dollars of annual (in perpetuity) monetary compensation of Native American nations by the U.S., seems quite challenging but nonetheless workable. Surely a reasonable person would not deny Native American nations *this* severely limited but significant right to secede from the U.S. I say "significant" because it would make Native Americans the sole sovereigns to their own respective territories. Moreover, the tribunal or court would likely impose realistic secession settlement (exit) costs *on the U.S.*, not on Native Americans, as the human rights violations and compensation for lands unjustly acquired by the U.S. from Native

---

[88] Given such circumstances the U.S. is, to use the Rawlsian term, an "outlaw" society (though Rawls himself fails to refer to the U.S. as an outlaw society). And Rawls' words concerning how outlaw societies ought to be dealt with apply:

> For well-ordered peoples to achieve this long-run aim, they should establish institutions and practices to serve as a kind of confederative center and public forum for their common opinion and policy toward non-well-ordered regimes. They can do this within institutions such as the United Nations or by forming separate alliances of well-ordered peoples on certain issues. This confederative center may be used both to formulate and to express the opinion of the well-ordered societies. There they may expose to public view the unjust and cruel institutions of oppressive and expansionist regimes and their violations of human rights (Rawls, *The Law of Peoples*, p. 93).

[89] This proposal is consistent with what Rawls argues: ". . . Gradually over time, then, well-ordered peoples may pressure the outlaw regimes to change their ways; but by itself this pressure is unlikely to be effective. It may need to be backed up by the firm denial of economic and other assistance, or the refusal to admit outlaw regimes as members in good standing in mutually beneficial cooperative practices" (Rawls, *The Law of Peoples*, p. 93).

Americans inflicted on great numbers of Native Americans by the U.S. would justify an *in perpetuity* settlement of billions of dollars annually. This fails to compensate adequately Native Americans for the fair market values of their respective lands, or for the fullness of the human rights violations against their forebears by the U.S. (for deserved punitive damages are not considered here as part of what the U.S. owes to Native American nations). But such a conservative settlement offer does make it more difficult for a reasonable person to argue that the more modest proposal for a secession settlement runs afoul of the concern for moral realism in secession undertakings. Yet it is a significantly high price for the U.S. to pay annually. To this settlement of complete sovereignty of existing Native American reserves and billions of dollars dispersed to them as a conglomerate annually might be added, by order of the tribunal, the cost to the U.S. of United Nations military installations around each reserve to protect the Native Americans from U.S. interference (This measure is justified given the lengthy history of illicit U.S. interference with Native American nations even until today). And this provision might be backed by the credible threat of significant international economic sanctions against the U.S.

It might be objected that the added cost to the U.S. of such U.N. military installations (along with significant international economic sanctions) is unrealistic and in violation of Lon Fuller's sixth rule of the "internal morality of law:" "To command what cannot be done is not to make law; it is to unmake law, for a command that cannot be obeyed serves no end but confusion, fear and chaos."[90] More philosophically, even the proposed mitigated secession settlement of the tribunal faces the "'ought' implies 'can'" problem. If it is, practically speaking, impossible for the U.S. to survive in living up to the tribunal's decision, then morality does not seem to support the conclusion that the secession settlement under consideration is required, or even justified.[91]

In light of these considerations, it might be argued that the gaining of total sovereignty rights of Native American nations to their existing reserve lands, along with payments by the U.S. to Native American nations in the billions of dollars per year in perpetuity, backed by the sincere and promised *threats* of U.N. military intervention and international economic sanctions against the U.S. on behalf of Native Americans should the U.S. default on its secession settlement or pose a realistic threat to Native Americans, would sufficiently enrich the lives of Native Americans economically that the various nations could (if they so chose) to purchase military protection (in

---

[90] Lon Fuller, "Eight Ways to Fail to Make Law," in Joel Feinberg and Hyman Gross, Editors, *Philosophy of Law*, Fifth Edition (Belmont, Wadsworth Publishing Company, 1995), p. 89.
[91] A version of the violation of the "'ought' implies 'can'" problem as it applies to secession is found in Moellendorf, "Liberalism, Nationalism, and the Right to Secede," p. 95.

the forms of troops, weaponry, etc.) in order to protect themselves from what has for the past two centuries been their most oppressive source. Thus with complete Native American sovereignty comes also economic ability to both secure a stable future for Native America – and all within U.S. borders.[92] This further mitigated proposal for a secession settlement seems rather practicable, even if it fails to serve the interests of strict retributive justice for Native American nations according to which compensation is paid in (rough) proportion to the cumulative harms committed against Native American nations by the U.S.

Thus even if Native American secession claiming all lands of the U.S. in the name of rectificatory justice is morally justified according to strict justice but falls prey to the moral realism criterion of secession, and even if U.S. financing of U.N. military presence along borders of Native American reserves (along with international economic sanctions against the U.S.) is too costly for the U.S. to afford, then the mitigated proposal of billions of dollars of annual compensation (in perpetuity) and total Native American sovereignty of existing reserves seems quite workable, supported by the viable threats of U.N. military intervention and international economic sanctions against the U.S. for noncompliance.[93]

Yet the implications of even the modest proposal for the Native American right to secede from the U.S. are staggering. To be sure, it would be costly enough for the U.S. citizens to compensate Native American nations as stated, and the complete territorial sovereignty of Native American reserves, coupled with the fact that such sovereignty would make Native Americans (due to their wealth) not very dependent on the U.S., means that the U.S. must somehow be ready to defend itself militarily from within its borders as well as from perceived or actual enemies external to its

---

[92] This proposal is intended to address Buchanan's concern that "Nor should it be assumed that full sovereignty is either feasible or desirable for the native peoples [the Crees]. For one thing, independent statehood for a very small population is a hindrance to positive self-determination in a world economy in which only large scale political units have a chance at survival" (Buchanan, "Quebec, Secession and Aboriginal Territorial Rights," p. 3). In reply to Buchanan's assertion, it might be pointed out that his claim rests on a notion of "survival" that is economic in character. Yet there are certainly other ways of surviving – even flourishing – without becoming a global economic power. The Diné Nation, Six Nations, First Nation and others survived for *centuries* rather well without becoming global economic powers (and causing untold environmental destruction as global economic powers tend to do). Yet each is a rather small nation of indigenous people(s).
[93] Note that recent and current harms to existing Native American nations are not included here. For a discussion of some such harms, see Ward Churchill, *Struggle for the Land* (Monroe: Courage Press, 1993), pp. 261-328; Ward Churchill, Editor, *Critical Issues in Native North America, Volumes 1-2* (Copenhagen, 1988-91).

outermost borders.[94] This too is likely to drive the U.S. to its economic knees.

Now in light of this significantly high economic probability, it might be argued that even the proposed modest secession settlement falls prey to the "'ought' implies 'can'" problem, and hence must be further reduced in size or amount and impact on the U.S. in order to comply with "morally realistic demands of justice." A utilitarian might add that severely crippling the U.S. in a secession settlement is likely to have tremendously damaging effects on the global economy, thereby harming unjustly third parties.

But there is another proposal that seems to take precisely this sort of consideration into account. That suggestion for the restoration of lands to Native Americans is called the *"Buffalo Commons"* proposal. This proposal allows not for monetary compensation for crimes, torts and contract violations against Native Americans by the U.S. Nor does it seeks complete restoration of all lands of the U.S. Rather, it seeks the partial but significant restoration of lands to Native Americans, lands that have, it is argued, never played an important role in the economic viability of the U.S. Thus the restoring of such lands to Native Americans would pose no real threat to the U.S. economy:

> . . . What you end up with is a huge territory lying east of Denver, west of Lawrence, Kansas, and extending from the Canadian border to southern Texas, all of it "outside the loop" of United States business as usual.
>
> The bulk of this area is unceded territory owned by the Lakota, Pawnee, Arikara, Hidatsa, Crow, Shoshone, Assiniboine, Cheyenne, Arapaho, Kiowa, Comanche, Jicarilla, and Mescalero Apache nations. There would be little cost to the United States, and virtually no arbitrary dispossession or dislocation of non-Indians, if the entire Commons were restored to these peoples.[95]

The reasons given in favor of the Buffalo Commons proposal are twofold. First, it provides Native Americans with a means of tangible self-determination. Secondly, it provides "alternative socioeconomic models" for possible adaptation by those who are not Native Americans.

Now the Buffalo Commons proposal for the restoration of lands to Native Americans can serve as a model for Native American secession. For instead of arguing for the claiming of all U.S. lands and resources in the name of strict justice, and instead of demanding a secession settlement from the U.S. which would render the U.S. non-viable as a country, a certain area of land with its resources can be claimed in secession by a coalition of

---

[94] Assumed here, of course, is the perpetual political paranoia exhibited by the U.S. government and citizenry concerning what they perceive as a threat to their own security and capital interests, and their fear of political units over which they can have no legitimate control.

[95] Ward Churchill, *From a Native Son* (Boston: South End Press, 1996), p. 529.

Native American nations, lands and their resources that have never played an important role in the U.S. economy. Thus Native Americans claiming them as their own in seceding from the U.S. would seem to pose no serious economic threat to the U.S., evading previous concerns with other more stringent proposals for Native American secession.

Moreover, before the "'ought' implies 'can'" argument reduces the problem (for the U.S.) of Native American secession to a compensation of convenience *for the U.S.*, it must be recognized that the U.S. and its citizenry have always been on land to/in which it (they) has (have) no valid moral claim and/or valid moral interest. And unless and until morality dictates that oppressive countries have valid claims to the territories of their oppressed subjects, it must not be presumed, or even assumed, that such oppressive countries have rights to life. In light of morality's demand for adequate justice to Native Americans, caution must be exerted that Native American rights are yet again overridden in the name of the alleged rights of the citizens of the country the incessant evils of which are precisely and largely causally responsible for the very problem of rectificatory justice of which is currently spoken. We must remain ever mindful of Immanuel Kant's claim that ". . . if justice goes, there is no longer any value in human beings' living on the earth."[96]

One must bear in mind that, not only has the proposal of only mildly strict retributive (and proportional) justice been twice modified (and then further by the Buffalo Commons proposal), but none of the above proposals even hint at compensation by the U.S. to Native American nations for *fair market value of the lands* unjustly taken by the U.S. from Native American nations. Nor do they involve provisions for compensation for *punitive damages* for the repeated U.S. refusal to recognize its need to bring itself to justice for its crimes against humanity. Nor do the proposals invoke provisions for monies paid for U.S. illegal land use during the past two centuries. In light of these sobering considerations, it seems appalling that the Buffalo Commons proposal for a secession settlement would be met with skepticism insofar as its being allegedly overly stringent on the U.S. Thus the Moral Realism Objection against the Territorialist Rights-Based Theory of Secession is not telling. It seems to be satisfied only in instances of rather inadequate secession settlements that are convenient for the U.S.

---

[96] Immanuel Kant, *The Metaphysics of Morals*, Mary Gregor, Translator (Indianapolis: Hackett Publishing Company, 1996), 6: p. 332.

THE IDENTIFICATION OF INDIGENOUSLY OCCUPIED LANDS OBJECTION

It might be argued that not even something like the Buffalo Commons proposal is justified because it is not possible to identify, for every acre of land unjustly acquired from Native Americans by the U.S. and its citizens, precisely which lands belonged to which Native American nations, many of which have been completely annihilated by the U.S. and cannot resettle their territories. Thus there seems to be no manner in which to decide to which Native American nation to award lands and resources, or even compensatory damages. This daunting difficulty suggests, it might be added, the impracticality of the said proposal for a legal system.

In reply to this objection, it might be argued that even if it turned out that *no* Native American nation could be correctly identified as the legitimate occupiers of land taken from them by the U.S., it hardly follows that the *U.S.* has *any* valid moral claim to *any* territories in the Americas, especially given its record of human rights violations. This would undercut *any* U.S. or U.S. constituent claim to such territory and secession based on it.

Moreover, extensive historical evidence (based on both U.S. civilian and military archives, Native American records, etc.) is clear in several cases as to which Native American nations occupied which territories, or ranges of territories in cases of nomadic nations, making the task of remedies or compensation manageable for a legal system. Where such remedies are considerably more complex, class action suits can receive remedies for coalitions of Native American nations.

Furthermore, it is unclear that what might be called the Identification of Indigenously Occupied Lands Objection is telling against the twice modified proposals outlined above. For those proposals simply state that existing boundaries of Native American reserves be taken as guidelines for the secessional borders of the Native American reserves. Thus on those proposals for Native American secession there is no need to decide the historical boundaries of each Native American nation. Thus the objection misses the point entirely. It is relevant only if the proposal were that Native American nations were to claim their respective historical territories as their own.

Thus the Identification of Indigenously Occupied Lands Objection is not telling, especially given the established records of U.S. conquests of such territories. Not unlike the Nazis who kept records of their genocidal acts, the U.S. military kept records of which Native American nations against which it conducted a holocaust. Oftentimes details of the most barbarous evils are given by U.S. soldiers who seemed to be proud of their deeds.[97]

THE NATIVE AMERICAN IDENTITY OBJECTION

Another concern with the Territorialist Rights-Based (Indigenous) Theory of Secession might be that there is a reasonable skepticism regarding the way in which Native Americans can be identified, thus making any secession settlement to Native American nations morally arbitrary in that some beneficiaries of the settlement might not be properly counted among some Native American nation. What is needed is an adequate way by which to identify members of Native American nations so as to reduce this moral arbitrariness.

In reply to this concern, it must be pointed out that the concern for moral arbitrariness and identity of membership faces any theory of secession, just as it faces any views of affirmative action and reparations. Nonetheless, it must be pointed out that there are analyses of ethnic identity[98] that purport to provide ways of dealing with this difficulty. And that Native Americans comprise a cluster of ethnic groups is not in question. Nonetheless, beyond the philosophical analyses of ethnic identity lies a history of the U.S. government's employing varying standards of percentages of ethnic identification (based on blood ties to what the government perceived as being necessary and sufficient for ones being a Native American) to various Native American nations for legal/public policy purposes. This failure of consistency on the part of the U.S. government has

---

[97] For historical accounts of some of the U.S. holocaust of Native American nations, see William L. Anderson, Editor, *Cherokee Removal* (Athens: University of Georgia Press, 1991); Garrick Bailey and Roberta Glenn Bailey, *A History of the Navajos* (Santa Fe: School of American Research Press, 1986); Robert Berkhofer, Jr., *Salvation and the Savage* (New York: Athenum, 1965); Dee Brown, *Bury My Heart at Wounded Knee* (New York: Henry Holt and Company, 1970); Angie Debo, *A History of Indians in the United States* (Norman: University of Oklahoma Press, 1970); *And Still the Waters Run* (Norman: University of Oklahoma Press, 1989); Dougherty, *To Steal a Kingdom: Probing Hawai'ian History*; John Ehle, *Trail of Tears* (New York: Anchor Books, 1988); Grant Foreman, *Indian Removal* (Norman: University of Oklahoma Press, 1932); Michael D. Green, *The Politics of Indian Removal* (Lincoln: University of Nebraska Press, 1982); Robert V. Remini, *The Legacy of Andrew Jackson* (Baton Rouge: Louisiana State University Press, 1988); David E. Stannard, *American Holocaust* (Oxford: Oxford University Press, 1992); Ian K. Steele, *Warpaths* (Oxford: Oxford University Press, 1994); Clifford E. Trafzer, *The Kit Carsen Campaign* (Norman: University of Oklahoma Press, 1982); Peter H. Wood, Gregory A. Waselkov and M. Thomas Hatley, Editors, *Powhatan's Mantle* (Lincoln: University of Nebraska Press, 1989); Grace Steele Woodward, *The Cherokees* (Norman: University of Oklahoma Press, 1963).
[98] Corlett, "Latino Identity;" "Latino Identity and Affirmative Action;" *Race, Racism, and Reparations*, Chapters 2, 3, and 7; Gracia, *Hispanic/Latino Identity*.

led to a number of problems within and between Native American nations.[99] Thus the Native American Identity Objection does not pose an insurmountable obstacle to the Territorialist Rights-Based Theory of Secession.

However, even if it is too Herculean a task to provide a plausible account of ethnic or collective identity for purposes of the law pertaining to secession,[100] a subjective account might be adequate in a state's acknowledging the desire for independence of one of its constituent collectives.[101] Although an adequate analysis of collective identity is important, it is not obvious that the want of one prohibits a state's ability to recognize either historic or newly formed collectives within its own borders that are seeking justified independence from its rule.

THE PROLIFERATION OF INDIGENOUS SECESSIONIST
MOVEMENTS OBJECTION

Yet another concern with the Territorialist Rights-Based (Indigenous) Theory of Secession might be that, if constitutionalized in national and international laws, it would lead to a proliferation of indigenous secessionist movements globally. This would in turn lead to the dissolution of states such as, not only the U.S., but Brasil, Canada, Mexico, South Africa, Australia, and many other existing states. The chaos that would result is unimaginable, and the result would likely be a state of nature among secessionist states and the respective states from which they secede.

In reply to this concern, it must be acknowledged that the *un*warranted proliferation of secessionist movements among indigenous peoples globally is certainly a problem, and international law ought to prohibit or discourage such movements. However, to the extent that indigenous claims to secede are valid is the extent to which such claims ought to be recognized, and supported by international law, even if it means the dissolution of existing states and *en masse*. Nonetheless, just as in the case of Native American nations in the U.S., a significantly modified version of something akin to strict proportional retributive justice is likely to be quite workable in such cases of global indigenous secessions. In such cases, in other words, each indigenous conglomerate might claim its existing territory along with total sovereignty over it, coupled with significant monetary compensation by its current state (i.e., in cases similar to Native Americans in the U.S.). The significance that such secessionist movements would have on respective

---

[99] M. Annette Jaimes, "Federal Indian Identification Policy: A Usurpation of Indigenous Sovereignty in North America," in Jaimes, Editor, *The State of Native America*, pp. 123-38.
[100] Buchanan, *Secession*, p. 49.
[101] Philpott, "In Defense of Self-Determination," p. 365.

national and global economies cannot be *over*estimated. But the harms of
those governments that would then pay compensation and relinquish control
over their conquered indigenous should not be *under*estimated. Thus
moderate compensation and granting of total sovereignty over existing
indigenous territories to indigenous peoples might well serve the
practicalities of retributive justice globally as it would in the cases of the
U.S. and Native American nations within its borders. So the Proliferation of
Indigenous Secessionist Movements Objection ought not to embarrass the
Territorialist Rights-Based Theory of Secession. What is truly embarrassing,
on moral grounds, is the very thought that indigenous peoples who have
valid claims to territory would in some way need to even contemplate for an
instant their *not* being justified in exercising their valid claims to territory by
way of secession, especially from existing oppressive states.[102]

THE IMPOSSIBILITY OF SECESSION OBJECTION

Finally, it might be argued that if the Territorialist Rights-Based
(Indigenous) Theory of Secession fails to proliferate secessions unjustifiably,
then it would follow from its construal of condition (2) that certain kinds of
cases of morally justified secession would be made impossible because those
seeking secession from, say, severe injustice, are not indigenous peoples and
only indigenous peoples have valid claims to territories. Yet this result
seems counter-intuitive, as we would think that under such conditions of
severe injustice secession is justified as long as conditions (1)-(3) obtain.

In reply to this concern, it should be noted first that the objection admits
that the Territorialist Rights-Based Theory of Secession hardly proliferates
secessionist movements unwarrantedly, as the previous objection suggests.
Moreover, even if no secessionist movements were justified because, say, no
indigenous peoples exist, it would not logically follow that no means of
political independence from oppression and tyranny are available to the
conglomerate. Revolution is a possibility in some cases even where
secession is not. Also, in instances where secessionist groups occupy lands
that were acquired justly, say, from indigenous peoples, a right to secede

---

[102] Those who favor a less desert-based and a more utilitarian-based reply to the objection at
hand might find more concurrent with Thomas Pogge's reply that once the backlog of
collectives seeking self-determination has been "worked down, . . . there may not be much
redressing activity as people will then be content with their political memberships, and most
borders will be supported by stable majorities" (Pogge, "Cosmopolitanism and Sovereignty,"
p. 70). Another perspective on this matter is that, though currently stable Native American
nations such as the Diné nation, the Lakota nation, and some others might well seek secession
from the U.S., other less viable Native American nations would "probably choose some type
of autonomy or federation with existing states, preserving rights to internal self-governance
and control as members of a larger state" (Morris, "International Law and Politics: Toward a
Right to Self-Determination for Indigenous Peoples," p. 79).

might be said to accrue to secessionists as long as conditions (1) and (3) also obtain.

However, the Territorialist Rights-Based Theory of Secession need not insist that only indigenous peoples can satisfy condition (2), except in the aforementioned instances. For it might hold that *just* conglomerates acquire valid claims to territories previously occupied by indigenous peoples, where the latter no longer exist and cannot claim their rights to occupy such territories, or where such territories are genuinely ceded to such non-indigenous peoples. But even in such cases, the U.S. would *not* have a valid claim to the land on which it resides. Should the U.S. and Native Americans no longer exist, then perhaps a morally *just* conglomerate *might* acquire a valid claim or occupancy to such lands.

Thus the Territorialist Rights-Based Theory of Secession does not fall prey to the Impossibility of Secession Objection. It would seem, then, that neither the Moral Realism Objection, the Identification of Indigenously Occupied Lands Objection, the Native American Identity Objection, the Proliferation of Indigenous Secession Objection, nor the Impossibility of Secession Objection poses a daunting challenge to the Territorialist Rights-Based Theory of Secession. Perhaps there are more plausible objections to the theory proposed herein. If so, then they ought to be registered and given our attention. If no such objections exist, then it behooves us to commence taking more seriously the rights of Native American nations in analyzing secession.

In sum, I have provided a theory of secession that satisfies each of the above desiderata of a theory of secession. The Territorialist Rights-Based (Indigenous) Theory of Secession adopts a standard definition of "secession," thereby satisfying the Definitional Desideratum of a Theory of Secession. It also argues that secession of colonized Native American nations is justified, something which is consistent with international law, and it seeks to influence constructively the law as is pertains to secession, thereby satisfying the Legal Desideratum of Secession. The Territorialist Rights-Based Theory of Secession seeks to avoid problems of secession arising out of rights to land and resources, and there appears to be no reason to believe that the problem of perverse incentives is a special difficulty for the theory. Thus the Territorialist Rights-Based Theory of Secession satisfies the Moral Desideratum of a Theory of Secession. Moreover, it recognizes and remains true to the distinction between legal and moral questions of secession, thereby satisfying the Desideratum of Clarification of a Theory of Secession. Finally, the Territorialist Rights-Based Theory of Secession satisfies the Desideratum of Fairness and Rationality of a Theory of Secession by insisting on, among other things, on the generalization of the conditions set forth and defended for the morality and constitutionality of secession.

I have explained the ways in which the Territorialist Rights-Based Theory of Secession differs from other leading theories of secession. One such way is that it more than any other theory of secession takes Native American valid claims to secede with unbiased seriousness, not limiting the Native American rights to secede by way of biased reasoning or reworking proposals for compensation to Native American nations to ones of convenience for the U.S. or other colonial powers. It also supports a no-fault model of secession, and grounds the right of Native American nations to secede primarily in their valid claims to territories in the name of rectificatory justice.[103] Even if total sovereignty and claiming of *all* lands of the U.S. is unrealistic, valid claims to total sovereignty of existing reserve territories (or to the Buffalo Commons territories, absent the monetary compensation) and significant amounts of monetary compensation to Native American nations by the U.S. in perpetuity seem to be workable, even if the costs of such a Secession Settlement forces U.S. citizens and their government to alter their ways of being to accommodate a significantly more costly lifestyle. This newly imposed restrictive lifestyle is the direct result of the *U.S.'s own injustices* of immeasurable proportions against Native Americans during the past two centuries, and would be imposed, it is assumed, with the support of cumulative military and economic powers, by the newly formed International War Crimes Tribunal and International Criminal Court.

There are, of course, numerous important questions about secession that remain. Practically speaking, does not the Territorialist Rights-Based Theory of Secession imply or make room for compensation to Native American nations by countries other than the U.S. that unjustly took lands and lives from Native Americans? This would include the Dutch, the British, the Spanish, and the French, among others. Would not history tell us that a Native American secession would include, not only a Secession Settlement from the U.S., but ones from those other European governments as well? Moreover, what should be said of the proposal that some have regarding African American secession? If such a right to secede is justified by morality and workable in law, then what implications might this have? Might this lead to the "balkanization" of not only the U.S., but of several other countries? Might the implications therein serve as a *reductio ad absurdum* of the position defended herein? Or, rather, is it possible that the problems of secession serve as a constant reminder of the deeper levels at which political philosophy must delve? Might we not need to arduously challenge and cease

---

[103] Note that nothing in my argument even hints that Native American nations *as such* have rights to secede, morally speaking. For arguments against the idea that nations *as such* have such rights, see Buchanan, "What's So Special About Nations?"

taking for granted certain assumptions about what is deemed political liberalism or what counts as a legitimate political regime?

What is clearer than ever before, I believe, is that adopting a Native American (or, more broadly, an indigenous) perspective in political philosophy challenges political philosophy to take seriously historic injustices to the extent that contemporary states require moral evaluation of an undauntingly and increasingly objective kind. Furthermore, "An important part of the morally relevant historical reality is the ignoble story of violence, conquest, deceit, theft, and broken promises and treaties with which we are all familiar. It is not sufficient to assume that we are all equal citizens and then move further from reality by treating individuals abstractly as members of a culture."[104] What is likely to follow from this new perspective on secession is a renewed or newfound respect for the injustices of the past, their need of adequate, albeit approximate, rectification, and what that rectification implies for those who have based their entire lives, knowingly or not, on the egocentric and ethnocentric presumption of self-preservation and happiness at the deadly costs to others.

It is correct to state that theorizing about secession provides us with a fresh and valuable perspective on political philosophy, revealing inadequacies in traditional approaches to political thought.[105] But I would add that adequate theorizing about secession demands that indigenous experiences and rights be taken seriously, absent anti-indigenous biases and *ad hoc* statutes of limitations on the extent to which such experiences and rights ought to be respected. When indigenous experiences and rights are given their proper consideration, it is likely that both ideal and non-ideal political philosophy will be shaken, perhaps as never before, at their foundations. The hope is that the foundations of political philosophy will, despite the shaking of its assumptions exclusive of indigenous experiences and rights, recover with an unbridled commitment to a more extensive and deeper analysis of truth and justice. When this occurs, then it will be acknowledged that "Ultimately, it is the people of any society that demand accountability and compel its government to act fairly and respectfully towards the rights of others."[106]

Now that the nature and moral justification of secession has been discussed, I now turn to a discussion of the nature and moral status of another salient form of political violence: terrorism.

---

[104] Danley, "Liberalism, Aboriginal Rights, and Cultural Minorities," p. 182.
[105] Buchanan, *Secession*, p. 7.
[106] Grand Council of the Crees, *Sovereign Injustice*, p. 6.

CHAPTER 5

CAN TERRORISM *EVER* BE MORALLY JUSTIFIED?

It is disappointing that much of what has been written that purports to deal with terrorism ends up not pertaining to terrorism at all, but only to particular forms of violent activity–either state[1] or individual. Perhaps this is due at least in part to writers not devoting sufficient attention to the exploration of the definitional conditions of terrorism. For example, in Leon Trotsky's work, *Terrorism and Communism*,[2] "terrorism" is not defined. Nor is terrorist activity contrasted with other significant forms of violence such as revolution, assassination, etc.[3] Although Trotsky argues that the communist revolution does not "logically" require the revolutionaries' employment of terrorism, it does require that any means necessary are to be used to secure revolutionary power, even by terrorism.[4] Terrorism, for Trotsky, is a form of justified violence[5] when it is a matter of self-defense[6] and is an act of intimidation[7] by revolutionary forces against an oppressive state:

> If human life in general is sacred and inviolable, we must deny ourselves not only the use of terror, not only war, but also revolution itself. . . . As long as human labor power, and, consequently, life itself, remain articles of sale and purchase, of exploitation and robbery, the principle of the "sacredness of

---

[1] For an interesting and informative discussion of state terrorism, see Jonathan Glover, "State Terrorism," in R. G. Frey and Christopher Morris, Editors, *Violence, Terrorism, and Justice* (Cambridge: Cambridge University Press, 1991), pp. 256-75.
[2] Leon Trotsky, *Terrorism and Communism* (Ann Arbor: University of Michigan Press, 1961). This work was originally published in the United States as *Dictatorship vs. Democracy* and in Great Britain as *The Defence of Terrorism*.
[3] Even though Trotsky, in his 1935 Preface to the Second English Edition, admits that it was the Editor's idea to include "terrorism" in the book's title, and that Trotsky's own concern is "not at all the defence of 'terrorism' as such," it leads to much confusion when he devotes an entire chapter to terrorism without either defining it or providing its justification (moral or otherwise).
[4] Trotsky, *Terrorism and Communism*, p. 58; Walter Laqueur, *Terrorism* (Boston: Little, Brown and Company, 1977), pp. 67-8.
[5] Trotsky, *Terrorism and Communism*, pp. 58-9.
[6] Trotsky, *Terrorism and Communism*, p. 62.
[7] Trotsky, *Terrorism and Communism*, p. 58.

human life" remains a shameful lie, uttered with the object of keeping the oppressed slaves in their chains.

. . . To make the individual sacred we must destroy the social order which crucifies him. And this problem can only be solved by blood and iron.[8]

This is as close to a definition of "terrorism" as Trotsky comes, though this lack of precision should not surprise us since Trotsky penned it on a military train during civil war–hardly ideal conditions for a record of his considered judgments on such a volatile issue! Although there seems to be no textual evidence that Karl Marx ever endorsed terrorism, there is also a lack of such evidence that he rejected it *tout court*.

Some writers seem to write of terrorism in a confusing or ambiguous way due at least in part to their failure to become attentive to the problem of carefully defining "terrorism." Others, however, sneak into the very definition of "terrorism" that which (by the lights of most) would clearly condemn any instance of terrorism, morally speaking.

My task in this chapter is to explore some philosophical conceptions of terrorism and work toward what I think is the best working definition of "terrorism." I do this in light of the fact that Walter Laqueur asserts that "no definition of terrorism can possibly cover all the varieties of terrorism that have appeared throughout history."[9] However, this is a strange claim since we must have an adequate definition of the term to begin with to know whether or not a proposed definition of the term includes all species of terrorism in history! With this sort of reasoning it is no wonder that Laqueur claims (at the *outset* of his book) that it is a "hopeless undertaking" to provide a "general theory" of political terrorism.[10] Worst still is his more recent insistence that "Such a definition does not exist nor will it be found in the foreseeable future. To argue that terrorism cannot be studied until such a definition exists is manifestly absurd."[11] However, the confusion inherent in Laqueur's words here becomes apparent when one understands that even if it were supposed that Laqueur were correct in his assertion (totally unsupported as it stands) that an adequate definition of "terrorism" does not exist, it surely does not follow logically that it cannot be "found" in the future! For this claim to have even a semblance of plausibility on logical grounds, it would have to be *shown* that such a definition is conceptually absurd, or impossible. Yet neither Laqueur nor anyone else of whom I am aware has done anything whatsoever to demonstrate that it is *impossible* to adequately define "terrorism." In fact, Laqueur has not even performed the

---

[8] Trotsky, *Terrorism and Communism*, pp. 62-3.

[9] Laqueur, *Terrorism*, p. 7.

[10] Laqueur, *Terrorism*, p. 6.

[11] Walter Laqueur, *A History of Terrorism* (New Brunswick: Transaction Publishers, 2002), p. 5.

Herculean task of demonstrating the problematic nature of proposed definitions of "terrorism," a task that he owes his readers if his claim that no such (adequate) definition exists is not to be construed as being premature, or simply naïve. Furthermore, Laqueur's claim that "terrorism cannot be studied until such a definition exists is manifestly absurd" is itself problematic in that if one does not have an adequate working definition of the nature of terrorism, then one's construal of terrorism will be replete with confusions about which acts of political violence amount to terrorism, and which ones do not. This will inevitably lead to the conflation of various acts of political violence, and an arbitrary categorization of certain acts under the rubric of terrorism, while others are arbitrarily classified under other categories.

Despite Laqueur's unfounded pessimism regarding a definition and theory of terrorism, I shall undertake to set forth a philosophical foundation of a theory of terrorism by: providing a working philosophical definition of "terrorism;" providing moral justificatory conditions for the employment of terrorist activity; stating the possible role of terrorism in society; and assessing some important philosophical objections to any view of terrorism which argues that terrorism is sometimes morally justified. By "morally justified" and its cognates, I mean "morally permitted or warranted, supported by the balance of human reason." I mean that the weight of moral reasons in favor of the employment of terrorism at a given time and in a given circumstance outweighs the moral reasons against the use of terrorism at that time and in that circumstance. Furthermore, as stated in the "Introduction," I mean to imply that if a particular act of terrorism is morally justified, then there is a moral right to the terrorism, implying in turn a moral duty of others to not interfere with those whose right it is to commit the terrorist act.

THE NATURE OF TERRORISM

It is crucial to separate three important philosophical problems about terrorism.[12] The first is the problem of the *nature* of terrorism. The second

---

[12] There is some recognition that the questions of the definition of "terrorism" and its justification need to be considered separately. For example, Virginia Held states that the definitional question is often confused with the matter of the *legal* justification of terrorism as a practice of political change [Virginia Held, "Terrorism, Rights, and Political Goals," in R. G. Frey and Christopher Morris, Editors, *Violence, Terrorism, and Justice* (Cambridge: Cambridge University Press, 1991), p. 59]. But this is not the same as pointing to the conflating of the questions of the definition of "terrorism" and its *moral* justification, as I argue. Moreover, R. G. Frey and Christopher Morris recognize that there exist two such separate questions, but they state that "they are hard to separate" (Frey and Morris, *Violence, Terrorism, and Justice*, p. 1). They do not, however, *insist* that the two questions be separated as a matter of analyzing terrorism, as I do. Finally, Terrence L. Moore argues that if we

concerns the *moral justification* of terrorism. The third concerns the possible *role* of terrorism. Some philosophers confuse these problems in their respective attempts to discuss terrorism. They do not see that the nature of terrorism and what makes it morally justified (or not) are different matters. For example, C. A. J. Coady writes,

> What is the lesson of this digression for our discussion of terrorism and revolutionary violence? Surely this, that we should continue to make a distinction between two broad types of revolutionary violence, that which is directed at what would be legitimate targets if the revolution were justified and that which is directed at non-combatants. We should reserve the term "terrorism" only for the latter and it can be unequivocally condemned.[13]

It is unsurprising, then, that such thinkers do not even consider the possible (positive) role of terrorism. For on their accounts, terrorism essentially involves harming innocent persons. For, "targeting of the innocent is the essential trait of terrorism, both conceptually and morally."[14] Yet this targeting of the innocent violates the fundamental moral intuition that innocent persons ought not to be targets or victims of violent physical attack.[15] How, then, can it be morally justified?[16] What possible role can terrorism have in society besides a negative one?

---

construe "terrorism" as by definition immoral, then inevitable disagreements about the morality of terrorism will surely lead to disagreements about what in fact terrorism amounts to [Terrence L. Moore, "The Nature and Evaluation of Terrorism," Ph.D. dissertation, University of Pittsburgh, 1987, p. 59]. My point, of course, is not simply that sneaking the harming of non-combatants or innocents into the definition of "terrorism" leads to further disagreements in discussing terrorism, but that doing so *begs the moral question* against terrorism. This point is recognized by G. Wallace. However, while Wallace attempts to avoid the problem of conflating the nature and justification of terrorism by "doing without a formal definition of terrorism," [G. Wallace, "Terrorism and the Argument From Analogy," *International Journal of Moral and Social Issues*, 6 (1991), p. 150], I set forth and explicate a definition of "terrorism" in distinguishing the questions of the nature, moral justification, and possible role of terrorism.

[13] C. A. J. Coady, "The Morality of Terrorism," *Philosophy*, 60 (1985), p. 65.

[14] Igor Primoratz, "What is Terrorism?" *Journal of Applied Philosophy*, 7 (1990), p. 133. It is noteworthy that in his critique of Igor Primoratz's definition of "terrorism," Walter Sinnott-Armstrong does not challenge Primoratz's idea that targeting the innocent is essential to terrorism [Walter Sinnott-Armstrong, "On Primoratz's Definition of Terrorism," *Journal of Applied Philosophy*, 8 (1991), pp. 115-120]. For another critique of Primoratz's definition of "terrorism," see Tony Dardis, "Primoratz on Terrorism," *Journal of Applied Philosophy*, 9 (1992), pp. 93-97.

[15] Michael Walzer, *Just and Unjust Wars* (Harmondsworth: Penguin Books, 1980), p. 145. Held argues that not only has ordinary language use wreaked havoc in defining the nature of terrorism, but it has also tended to build into such definitions of terrorism a moral (pre)judgment against it. Such biases make it impossible to even question, philosophically, whether or not terrorism can ever be morally justified. Even thinkers as well respected as Michael Walzer have assumed that terrorism is morally wrong without offering arguments against its immorality (See Held, "Terrorism, Rights, and Political Goals," p. 65).

Terrorism has been understood in a variety of ways:

(a) "A political act, ordinarily committed by an organized group, which involves the intentional killing or other severe harming of non-combatants or the threat of the same or intentional severe damage to the property of non-combatants or the threat of the same."[17]

(b) "The expression of disdain for the institutions of civil society in general and, specifically, for the goal of limiting the practice of violence."[18]

(c) "A political action or sequence of actions. . . . to inspire the 'target' population with terror, by means of random acts of violence. . ."[19]

(d) A terrifying act which is used to coerce with the threat of great harm of one or more persons if the threat is not heeded.[20]

(e) "Terrorism is the use of coercive means aimed at civilian populations in an effort to achieve political, religious, or other aims."[21]

The difficulty with these conceptions of terrorism is that they unwarrantedly sneak into the construal of terrorism (by implication or more directly) a feature which is obviously (by the lights of most) either morally problematic or unjustified. "Harming of non-combatants" in (a), "disdain, . . . for . . . limiting . . . violence" in (b), "random acts of violence" in (c), the vagueness of the referent of "persons" in (d) [as well as the fact that (d) does not

---

[16] Another position against the moral justification of terrorism is articulated in Haig Khatchadourian, "Terrorism and Morality," *Journal of Applied Philosophy*, 5 (1988), pp. 131-45; *The Morality of Terrorism* (New York: Peter Lang Publishing, 1998), Chapters 2-4. It is noteworthy, however, that even if intentionally harming innocent persons turns out to be essential to terrorism, it is not obvious that terrorism would always be morally unjustified, as is argued in Gerry Wallace, "Area Bombing, Terrorism and the Death of Innocents," *Journal of Applied Philosophy*, 6 (1989), pp. 3-15.

[17] Coady, "The Morality of Terrorism," p. 52. Another of those who seeks to conflate the two questions of the definition of "terrorism" and the moral justification of terrorism is Martin Hughes, "Terrorism and National Security," *Philosophy*, 57 (1982), p. 5.

[18] Loren Lomasky, "The Political Significance of Terrorism," in R. G. Frey and Christopher Morris, Editors, *Violence, Terrorism, and Justice* (Cambridge: Cambridge University Press, 1991), pp. 100, 104.

[19] Jan Narveson, "Terrorism and Morality," in R. G. Frey and Christopher Morris, Editors, *Violence, Terrorism, and Justice* (Cambridge: Cambridge University Press, 1991), p. 119.

[20] Carl Wellman, "On Terrorism Itself," in Joe P. White, Editor, *Assent/Dissent* (Dubuque: Kendall/Hunt Publishing Company, 1984), pp. 254-5.

[21] Noam Chomsky, *9/11* (New York: Seven Stories Press, 2001), p. 57.

recognize that property may be a terrorist target], and "aimed at civilian populations" in (e) each write into the definition of "terrorism" or the conception of terrorism the idea of either adversely or unjustifiably affecting innocent persons (understood to be non-legitimate/civilian/non-combatant targets).[22] It is no wonder that most philosophers who have written on this topic do not believe terrorism can ever be morally justified.

Perhaps some philosophers construe terrorism as necessarily harming or threatening terrorist harm to non-combatants or innocents out of a conviction that terrorism results from motives or reasons which do not take seriously the idea that innocents should not be harmed whenever possible. But even if terrorism is unconcerned with the harming of innocent persons, it hardly follows from this supposition that terrorism *must be* directed at innocents. Indeed, most terrorist activity, whether morally justified or not, is aimed at a perceived wrongdoer or group of wrongdoers. In this way, terrorism contains, or may plausibly be argued to contain, an essential element which would seek to *avoid* innocents as targets. The very plausibility of construing some terrorists as acting out of certain motives against those who are perceived as guilty of significant wrongdoing, then, suggests that terrorism by nature need not entail the targeting of innocents.

An understanding of terrorism is needed which captures all or most of the essential features of it while not begging the question against the moral justification of terrorism. Consider the definition of "terrorism" offered by Burleigh T. Wilkins:

(f) "Terrorism is the attempt to achieve political, social, economic, or religious change by the actual or threatened use of violence against persons or property; the violence employed in terrorism is aimed partly at destabilizing the existing political or social order, but mainly at publicizing the goals or cause espoused by the terrorists; often, though not always, terrorism is aimed at provoking extreme counter-measures which will win public support for the terrorists and their cause, . . ."[23]

---

[22] Furthermore, Chomsky's definition of "terrorism" wrongly ignores the fact that terrorism can be aimed at military targets, such as the cases of the 11 September 2001 attack on the U.S. Pentagon Building, the Jewish resistance (terrorist) attacks on the Nazi military during World War II, or even Native American terrorist attacks on the U.S. military during the U.S. military anti-Indian campaigns during the 19th Century.

[23] Burleigh Taylor Wilkins, *Terrorism and Collective Responsibility* (London: Routledge, 1992), p. 6. Coady agrees that one of the distinctive points of terrorism is to destabilize social relations (Coady, "The Morality of Terrorism," p. 53). However, Coady sees this as a matter of the sociology of terrorism, rather than as a point about the definition of "terrorism."

Not only does Wilkins' definition serve as a corrective to (a)-(e), it also improves upon the attempts by Annette Baier and Virginia Held (respectively) to clarify the nature of terrorism. Among other things, Baier says, terrorism "endangers human life" by "violent or coercive action," that it is done "publicly," and "randomly."[24] Held argues that, among other things, "violence seems an inherent characteristic of terrorism."[25] And Alan Ryan states that terrorism is distinguished by two factors: it uses methods of violence which deprive its victims of the power of a graduated, rational response, and it expresses the unwillingness of terrorists to abide by any restraints.[26] But surely Wilkins' definition of "terrorism" best captures what is essential to terrorism: it need not be violent, but pose only a threat of violence. Nor must it target the innocent ("non-combatants," "non-legitimate targets," etc.) or those undeserving of harm through the random acts of violence. Nor must terrorism be unrestrained, as the madness of an uncontrolled animal. Surely the terrorist may be one who seeks to negotiate with the primary targets of terrorism, providing politicians and legal authorities the opportunity to reason with the terrorists toward a fair and equitable solution to the problem which, presumably, led to the perceived need for terrorism in the first place. If Gregory S. Kavka is correct, then self-defense may sometimes justify (morally speaking) the taking and holding of hostages by terrorists.[27] But this in no way shows unrestraint by the terrorist. Nor does it demonstrate an unwillingness to permit a graduated, rational response by the victims of terrorism. Wilkins' definition of "terrorism" is one of the few by a philosopher of which I am aware which does not in some significant way beg the moral question against the practice of terrorism. Thus it is a good philosophical propaedeutic.

However, Wilkins' otherwise incisive understanding of the nature of terrorism is lacking in the following respects. First, it assumes, with his use of the locution "publicizing the goals or cause espoused by the terrorists," that terrorists espouse a certain political, social, economic, or religious view which fuels the terrorist act against a certain powerful group. Although this truly describes many terrorists, other terrorists can be "hired" to perform an act which a certain group is either unwilling or unable (for whatever reasons)

---

[24] Annette Baier, "Violent Demonstrations," in R. G. Frey and Christopher Morris, Editors, *Violence, Terrorism, and Justice* (Cambridge: Cambridge University Press, 1991), pp. 33-7.

[25] Held, "Terrorism, Rights, and Political Goals," p. 60.

[26] Alan Ryan, "State and Private: Red and White," in R. G. Frey and Christopher Morris, Editors, *Violence, Terrorism, and Justice* (Cambridge: Cambridge University Press, 1991), pp. 230-55; Frey, R. G. and Christopher Morris. "Violence, Terrorism, and Justice," in R. G. Frey and Christopher Morris, Editors, *Violence, Terrorism, and Justice* (Cambridge: Cambridge University Press, 1991), p. 15.

[27] Gregory S. Kavka, "Nuclear Hostages," in R. G. Frey and Christopher Morris, Editors, *Violence, Terrorism, and Justice* (Cambridge: Cambridge University Press, 1991), pp. 276-95.

to commit. In such cases it is the oppressed members of the *group* who espouse certain goals, have certain causes, etc., not the terrorist herself. Second, Wilkins' definition does not account for the possibility that terrorism may have as its aim to *prevent* change, as in the case where state terrorism is used to squelch an uprising by citizens.[28] The former South African government comes to mind here, as do counter-terrorist attempts by Israel to prevent the establishment of a Palestinian state partly by way of revolutionary terrorism by certain Palestinians. Indeed, some have argued that the FBI is responsible for terrorist acts on certain members of the Black Panther Party in the 1960's. Whether or not such an act is morally justified, it is important to include these sorts of acts in the definition of "terrorism." Moreover, non-state terrorism may also seek to prevent change, such as when a group of citizens uses terrorism to keep the status quo on a certain matter, even though the rest of the country seeks a drastic change. Many U.S. segregationists, including many members of the KKK, committed terrorist acts against African Americans and their supporters who sought to integrate the U.S. south prior to 1970. Indeed, such acts of terrorism against African Americans continued for generations without serious intervention by the U.S. government. In such cases, terrorism might be used to try to influence the majority to have things *remain* as they are. Such terrorist activity, then, might be plausibly construed as terrorism from the political right.

But (f) can be modified to accommodate my concerns:

(f') Terrorism is the attempt to achieve (*or prevent*) political, social, economic, or religious change by the actual or threatened use of violence against other persons or other persons' property; the violence (or threat thereof) employed therein is aimed partly at destabilizing (or maintaining) an existing political or social order, but mainly at publicizing the goals or causes espoused by the agents *or by those on whose behalf the agents act*; often, though not always, terrorism is aimed at provoking extreme

---

[28] Gordon Graham argues that "terrorists are enemies of the established state" and are "aimed against the state" [Gordon Graham, "Terrorism and Freedom Fighters," *Philosophy and Social Action*, 11 (1985), p. 46]. However, as Bat-Ami Bar On states concerning the etymology of "terrorism,"

> 'terrorism' as a negative term was coined in 1795 by the French Directory to refer specifically to the repressive measures practiced by Robespierre's government. It was later used to describe the activities of nineteenth-century clandestine oppositional groups in Russia. Not surprisingly, because these groups were considered revolutionary, 'terrorism' retained its negative connotations in the dictionaries of the time even though these groups were different from the French revolutionaries, and their ends differed also [Bat-Ami Bar On, "Why Terrorism is Morally Problematic," in Claudia Card, Editor, *Feminist Ethics* (Lawrence: University of Kansas Press, 1991), pp. 109-110].

counter-measures which will win public support for the
terrorists and their goals or causes, . . .

I offer (f') as a working definition of "terrorism."[29] It is what Gerry Wallace
refers to as a "neutral" definition of "terrorism," one which rests on the
possibility of separating questions about the nature of terrorism from
questions about its morality."[30] Although it may not capture all sorts of
terrorist acts, it captures most, and it evades the several problems of
definition which plague the above-mentioned construals of terrorism. It
assumes that terrorism requires (at the very least) a subject, an object, and an
audience. (f') also remains consistent with the idea that many acts of
terrorism involve some element of surprise from the standpoint of the targets
of terrorism. It also can accommodate the idea that terrorism can also be, at
least partly, a declaration or re-declaration of war by terrorists on their
respective targets. It might even be part (or all) of a terrorist group's battle
plan when waging war on its enemy. In any case, (f') is meant to capture
primarily, though not exclusively, acts of revolutionary and/or retributive
terrorism as defined in the "Introduction."

---

[29] Compare this definition of "terrorism" to Jenny Teichman's:

> Terrorism consists of violent actions carried out for political or other social purposes,
> including some large-scale mercenary purposes, by individuals or groups, having an aim
> which might be good or bad, but carried out by means of either or both of the following:
> 1, attacks on innocent or neutral or randomly chosen people, or 2, using means which
> involve atrocities, e.g., torture, cruel killings, or mutilation of the living or the dead,
> committed against randomly or non-randomly chosen people who may be innocent or
> not [Jenny Teichman, "How to Define Terrorism," *Philosophy*, 64 (1989), p. 513].

Note that Teichman's definition, unlike (f'), does not count certain *threats* of violence as
terrorism. Nor does her definition allow for one party to commit an act of terrorism on behalf
of another. Finally, Teichman's definition does not allow that property can be used as an
object of terrorism to address a person or set of persons as the primary target of terrorism. On
Teichman's definition of "terrorism," then, if a political group secured a quite valuable
artifact of a government (perhaps some "top-secret" documents, "national treasures," etc.),
threatening to destroy it unless that government released certain political prisoners all of
whom constitute a third party to this act, this act would *not* be a terrorist one. Whether or not
this sort of action is in the end effective, there is little question that Teichman's definition has
failed to capture some important features of the nature of terrorism.

Nonetheless, (f') shares the following commonalties with Teichman's definition of
"terrorism." First, both are what Teichman refers to as "narrow stipulative definitions" of
"terrorism." Secondly, (f') and Teichman's definition agree that one "ought not to begin by
defining terrorism as a bad thing" (Teichman, "How to Define Terrorism," p. 507).

Also note the stated goals of terrorism as being political, social, economic or religious.
Such goals are discussed as possible *motivations* in Jessica Stern, *The Ultimate Terrorists*
(Cambridge: Harvard University Press, 1999), Chapter 5.

[30] G. Wallace, "The Language of Terrorism," *International Journal of Moral and Social
Issues,* 8 (1993), p. 125.

Under (f') would fall events such as the one which took place at the 1972 Olympic Games in Munich, where certain Palestinians held hostage and killed some members of the Israeli Olympic Team, the 1995 bombing of the Federal Building in Oklahoma City, OK, the several years of Unabomber bombings, the 1998 bombings of the U.S. embassies in Nairobi and Tanzania, the 1997 seizure of the Japanese embassy in Lima, Peru by MRTA, the 2001 attacks on the World Trade Center and the U.S. Pentagon building, as well as the several acts of Palestinian (HAMAS) terrorism, suicidal or otherwise, against Israel and terrorism by the Israeli government against Palestinians. Clearly there were political causes that were made public, and the terrorists involved had in mind (or represented those who did), at least as a partial goal, the destabilization of an oppressive government or the gaining of justice. There are, of course many other historical examples of what would count as terrorist activity under (f'). But let us turn to other important philosophical and ethical questions about terrorism.

THE QUESTION OF MORAL JUSTIFICATION

As Kai Nielsen notes, "political violence, like violence generally, is in need of very special justification indeed."[31] Can terrorism, being a species of political violence and understood in terms of (f'), ever be morally justified? In posing this question it is crucial to point out that I am *not* asking whether or not an act of terrorism is "justified" merely in the mind of the terrorist, subjectively speaking. On the contrary, I am asking whether or not an act that satisfies the description in (f') is supported by the balance of human reason, *all things and persons considered.* Nor am I asking whether or not *every* act or event that satisfies the description in (f') is morally justified. On the contrary, I am asking whether or not *some* such acts or events are morally justified. Indeed, I am also asking whether or not certain *aspects* of specific terrorist activities are morally justified, and why. For not unlike other moral issues, the moral status of terrorism admits of *degrees* of moral justifiedness or unjustifiedness, as the case may be, all things and persons considered in the light of the balance of human reason. That is to say, a terrorist act might be morally justified to one extent or degree or another, contingent on the degree to which it satisfies the conditions necessary and sufficient for justified terrorism. Such an act might satisfy each condition of morally justified terrorism, but not with equal strength. In other words, the terrorist might respond to a context of severe and persistent oppression and target those most guilty of the oppression, but not be sufficiently careful to

---

[31]   Kai Nielsen, "Political Violence and Ideological Mystification," *Journal of Social Philosophy*, 13 (1982), p. 25.

guard against the harming of innocents. Or, a terrorist might satisfy conditions of responding to severe injustice, targeting only those deserving of harm, but act terroristically in a manner that is quite disproportional to the level(s) of oppression to which her terrorism is a response. Or, a terrorist might target proportionally those most responsible for the severe oppression to which the terrorism is a response, but without much planning in order to best achieve the overall best results of overcoming the oppression. Thus an act of terrorism might be morally justified, if it is justified at all, to one degree or another contingent on the extent to which it actually satisfies the conditions (or analysis) of what would indeed justify terrorism on moral grounds.

Whatever conditions, if satisfied and to whatever extent they are satisfied in a given instance of terrorism, would morally justify terrorism vitiate against the idea that a terrorist's mental state (intent, knowledge, etc.) counts as a necessary condition of what would morally justify terrorism. There is a difference between an *act of terrorism* being a morally justified one versus a *terrorist's* being morally justified in committing such an act. Suppose there is an evil group of people who in virtue of their history of unwarranted domestic and foreign oppression deserves to be victimized by horrendous acts of deadly terrorism. In this instance, it would not matter at all that a group of terrorists targeted the oppressive group for the reason of, say, merely insulting another group on the basis of race or ethnicity. The act of terrorism directed at the oppressive group is morally justified (other conditions obtaining) regardless of the terrorist group's reasons for employing terrorism against the oppressive group. The fact is that the terrorism in question was *deserved*. My analysis of the moral status of *acts of terrorism* does not require that the terrorist possess an adequate reason for targeting a particular person or thing. However, insofar as the question of whether or not the *terrorist* herself is morally justified in engaging in terrorist activity is concerned, her blameworthiness or praiseworthiness (or both) is quite contingent on the content of her mental states and reasons for action, inaction, or attempted action, as the case may be.

This distinction between an *act of terrorism* being morally justified (or not) versus a *terrorist's* being morally justified (or not) in employing terrorism suggests the following possible scenarios concerning terrorism and its possible moral justification. First, an act of terrorism might be to some meaningful extent morally justified where the terrorist herself is also morally justified. Second, an act of terrorism might be to some meaningful extent morally justified while the terrorist herself is morally unjustified. Third, an act of terrorism might be unjustified where the terrorist herself because of her mental state is to some meaningful extent morally justified. This kind of scenario would obtain under conditions such that a terrorist acted intentionally, with knowledge of why the prospective terrorist activity is morally justified and voluntarily, and even executed the terrorist plan rather conscientiously, but where due to a fluke innocent persons were inadvertently victimized instead of deserving ones. Fourth, both an act of terrorism and the terrorist herself might be morally unjustified. While many would assert that all terrorist contexts constitute instances of the fourth category, such a claim, unsupported by the balance of human reason, amounts to mere shibboleth motivated by presumptuous and dogmatic ideology. What is needed, then, is a philosophical analysis and assessment of the conditions under which an act of terrorism could ever be morally justified. Only then can specific or prospective acts of terrorism or terrorists themselves be judged reasonably as being morally justified or not. *Reason, not mere emotion or blind ideology, must be our guide.*

Now the arguments against the moral justification of terrorism are many. Carl Wellman has argued that terrorism is *prima facie* unjustified (morally speaking) because it: (i) is harmful; (ii) uses terror; (iii) unduly harms the innocent; (iv) is necessarily coercive; and (v) infringes rights.[32] However, (i) may be neutralized to the extent that terrorism significantly harms only those who deserve it (minimizing harm to innocent persons). Moreover, terrorism's resulting in harm (or potential harm) cannot in itself render terrorism morally problematic. Terrorism is morally problematic to the extent that it targets or results in the harming of innocents. But simply that it is a means of harming (or threatening harm to) others is insufficient reason to render it morally dubious. Otherwise, punishment would be morally unjustified in that it brings harm to wrongdoers. (ii) is neutralized to the extent that, as Wellman himself states, "the concept of terror that defines 'terrorism' is that of 'great fear, dread or anxiety' where the greatness of the fear or dread is measured either by the intensity of the emotion felt or by the magnitude of the harmed feared."[33] But surely this sort of terror cannot be what makes terrorism even *prima facie* morally unjustified, that is, unless one is willing to concede that the great fear, dread or anxiety many segregationists in the U.S. south felt in the face of civil disobedience and non-violent direct action is what renders the civil disobedience and non-violent direct action *prima facie* morally unjustified. Wellman might argue that such civil disobedience and non-violent direct action were in fact *prima facie* morally unjustified. However, in light of the strong intuition that segregationism was morally wrong, coupled with the arguments *against* there being even a *prima facie* moral obligation to obey the law,[34] it would seem that Wellman has the burden of argument in demonstrating that, say,

---

[32] Wellman, "On Terrorism Itself," pp. 254-5.
[33] Wellman, "On Terrorism Itself," p. 253.
[34] Joel Feinberg, "Civil Disobedience in the Modern World," *Humanities in Society,* 2 (1979), pp. 37-68; Richard Wasserstrom, "The Obligation to Obey the Law," *UCLA Law Review*, 10 (1963).

the civil disobedience to segregationism was even *prima facie* morally unjustified. Lacking such argumentation, it would appear both that civil disobedience to segregationism created terror in the minds of many segregationists and that such civil disobedience was *prima facie* morally justified. If this is true, then the mere fact that terrorism employs terror or the threat thereof is hardly sufficient reason to render it *prima facie* morally unjustified. (iii) does not clearly count against the use of terrorism in that it is neither obvious who the legitimate targets of terrorism are nor that terrorism must always inflict violence or the threat thereof on truly innocent parties. I shall return to this point later. (iv) does not serve as a reason why the use of terrorism is *prima facie* unjustified because even civil disobedience is sometimes coercive. In his "Letter from Birmingham Jail," Martin Luther King, Jr. argues that power is never simply given from the oppressor to the oppressed; such power must be forced from the hand of the oppressor (however non-violently). To argue, as Wellman does, that terrorism is *prima facie* unjustified because it is coercive would be to imply that other forms of coercion, such as civil disobedience and non-violent direct action, are unjustified. Or, Wellman owes us an argument as to why terrorist coercion is a special case and requires condemnation on moral grounds. (v) cannot serve as a sufficiently good reason why terrorism *per se* is *prima facie* wrong in that terrorism against one who presumably deserves it is not an unwarranted infringement of *that* person's right to be treated as a human being.[35] For Wellman to push this point he would seem to have to challenge the claim that retributive justice itself violates the Kantian dictum that persons should be treated *as* human beings. But as Kant himself states, when an individual or group violates the rights of others, retribution is required.[36] Terrorism might be the retributive means (or one such means) by which to inflict justice on such persons. Thus that terrorism infringes rights is not clearly a sufficient reason to condemn it (as Wellman does).

Wellman's reasoning aside, there are other arguments that might be proffered against terrorism's moral justification. R. M. Hare poses a consequentialist objection to terrorism: it is not very likely to be in the

---

[35] Elsewhere Wellman minimizes the strength of the moral rights objection to terrorism because of related considerations. See Carl Wellman, "Terrorism and Moral Rights," in John Howie, Editor, *Ethical Principles and Practice* (Carbondale: Southern Illinois University Press, 1987), pp. 128-53.

[36] Immanuel Kant, *The Metaphysical Elements of Justice*, John Ladd, Translator (London: Macmillan, 1965); Jeffrie G. Murphy, "Does Kant Have a Theory of Punishment?" *Columbia Law Review*, 87 (1987), pp. 510-32; "Kant's Theory of Criminal Punishment," in Jeffrie G. Murphy, Editor, *Retribution, Justice and Therapy: Essays in the Philosophy of Law* (Dordrecht: D. Reidel, 1979), pp. 82-92; *Kant's Philosophy of Right* (New York: St. Martin's, 1970); J. Angelo Corlett, "Foundations of a Kantian Theory of Punishment," *The Southern Journal of Philosophy*, 31 (1993), pp. 263-83; *Responsibility and Punishment* (Dordrecht: Kluwer Academic Publishers, 2001), Chapter 4.

greatest interest of all those affected by its employment.[37] There are a number of problems with Hare's consequentialist position on terrorism and its possible justification.[38] One which has yet to be articulated is that Hare's consequentialist view of terrorism does not consider the possibility that some circumstance might indeed yield a greater net balance of good for society by the use of terrorism than if terrorism is not employed. Of the use of terrorism, Hare writes that

> the question is, though, whether such particular cases are *likely* to be encountered in the world as it is, and whether, therefore, the world in general *is* such that the principles of the terrorist have a higher acceptance-utility than those which most of us embrace.[39]

But this surely is *not* "the question." The normative question, morally speaking, is whether or not terrorism can ever be morally justified. All that is needed is some hypothetical case which satisfies the conditions sufficient for morally justified terrorism, whether or not any actual case (to date) has satisfied such conditions. As Walzer observes, "It is at least possible to imagine oppression so severe that terrorism aimed systematically at political division might be morally defensible."[40] Furthermore, some future instances of terrorism can be morally justified even if no actual instance of it (to date) is morally justified.[41] Nonetheless, Chapter 6 is devoted to a philosophical and moral analysis of some recent incidents of terrorism.

---

[37] R. M. Hare, "On Terrorism," in Joe. P. White, Editor, *Assent/Dissent* (Dubuque: Kendall/Hunt Publishing Company, 1984), pp. 247f. An alternative consequentialist analysis of the moral status of terrorism is found in Stephen T. Davis, "Is Terrorism Ever Morally Justified?" in *Terrorism, Justice and Social Values*, Creighton Peden and Y. Hudson, Editors (Lewiston: The Edwin Mellen Press, 1990), pp. 385-90.

[38] Wilkins, *Terrorism and Collective Responsibility*, pp. 33-41.

[39] Hare, "On Terrorism," p. 248.

[40] Michael Walzer, *Obligations* (Cambridge: Harvard University Press, 1970), p. 67.

[41] The analysis of morally justified terrorism provided in this section is not set forth as an analysis of certain historical cases of morally justified terrorism. One difficulty with either defending or condemning particular historical instances of terrorism is the media's biases in presenting the "facts" of a given terrorist act or event. Much of what counts as news reports on terrorism amounts to little more than propaganda and is of little use to philosophers in their attempts to judge the moral status of such terrorist actions. Few, if any, reports of terrorism will attempt to provide information about the possibility that the action or event was a response to significant injustice, or that the terrorists were conscientious in selecting targets, and so forth. In light of these factors, then, the following analysis is set forth and defended as one pertaining to the *possibility* of morally justified terrorism. Its significance lies in the fact that it stands as a challenge to what Wallace calls "non-neutral" definitions of "terrorism," ones which "either assert or recommend that moral wrongness is built into the definition of terrorism" (Wallace, "The Language of Terrorism," p. 127).

What would such an analysis of justified terrorism look like? Let us begin with Wilkins' insightful analysis of morally justified terrorism. One is morally justified, on his view, in engaging in terrorist activity when:

> (1) one is defending oneself;
> (2) one is selective whenever possible; and
> (3) one directs terrorist activity only against those guilty of injustice.[42]

However, there are weaknesses in Wilkins' view [(1)-(3)] of what might morally justify an act of terrorism. Although, contrary to Primoratz,[43] terrorism's moral justification requires (among other things) that it is a means of self-defense in some cases, (1) is problematic since terrorism might be justifiably employed by those *defending others*. Certainly if terrorism is justified at all it is justified in cases where an oppressed group that cannot defend itself asks for another group to aid through terrorist activity. (2) and (3) seem plausible, as stated. However, there remain other shortcomings regarding Wilkins' otherwise helpful analysis. First, in general, terrorism should not be engaged in until other means of change have been attempted in good faith (though, I might add, such means need not be exhausted). I use the locution, "in general" because there may be circumstances in which the immediate use of "militancy" is justified, as John Rawls admits in his discussion of civil disobedience.[44] Second, terrorist activity should be *well-planned* so that it is more likely than not to satisfy its goal(s) (revolution, freedom, prosperity, etc.), and so that harm to innocent or illegitimate targets is minimized. Third, the use of terrorism should be *generalizable*. That is, if it is morally justified for someone or some group to employ terrorism of a certain kind and a given time and in a certain circumstance, then it is morally justified for anyone else in relevantly similar circumstances to employ similar terrorist acts.

In light of the above considerations, then, I offer the following analysis of morally justified terrorism: S is morally justified in employing terrorism, T, in a certain circumstance, C, and at a given time, t_1, to the extent that:

> (1') S, being morally innocent, is defending herself or another morally innocent individual or group of moral innocents in the face of a significant form of injustice in C at

---

[42] Wilkins, *Terrorism and Collective Responsibility*, p. 7. Wilkins admits that he is offering a partial analysis of morally justified terrorism.

[43] "Terrorism is different, both conceptually and morally, from violence employed in self-defense" (Primoratz, "What is Terrorism?" p. 133).

[44] John Rawls, *A Theory of Justice* (Cambridge: Harvard University Press, 1971), p. 373.

t_1, and concerning which injustice S [or the one(s) defended by S] is (are) morally innocent;

(2') S is as conscientiously selective as possible in her choice of terrorist targets in C at t_1-t_n;

(3') In C at t_1, S directs terrorist activity both proportionately and only against those clearly guilty of committing acts of significant injustice;[45]

(4) If time and circumstance permit, S attempts non-violent means of political, social, economic, or religious change in good faith;

(5) S plans T so as to best achieve the cessation of the conditions of injustice which might justify the use of T in the first place; and

(6) It is morally justified for others in relevantly similar circumstances to engage in T.

The locution, "to the extent that" implies that there are degrees of moral justification when it comes to terrorism (as with several other actions having moral implications) contingent on the extent to which the above conditions are satisfied in a given instance of terrorism, all things and persons considered. For example, to the extent that a case of terrorism involves terrorists whose moral "hands" are sufficiently clean, satisfying (1'), who conscientiously selects only those most directly responsible for significant wrong doing as her targets, satisfying (2')-(3'), attempts other normal means of political, social, economic change, satisfying (4), plans her terrorist act(s) so as to best achieve the cessation of the injustice that is being addressed by way of terrorism, satisfying (5), and is generalizable, satisfying (6), a particular act of terrorism is morally justified.

In assessing morally an act of terrorism, then, the following factors are relevant: the level(s) of *responsibility* of those targeted and affected by the terrorism, the *proportionality* of the terrorist violence or threat thereof in light of the harm(s) being addressed by the terrorism, the degree, if any, to which a target of terrorism genuinely *deserves* to be its target, and the degree to which the terrorist herself has *clean moral hands*. It is noteworthy that (2')-(3') are consistent with Thomas Hill, Jr's construal of Immanuel Kant's notion of morally justified political violence, as discussed in Chapter 3. Recall that the first such Kantian condition is that "killing and maiming human beings is worse... than damaging property," and the second condition

---

[45] This condition renders implausible the objection that (1')-(6) war qualifies as terrorism. However, terrorism may be an "act of war."

is that "political violence targeted specifically against the grossly unjust is better than random political violence."

But what does it mean to say that a terrorist is as "conscientiously selective as possible"? At the very least, it means that she must not intend harm to either innocents or non-combatants [which is implied in (3')].[46] However, the sincerity of her intent might require, at least in some circumstances, that she run some significant risk of harm to herself in her attempt to avoid harming such persons. After all, if (1') is satisfied in the sense that the terrorist is defending others (innocents) against injustice, then at least some of the innocents are those for whom the terrorist is "fighting."[47] In at least some circumstances, this means that the terrorist will need to consider and use, say, a lesser caliber weapon so as not to endanger innocent persons. Detonating a powerful explosive in a building during business hours would endanger many innocent persons, whereas posing a terrorist threat of violence to certain individuals in specific offices within that building, perhaps by holding them as hostages and at gunpoint, would be a less harmful, and, other conditions obtaining, more morally justified, form of terrorism. Note that the latter form of terrorism poses a more dangerous situation for the terrorist herself, while is clearly poses a less severe risk of harm to innocent persons.[48]

(3') requires that terrorists employ terrorism "proportionately." This means that, pursuant to (1') wherein the terrorism is a response to a significant form of injustice, that the levels and kinds of harms that the terrorism inflicts are only on those guilty of such injustice and therefore deserving of a proportional terrorist response. The notion of guilt in (3') presupposes a cluster concept of responsibility sufficient to ground a deserving and proportional terrorist response to the injustice in (1'). This requirement of proportionality rules out the moral justification of terrorism altogether in cases where a harsh terrorist response clearly outweighs the oppression to which the terrorism is a response, say, where a terrorist detonates a bomb in a court room simply because she did not approve of the verdict and where the case has significant political, religious, etc.

---

[46] This point is directed at Michael Walzer's concern that the employment of terrorism is unjustifiable in that it fails to distinguish between combatants and non-combatants [Michael Walzer, *Just and Unjust Wars,* Third Edition (New York: Basic Books, 2000)].

[47] (1') is consistent with Robert Audi's first point of analysis of what morally justifies political violence, as stated in Chapter 3.

[48] Although Robert Young's defense of the use of terrorism is, like mine, based for the most part on the "just war" tradition, our respective accounts differ in significant respects. First, I do not require that terrorism's moral justification be a tactic of final resort, as Young's account does. Nor does my view make use of an economic analysis of terrorism as Young's does. Finally, my analysis of morally justified terrorism is far more dependent on the notion of a terrorist's *not* harming innocents than is Young's [Robert Young, "Revolutionary Terrorism, Crime, and Morality," *Social Theory and Practice,* 4 (1977), pp. 287-302].

implications, such as a case dealing with abortion. It also rules out indiscriminate "terrorist" attacks, such as the bomb detonated at the Olympic Park during the summer Olympic Games in Atlanta, GA in 1996. The moral requirement of proportionality means that terrorism is morally justified, among other things, only to the extent that the kinds and levels of force used are in proportion to the injustice to which the terrorism is a response. The significance of this condition of proportionality is that it holds terrorists to the requirement of proportional infliction of harm on others, which is the same kind of requirement to which courts are bound when punishing those who deserve it. Insofar as many terrorists construe themselves as inflicting retribution on those who deserve it, my analysis of morally justified terrorism holds them to the standard of proportional "punishment" or retribution. Without the terrorists' conformity with this moral consideration, there is no hope whatsoever that an act of terrorism can be justified.

Note, however, that (1') does not require that a terrorist *herself* be justified in the sense of having a reason for engaging in terrorism against a target that constitutes, all things and persons considered, an adequate one. For it could turn out that S targets a well-deserving group, but for the "wrong" reasons. In such a case, the terrorist herself is not morally justified, but the *act of terrorism* against the deserving group is. Thus an act of terrorism itself can be morally justified even though the terrorist herself might not be praised for the act, perhaps in that the terrorism targeted deserving parties accidentally, or because the terrorist targeted the deserving parties but for the wrong reasons.

Another important question is, of course, whether or not these conditions are ever jointly satisfied in a given case. Hare seems to think not. For (1')-(6) require the terrorist to be a rational agent, considerate of the moral innocence of some in the midst of the evil of others in the world. But Hare insists that:

> Of course most terrorists are not as clear thinking as is required in order to engage in the sort of argument we have been having. They have an extremely selective view of the facts; they do not pay much attention to the facts on which we have been relying, such as the suffering they are inflicting on others, and the rather dubious and over-optimistic nature of their own predictions. They give play to particular emotions to an extent which makes them incapable of logical thought. The philosopher cannot say anything that will help further an argument with such people; for he can only reason, and they will not.[49]

---

[49] Hare, "On Terrorism," p. 249. For a similar view of terrorism, see Paul Wilkinson, *Terrorism and the Liberal State*, Second Edition (New York: NYU Press, 1986), p. 56, where "terrorism" is defined as "the systematic use of murder and destruction, and the threat of murder and destruction, to terrorise individuals, groups, communities or governments into

Is Hare correct in his estimation of the terrorist? Is the terrorist "incapable of logical thought," as Hare states? Are terrorists unwilling to engage in rational thought?

While one might be tempted to brush aside Hare's words about terrorists as Hare's unwillingness to treat the moral problem of terrorism in an analytical and non-affective manner, his statements might be taken seriously in order to grasp a different portrait of the terrorist. Alternatively, Hare's description might be seen as a challenge to terrorists to indeed satisfy the justificatory conditions of terrorism whenever terrorism is used.

Be this as it may, terrorists often and typically do show a significant degree of certain kinds of rationality.[50] Often, if not nearly always, terrorists are reacting to a perceived injustice with the experienced retributivist emotions or reactive attitudes (such as hatred, anger, resentment, etc.). Surely this is one sign of rationality. Another sign of rationality is that the terrorist knows to publicize the act of terrorism in order for terrorism to have some chance of becoming effective. Yet another sign is that the terrorist often purposefully chooses arenas in which terrorism is to some extent catastrophic: airports, large public squares, etc. In fact, these are precisely the kinds of rationality exhibited, for better or for worse, by Osama Bin Laden and the al-Qaeda network of terrorists in their recent attacks on the U.S. for its support of Israel over the past several decades. Furthermore, the level of planning and coordination involved in the 11 September 2001 attacks on the World Trade Center and the U.S. Pentagon buildings was so extensive that it is disingenuous to think even for a moment that such terrorism is irrational. If the terrorist is "incapable of logical thought," as Hare avers, then few or none of these sorts of choices would be made by the terrorist. Instead, the terrorist would choose the countryside as an arena, with no humans to witness the spectacle, and for no particular reason! Indeed, there is some rationality and "logic" to terrorism, whether or not a particular instance of it is morally justified. As Primoratz correctly argues, "the terrorist does not strike blindly and pointlessly, left and right, but rather plans his actions carefully, weighing his options and trying for the course of action that will best promote his objective at the lowest cost to himself."[51] This description of the terrorist is, notably, consistent with condition (5) of

conceding to the terrorists' political aims. . . . terroristic violence is characterized by its indiscriminateness, inhumanity, arbitrariness and barbarity."
[50] For an alternative account of the rationality of terrorism, see Robert Holmes, "Terrorism and Violence: a Moral Perspective," in *Issues in War and Peace: Philosophical Inquiries*, J. C. Kunkel and K. H. Klein, Editors (Wolfeboro: Longwood, 1989), p. 116.
[51] Primoratz, "What is Terrorism?" p. 130. Also see Jenny Teichman, "How to Define Terrorism," p. 510: "Modern terrorism is not necessarily arbitrary in its choice of victims." Perhaps the modern terrorist's (sometimes) choice of specific victims is yet another sign of her sometimes rational behavior.

my analysis of morally justified terrorism.   That terrorism *per se* is unreasonable is a judgment that can only be evaluated in light of reason and critical analysis. But that terrorism is irrational is itself an unreasonable assertion. The very fact that, according to (e'), the terrorist seeks political, religious, economic, etc., reform is itself some significant sign of the terrorist's rationality.

It is crucial to see that my analysis of justified terrorism also differs from Wilkins' concerning justified targets of terrorism. Wilkins argues that collectives of certain kinds can be vicariously and morally liable for harms such that they might be justified targets of terrorism.[52] He bases his view on Joel Feinberg's notion of collective responsibility (where liability is not distributive, but collective).[53]

But there are some problems with Wilkins' proposal. First, Feinberg's analysis of collective responsibility concerns, on Feinberg's own admission, *legal* liability only, not collective moral responsibility. For what counts as collective legal responsibility (in a liability sense) does not always count as a case of collective moral responsibility (in a liability sense), and vice versa. Second, Feinberg has since recanted his view on the matter of collective liability where there is no individual or distributive liability.[54] For as I have argued elsewhere,[55] Feinberg's example of a random collective's being collectively liable for a harm (inflicted on it by the Jesse James gang of thieves) is problematic in a number of ways. One problem with it is that it confuses a causal sense of responsibility with a liability sense of the same. Just because those in the random collective could have acted differently in changing the outcome of the Jesse James train robbery does not mean they are, collectively or individually, morally responsible (in a liability sense) for not acting. There is a crucial difference between causal and liability responsibility. Moreover, to act in a way which would make it liability responsible for the harm the group would have had to be a decision-making entity. But it is a random collective (by stipulation), and random collectives do not make decisions. So how can a random collective be guilty of anything when guilt can be the result only of a choosing or deciding agent? To the extent that Wilkins' view is contingent on Feinberg's earlier notion of collective (but not distributive) responsibility, it is problematic.

Was the terrorism at the 1972 Olympic Games in Munich morally justified? Even if we assume, for the sake of argument, that the Palestinian terrorists in Munich satisfied (1')-(2'), and (4)-(6) and that Palestinians have

---

[52] Wilkins, *Terrorism and Collective Responsibility*, Chapter 7.

[53] Joel Feinberg, *Doing and Deserving* (Princeton: Princeton University Press, 1970), p. 249.

[54] Feinberg has made this point to me in private on more than one occasion.

[55] J. Angelo Corlett, "Collective Moral Responsibility," *Journal of Social Philosophy,* 32 (2001), pp. 573-84. Also see J. Angelo Corlett, *Responsibility and Punishment* (Dordrecht: Kluwer Academic Publishers, 2001), Chapter 7.

been significantly wronged by Israel, it seems that the terrorist activity in question fails to satisfy (3'). For those terrorists harmed certain Israeli *athletes* who represented Israel at the Olympic Games. But it is far from obvious that the athletes are genuinely and significantly deserving of becoming the targets of terrorism. It is doubtful that the Israeli athletes had very much, if anything, to do with the sorts of political decisions that led to or sustained the "Palestinian Problem." The athletes, then, were secondary targets of terrorism. Yet secondary targets are not to be treated by terrorists, *if they are justifiable targets at all*, in the same ways that primary targets might be justifiably treated in a given case.[56] Thus it is doubtful that the terrorism at the 1972 Olympic Games was morally justified. More precisely, the degree to which that instance of terrorism is morally justified is significantly mitigated in light of the terrorists using secondary targets in a violent way. To the extent that the Israeli athletes were innocent non-combatants in regards to any wrongs committed against Palestinians by Israel, the athletes were not the legitimate targets of terrorism.

However, it is not far-fetched to imagine a terrorist group the members of which satisfy conditions (1')-(6). It is possible to imagine a group of conscientious, politically, socially, economically and religiously sensitive persons who themselves have for years engaged in various forms of non-violent protest in good faith, but who have found their oppressors to be unmoved and unconcerned. Further, it is easy to imagine this group carefully planning and executing a terrorist plan against those in power (officials) or their property, an act which is distinct from assassination (the actual killing of such officials for mainly political reasons). And it is not far-fetched at all to imagine such terrorists doing all they can to minimize harm to non-legitimate targets of terrorism. What is so distinct about the terrorist that she cannot, like the revolutionary (at times), distinguish between legitimate and non-legitimate targets? Even some assassins, as we read in Albert Camus' play "The Just Assassins," can and are willing to forego their deeds of violence when innocent parties such as small children are endangered. Camus has one such person utter, "Even in destruction, there's a right way and a wrong way – and there are limits."[57] Not all terrorists are like the infamous cocaine cartel lord Pablo Escobar, who in seeking to assassinate a

---

[56] The helpful distinction between primary and secondary targets of terrorism is made by Wellman. A *primary target* of terrorism is the person who is or is perceived to be the main political addressee of the terrorist activity, while a *secondary target* is a person or thing which is used as a means to address the primary target. See Wellman, "On Terrorism Itself."

[57] Albert Camus, "The Just Assassins," in *Caligula and Three Other Plays*, Translated by Stuart Gilbert (New York: Alfred A. Knopf, 1958), p. 258. That terrorists can and do discriminate between possible targets is discussed in Che Guevara, *Bolivian Diary*, translated by Carlos P. Hansen and Andrew Sinclair (London: Jonathan Cape/Lorrimer, 1968); and Michael Walzer, *Just and Unjust Wars* (London: Allen Lane, 1978), p. 199.

political leader in Bogata, Colombia, by having a passenger aircraft blown to pieces (only to discover subsequent to over 100 persons dying in the blast) that his target of terrorist assassination was *not* on board the aircraft after all. Perhaps terrorists hijack some aircraft transporting only officials who are clearly responsible (in a liability sense) for significant injustice, demanding rectification, retribution, etc. Surely this sort of act, if generalizable, is morally justified. Surely, moreover, it is a terrorist act. Thus we have an imaginable case where terrorism is morally justified. Perhaps if we look beyond the media reports of terrorism, we might begin to see that at least some acts or events are in some significant measure morally justified. Great attention will be devoted to some such events in the following chapter.

Does it follow from the supposition that terrorism is sometimes morally justified that there is in such cases a moral *right* to employ terrorism? A moral right,[58] if it does exist, is conferred on a right holder by the balance of human reason or the principles of an enlightened conscience.[59] Moreover, such a right is correlated with the moral duty of others to not interfere with the exercise or enjoyment of such a moral right by the right holder. Such a right has both a subject (the right holder) and an object (those against the right holds to a duty). A moral right is a valid moral claim to and/or interest in something.

Is there a moral right to employ terrorism? Certainly an individual or group may have a moral *choice* to and/or an *interest* in doing so. For example, a group may have a moral choice or freedom to preserve itself from unwanted intrusion or oppression, even if it means that violence is needed as a means of self-defense. Or, it might have an interest in doing so. But a moral right is not a mere choice and/or a mere interest; it is a *valid* moral claim, i.e., a *legitimate* moral choice and/or a *legitimate* moral interest which binds other parties to a moral duty to not interfere with the use of terrorism under such circumstances. I argue that there is a moral right to employ terrorism to the extent that the act of terrorism satisfies (1')-(6), above.

THE POSSIBLE ROLE OF TERRORISM

This brings us to the possible (positive) role of terrorism. What might the possible role of terrorism be? Of course, when (if) terrorism is not

---

[58] Moral rights are sometimes referred to as "natural" or "human" rights. They are, unlike legal rights, non-conventional in nature. They are grounded in human reason quite independently of conventional norms [See Carl Wellman, *A Theory of Rights* (Totowa: Rowman and Littlefield Publishers, Inc., 1985)].

[59] Joel Feinberg, *Social Philosophy* (Englewood Cliffs: Prentice-Hall, 1970); *Rights, Justice, and the Bounds of Liberty* (Princeton: Princeton University Press, 1980); *Freedom and Fulfillment: Philosophical Essays* (Princeton: Princeton University Press, 1992).

morally justified, its role is unclear. But morally justified instances of
terrorism, when or if they do obtain, have the role of helping victims of
significant forms of injustice to revolt against their oppressors, thereby
enabling the group to establish or re-establish itself as a free and equal
society. Indeed, terrorism may serve the same purpose as Rawls says civil
disobedience serves in a nearly just democratic society: it can maintain and
strengthen just institutions. The difference, most would hold, is that
terrorism utilizes violence or the threat thereof, while civil disobedience
(traditionally construed) does not. This may surprise some in that a violent or
potentially violent activity is seen as having a possibly positive role in a
democratic society. But perhaps this is partly because some find it difficult
to accept that violence does not *always* beget violence only, but sometimes
peace, solidarity, democracy and justice. Although in some cases non-violent
means of social change are more likely than terrorism to permit the *mending
of enemies* in a state, terrorist violence of a revolutionary nature can more
easily *remove forces of oppression* from a state, it would seem.

OBJECTIONS AND REPLIES

Thus far I have considered some of the conceptions of terrorism and
proposed assessments of its moral justifiedness. I have also set forth my own
analyses of the nature and justification of terrorism. But it is incumbent on
me to defend my analyses against at least two general lines of moral
objections to it. One concerns the neutral definition of "terrorism" [(e')]. The
other focuses on the analysis of morally justified terrorism [(1')-(6)].

AN OBJECTION TO THE NEUTRAL DEFINITION OF "TERRORISM"

Wallace argues that a neutral definition of "terrorism" faces a basic
problem of there being a rarity of self-declared terrorists: "Might not the
explanation be that the moral wrongness *is* written into the concept and that
to admit to terrorism is to repudiate those deeds?"[60]
However, there might well be a better explanation for a terrorist's
unwillingness to admit to or declare her actions than Wallace's suggestion
that "moral wrongness *is* written into" the very concept of terrorism. For
such a declaration by the terrorist would bring sure retaliation, and
punishment if caught. Why should the terrorist believe that her targets are in
a moral position to judge her actions? Thus it need not be the case that a
terrorist's not declaring her actions implies the moral wrongness of her
terroristic deeds, contrary to Wallace.

---

[60] Wallace, "The Language of Terrorism," p. 126.

It might also be objected that I have been unfair in my assessment of those conceptions of terrorism which include violence to innocents as an essential feature of terrorism. For instance, Primoratz understands terrorism as "the deliberate use of violence, or threat of its use, against innocent people, with the aim of intimidating them, or other people, into a course of action they otherwise would not take."[61] Furthermore, he insists that his construal is "morally neutral," "not a definitional *fiat* that begs the moral question at issue . . . it does not make the moral condemnation analytically true, or the question about its moral standing a self-answering one."[62]

But I have already explained how a terrorist might, by satisfying conditions (1')-(6), be morally justified in employing terrorism. Yet nothing in the definitional (e') or justificatory (1')-(6) conditions of terrorism logically requires the harming of innocents by terrorists. Certainly if, as Primoratz himself admits, terrorists can and do plan their actions carefully to achieve their objectives, then why cannot such planning and care be taken in the selection of terrorist targets? As I have argued, to the extent that the terrorist accomplishes this aim, she is morally justified in her terrorism, other things being equal. It is simply question-begging to write into the definition of "terrorism" the harming of innocents. For the terrorist might target only primary targets, who on Primoratz's own admission might not be innocent.[63] So as long as it is possible for a terrorist to select only primary targets who are *not* innocent, then the claim that terrorism is morally wrong because it harms the innocent is incorrect.

THE NON-CONSEQUENTIALIST OBJECTION TO TERRORISM[64]

As noted earlier, Wellman objects that terrorism is *prima facie* unjustified because it violates the right of others to be treated as humans. But let us modify this objection to say that terrorism is morally unjustified because it infringes rights which are inviolable, such as the right to be treated as a human being, i.e., the right to not be treated (violently) as a mere means to an end. Is this objection sound? To argue that terrorism is morally unjustified because it violates some such right is to beg the moral question against the use of terrorism. For it must be shown, by independent argument, that at least two things are true. First, it must be shown that there exist moral rights which are in fact inviolable (such as the right to be treated as a human being, etc.). Second, it must be shown that terrorism *necessarily* infringes such rights.

---

[61] Primoratz, "What is Terrorism?" pp. 129, 135.

[62] Primoratz, "What is Terrorism?" p. 136.

[63] Primoratz, "What is Terrorism?" p. 131.

[64] As noted earlier, Wellman brings this concern to the fore (Wellman, "On Terrorism Itself," pp. 156-60).

But what is so special about terrorism such that the harm it inflicts on others is morally prohibitive? Is it not true, as Camus writes, that "freedom can be a prison, so long as a single man on earth is kept in bondage"? And if those who unduly keep others in bondage become the victims of terrorism (at least partly as a matter of retribution), what moral *right* have they which might bind *anyone* to a moral duty to not infringe their claim to remain *un*harmed? Is it not true that a criminal's claim to not be harmed (in certain ways) is sometimes or to some extent invalid insofar as the criminal justice system, having found the person guilty through a procedure of due process, takes pains to punish her? How is it, then, that an oppressor has a right not to be terrorized, especially by those whom he has abused? How much weaker is the oppressor's claim to not be a victim of terrorism when that oppressor has already victimized others by way of terrorism? Is a state that unjustifiably inflicts terrorism on its citizens entitled, as a matter of moral right, to protection from non-state terrorists who engage in terrorism according to (1')-(6), above? I think not. There are some instances where terrorism is morally justified, where terrorism overrides another's claim to be treated "as a human being." For there is no absolute, non-conflictable, inviolable moral right to be treated "as a human being."

Thus it seems that there is no inviolable or absolute and non-conflictable moral right to not become a victim of terrorist action, unless, of course, one is truly innocent of harming the terrorist and/or her property, or someone on whose behalf the terrorist chooses to act. The only ones who are truly morally exempt from the horrors of terrorism are the morally innocent, or nonlegitimate targets. The morally guilty enjoy no such luxury.

THE CONSEQUENTIALIST OBJECTION TO TERRORISM[65]

Kai Nielsen sets forth the consequentialist objection to the use of terrorism:

> Thus we are not justified in rejecting political assassinations and terroristic activity out of hand simply because they involve violence for sometimes a resort to violence is justified; but, generally speaking, they are not justified because they are ineffective and are very likely to enhance the oppression of the oppressed classes in the society in whose name they are carried out.[66]

However, as Wilkins so eloquently argues,

---

[65] For an enlightening treatment of this sort of objection, see the critique of the respective consequentialist views of Hare, Kai Nielsen, and Ted Honderich in Wilkins, *Terrorism and Collective Responsibility*, Chapter 2; Held, "Terrorism, Rights, and Political Goals," p. 70f.; and Frey and Morris, "Violence, Terrorism, and Justice."

[66] Kai Nielsen, "On Terrorism and Political Assassination," in Joe P. White, Editor, *Assent/Dissent* (Dubuque: Kendall/Hunt Publishing Company, 1984), p. 312.

from a strictly consequentialist point of view it would seem that where human suffering is concerned the additional suffering caused by terrorism might be but a drop in the bucket, a drop which would seem justifiable if there were any chance at all that it might alleviate the wider human suffering to which it is a reaction.[67]

Thus it is far from obvious that the actual or prospective or foreseeable results of terrorism can never outweigh the prospective benefits of a subgroup of significantly and continually oppressed individuals, especially where (1')-(6) are satisfied.

This does not mean, however, that consequentialist considerations do not figure into the moral justificatory status of a terrorist act. It simply means that the above sort of consequentialist objection to the use of terrorism cannot rightly serve as a general defeater to the use of terrorism under conditions (1')-(6). That is, the terrorist, in seeking to satisfy (1')-(6), should consider the likely results of her action for herself and others. For such a consideration might very well play a role in deciding to what extent terrorism ought to be utilized in a given circumstance.

So neither of these objections to my positions on the definition, justification and possible role of terrorism is telling. What counts as terrorism must be considered in light of (e'), and the possible moral justification of specific acts of terrorism must be debated in terms of (1')-(6), above. Confusion about terrorism's moral status often results from not distinguishing these two distinct problems: the problem of definition and the problem of justification.

FURTHER THOUGHTS ON TERRORISM

Having analyzed philosophically the nature and moral justification of terrorism, it is helpful to provide critical dialogue with two important contemporary philosophers on the problem of terrorism. Each of these thinkers subscribes to a position which is markedly different from the one set forth and defended above.

HELD ON TERRORISM

Violence, Held argues, is essential to the nature of terrorism, and so she argues that it is wrong to imply that even non-violent acts can amount to terrorism. She also argues that it is wrong to think that terrorism does not necessarily have as its goal coercion. For terrorism may have a variety of goals: punishment, or to call attention to a problem even where there is no

---

[67] Wilkins, *Terrorism and Collective Responsibility*, p. 48.

ability to coerce anyone: So for Held, violence is essential to terrorism, but coercion is not.[68]

But are there not instances of terrorism that do not involve violence? Although failed acts of terrorism might count only as *attempted* acts of terrorism, what about terrorist *threats*?[69] And there can be various kinds of threats: *direct and intentional threats*, where the terrorist states to the targets that she will hijack an airplane unless the target does such and such or unless it does *not* do such and such. There are also *indirect and unintentional threats*, where a terrorist does something which itself is not intended to be a threat to a target, but what the terrorist does ends up counting as a threat in the minds of the targets. For example, if HAMAS decided to attend peace talks with the Israeli government, to many that would constitute a terrorist threat even if all HAMAS wanted to do is to participate peacefully in the process of negotiations. HAMAS in no way, let us assume, intends to make a threat, but its mere attending the meetings, given its history of violent terrorism, constitutes an unintended and indirect threat to many others.

Thus there are various sorts of terrorist threats. Although we would not want to include the indirect and unintentional category of terrorist threats as themselves being terrorism, it seems to make good sense to say of the threat to hijack case that it is an instance of terrorism as long as certain other conditions are satisfied. If this is plausible, then the claim that terrorism must be violent (i.e., that violence is essential to terrorism) is dubious. For some terrorism involves no violence, but the threat thereof.

Held concurs with Coady that intentionality is essential to terrorism. However, Held is careful to note that we need to specify precisely at what the intentionality is directed in terrorist activity. Without intentionality, it might be difficult to make sense of a terrorist's having certain political motivations. However, Coady insists that the "intentional harming of non-combatants" is a necessary condition of terrorism.[70] But Held correctly argues that this would exclude terrorist acts which target only combatants or the guilty. I would add that Coady's definition of terrorism as necessarily involving intentional harm to non-combatants begs the question against the morality of terrorism insofar as it is unjust to target or harm the innocent, assuming here that non-combatants and innocents are the same.

---

[68] Held, "Terrorism, Rights, and Political Goals," pp. 60-1.

[69] Jan Narveson admits that terrorism need not employ violence, but the threat thereof [See Jan Narveson, "Terrorism and Morality," in R. G. Frey and Christopher W. Morris, Editors, *Violence, Terrorism, and Justice* (Cambridge: Cambridge University Press, 1991), p. 117. In fact, a serious threat of terrorism is sufficient for it on Narveson's account.

[70] Coady, "The Morality of Terrorism," p. 60.

For Held, terrorism is violent, political, and usually creates fear. It intentionally targets for harm persons rather than property.[71] But she also argues that "we should probably not construe either the intention to spread fear or the intention to kill non-combatants as necessary for an act of political violence to be an act of terrorism. It does seem that both are often present, but not always."[72] She goes on to aver that "perhaps when either the intention to spread fear or the intention to harm non-combatants is primary, this is sufficient [for an act of political violence to be an act of terrorism]."[73]

Is intentionally harming non-combatants always wrong, and is terrorism wrong because it involves this? Held's answer to these questions is that terrorism is *not* necessarily morally wrong even if it sometimes involves the intentional harming of non-combatants. As she argues, *if* the terrorist violence is morally justified on other grounds, then it is not always easy to differentiate those who are conscript combatants from ordinary citizens. This collapses the distinction between combatants and non-combatants, at least in some cases. The point she is making is not that there is no helpful and sound distinction to be made between combatants and non-combatants. Rather, Held is arguing that where the distinction is very hard to make, or not a substantive one, then if terrorism is morally justified against a repressive regime, then the terrorist's intentionally harming non-combatants does not seem to be a powerful objection to the terrorism in question.[74]

One nuance that Held adds to Wilkins' attack (above) on the consequentialisms of Hare, Nielsen and Honderich is that each of those philosophers assumed that consequentialist considerations would render morally unjustified terrorism against the state. But Held points out that if the consequentialist calculus is at all telling against terrorism, it is as telling against state terrorism of its citizens or of another state as it is against anti-state terrorism, or what Nielsen referred to as "revolutionary terrorism."[75]

Of course, Held's point is not to embrace the inadequacies of a consequentialist ethics. Instead, it is to argue that "we cannot adequately evaluate social action in consequentialist terms alone."[76] We must, she insists, evaluate terrorism's moral status in terms of rights also. Wellman argues that terrorism is morally wrong because it violates rights, namely, the rights of the targets of terrorism.[77] But Held points out that, though rights are indeed an important consideration in assessing terrorism morally, this does

---

[71] Held, "Terrorism, Rights, and Political Goals," p. 64; "Violence, Terrorism, and Moral Inquiry."
[72] Held, "Terrorism, Rights, and Political Goals," p. 64.
[73] Held, "Terrorism, Rights, and Political Goals," p. 65.
[74] Held, "Terrorism, Rights, and Political Goals," p. 69.
[75] Held, "Terrorism, Rights, and Political Goals," p. 71.
[76] Held, "Terrorism, Rights, and Political Goals," p. 72.
[77] Wellman, "On Terrorism Itself," pp. 250-58.

not mean that terrorism can never be morally justified.[78] This means, however, that an adequate assessment of the moral status of terrorism or of a particular instance of it must take rights seriously. But what about cases where rights conflict? How can we determine the moral status of terrorism if we need to consider rights, but where rights conflict? Held argues for a particular way of trying to deal with such problem cases when it comes to terrorism and rights:

> Where rights conflict, we may order them by priorities or stringency; this, however, is not a matter of maximizing, but of seeking consistency. Some rights may be deemed to have priority over others, but our aim is not to engage in trade-offs. We seek, rather, to arrive at a consistent scheme in which all the rights of all persons can be respected and none need be violated.[79]

Unlike Robert Audi who proposed a prioritizing of freedom, justice and welfare concerns when calculating whether or not political violence might be justified, and unlike Nielson who provided a consequentialist calculation of how to discern the justifiability of political violence,[80] Held argues for a primarily rights-based approach. Of course, held does not purport to provide a full-blown theory of rights here. But she suggests that to the extent that terrorism's moral status is contingent, at least in part, on considerations of rights, we must assess particular cases of terrorism in terms of "all things considered" judgments about which rights trump others in certain circumstances.

However, Held does provide some guidance for us on the conflicts of rights and terrorism. She seems to be arguing that there is always a *prima facie* reason to not resort to political violence. This means the same thing that it did when we discussed the putative *prima facie* moral duty to obey the law. In that context, it meant that, if such a duty obtains, then it could be overridden by moral considerations that, all things considered, made breaking the law by way of civil disobedience, pacifism, or non-violent direct action, necessary for reasons of justice. This same point is now being used by Held to suggest that terrorism as a species of political violence has a special burden of proof to bear.[81] This is another way of conveying that terrorism is morally justified only in very special circumstances indeed. Held states that one ought to attempt non-violent means of social change, and she discusses the views of Mohandas Gandhi along these lines.

All of this sounds well and good, especially since Held agrees that in some very special cases that terrorism could be morally justified where non-

---

[78] Held, "Terrorism, Rights, and Political Goals," p. 72.
[79] Held, "Terrorism, Rights, and Political Goals," p. 73.
[80] See Chapter 3 of this book.
[81] Held, "Terrorism, Rights, and Political Goals," p. 76.

violence is not an option that presents much or any hope of successful change in a dreadful situation of injustice. Her main argument is that *if we must have rights violations, a more equitable distribution of such violations is better than a less equitable distribution.*[82] And she goes on to conclude that "though non-violence is always better than violence, other things being equal, terrorism carried out by the group that has reason to believe it can only thus successfully decrease the disregard of rights where such disregard is prevalent is less morally unjustifiable than terrorism carried out by the group that maintains such disregard."[83] So Held seems to be arguing that terrorism that respects rights is better than terrorism that does not, and neither a consequentialist nor a rights-based analysis fully rules out terrorism's moral justification in some cases.[84]

But if it is plausible to hold, consistent with Feinberg,[85] that a moral right is a valid moral claim based on a valid moral interest and/or a valid moral choice, then perhaps what cases of conflicts of rights boils down to is, say, the interest and/or choice of a state to treat some or all of its citizens in a certain way versus those citizens' interest and/or choice to not live under such conditions. In such a case, there is a genuine conflict of moral interests and/or choices, and yet only one set of them can be the valid ones, all things considered. And it is precisely that set of moral interests and choices that bears the moral rights, a right that trumps all other moral considerations, many would argue. This brief sketch of the nature of a moral right sheds some light on the complex moral assessment of terrorism. We must, then, seek to identify the moral legitimacy statuses of moral interests and/or choices of each party to terrorism, of the terrorists and of their targets, and only then can we begin to make an adequate moral assessment of a particular case of terrorism.

NARVESON ON TERRORISM

When it comes to the moral justification of political violence, Narveson argues that there are four kinds of cases that would justify it: (i) preventing immediate injury to self; (ii) preventing immediate injury to others; (iii) preventing longer-range threats to life, self or others; and (iv) preventing or rectifying loss of legitimate liberty by self or others. These are, he argues, the *ends* for which political violence might be justified.[86]

---

[82] Held, "Terrorism, Rights, and Political Goals," p. 80.
[83] Held, "Terrorism, Rights, and Political Goals," p. 80.
[84] Held, "Terrorism, Rights, and Political Goals," p. 81.
[85] Joel Feinberg, *Freedom and Fulfillment* (Princeton: Princeton University Press, 1992), Chapters 8-10.
[86] Narveson, "Terrorism and Morality," pp. 130-31.

With these points in mind, Narveson discusses the morality of terrorism as a species of political violence. There are at least two sorts of reasons that are given to justify terrorism, according to Narveson. First, terrorism might be seen as a form of punishment for oppression or such.[87] Note that Narveson's reply to this line of reasoning takes the form of assuming that terrorism eventuates in death. For both of his replies to terrorism as punishment involve discussions of capital punishment and execution. But what about terrorism that eventuates in neither of these two things, such as the case of a terrorist bomb threat, or the MRTA taking hostages in Lima, Peru? Cannot punishment by terrorism be inflicted on a society in the form of real threats and destruction of property and such, with no death to persons? Had the U.S. Federal Building in Oklahoma City been bombed but with no one in or around it to be harmed, would it not, other things being equal, amounted to a terrorist act? Could not the same be said of various other terrorist attacks which eventuated in harm to others?

Terrorism might also be justified by saying that it is a means of social change. To this point Narveson raises the just war tradition's question of whether or not the terrorism is done for a just cause. Moreover, he asks, is the terrorism done discriminately and proportionately?[88] Even if the terrorist has a just cause, Narveson argues, she hardly commits her act of terrorism proportionately and discriminately. And it is here where Narveson raises three important questions for terrorism. The first point requires that terrorism be a necessary means to a particular end. The second one asks if terrorism is an effective means to social change. However, what is meant by "effective?" Terrorism can be effective if it raises consciousness where nothing else did before. Moreover, cannot something be effective in raising consciousness or being the right thing to do to thwart evil, all the while being condemned by a naïve or brainwashed public? The third concern is whether or not terrorism is morally permissible, or whether we could or should simply tolerate a particular injustice.[89]

Narveson does not believe it is easy to make the moral case for terrorism in a democratic context. But he even thinks that it is hard to make in a non-democratic one as well.[90] Yet Narveson argues that terrorism deliberately inflicts violence on innocent persons.[91] But we know that terrorism need not do this, nor does all terrorism do this. It appears that Narveson has violated a point made above, namely, that targeting innocents is not an essential feature of terrorism, it is an accidental or contingent feature of it. In fact, morally justified terrorism, as analyzed above, requires

---

[87] Narveson, "Terrorism and Morality," p. 138.
[88] Narveson, "Terrorism and Morality," p. 140.
[89] Narveson, "Terrorism and Morality," p. 144.
[90] Narveson, "Terrorism and Morality," p. 147.
[91] Narveson, "Terrorism and Morality," p. 151.

that the terrorist risk substantial harm to self in order to avoid risking the lives of innocents. In light of this, then, it would appear that Narveson's argument against the morality of terrorism begins to weaken. For he has not shown that terrorism cannot be morally justified in precisely the same kinds of cases that he cites for the justification of political violence in general: by preventing immediate injury to self; by preventing immediate injury to others; by preventing longer-range threats to life, self, and others; and/or by preventing or rectifying loss of legitimate liberty by self or others.

Concerning terrorism and public sentiment of the targets of terrorism, Narveson writes:

> Thus one must conclude that terrorism is extremely difficult to justify on strategic grounds, in the nature of the case. If its causes were plausible, terrorism as a means to promote them would be unnecessary, and when it is used, it is virtually assured of failure except for the most limited and immediate of purposes. Of course it will also produce hatred and suspicion of the terrorist group, rather than sympathy and support – another major factor working to ensure nonsuccess. Yet all of these factors are fairly obvious, and must surely be known to any terrorist groups that pause to reflect. Which, evidently, they do not.[92]

But it would seem that these remarks confuse the public's view of terrorism against itself with the question of whether or not terrorism is morally justified. As Narveson himself argues, terrorism might be justified on moral grounds in that it seeks to rectify loss of legitimate liberty by self or others. Yet cannot the public be wrong about whether or not it deserves terrorism inflicted on it, especially if it would have to admit that it was responsible for horrendous evil or wrong doing? Cannot the public be wrong about whether or not any act of terrorism is morally justified in such a case? The real issue here is not whether or not terrorism is sound strategically, say, in gaining the support of the public. If the public is evil enough to deserve to be a target of terrorism, then why is it relevant if the public supports terrorism in such a case? Terrorism is not bound to address the sense of justice of the society which is its target. This is optional for terrorism. For terrorism, unlike civil disobedience, might seek to replace or simply destroy an evil empire. And if the empire is genuinely evil or sufficiently bad, then it makes no sense to think that turning that society of outlaws against them ought to give pause to the terrorist group. At least, this seems to hold in contexts of morally justified revolutionary terrorism.

Finally, in the above quotation from Narveson it is mentioned that when terrorism is used, it is "virtually assured of failure." This belief, or something akin to it, is shared by most everyone in the world. But it bears noting that nothing could be further from the truth. If one thing is true about the 11

---

[92] Narveson, "Terrorism and Morality," p. 150.

September 2001 terrorist attacks on the World Trade Center and the U.S. Pentagon building, it is that one act or series of acts of terrorism can have cascading and lasting adverse effects on even one of the strongest economies in the world! Even almost two years subsequent to the attacks, the U.S. economy is faltering as millions of U.S. citizens struggle in terms of employment terminations, finding employment, staggering investment losses, etc. To think for even a moment that terrorism cannot succeed is to sustain a kind of blindness to its sometimes obvious effects. Of course, there are the long-term economic effects of the U.S. economy's having to somehow take account of the tremendous military costs of an ongoing "war on terrorism" and the heightened security that accompanies it, coupled with a regime's promise to somehow not increase taxes! Indeed, the adverse effects of the attacks seems phenomenal, as it even has ripple effects throughout much of the global economy.

I have provided a working definition of "terrorism," set forth the conditions under which it is morally justified, and stated the possible role of justified terrorism. I have not (yet) claimed that any specific case of terrorism is justified. Rather, I have set forth the foundations of how we might begin to judge terrorist activity, morally speaking. My estimation is that more terrorist acts than those who condemn it out of hand think are morally justified, and fewer instances of terrorism than terrorists think are morally warranted, though both reason and history must help us to assess this claim.

Now let us turn to a moral assessment of some recent acts of terrorism in the world, using as our basis for assessment the analyses found in this and the previous chapters.

CHAPTER 6

THE MORAL STATUS OF TERRORISM:
SOME RECENT CASES

In the previous chapter, I analyzed philosophically the nature of terrorism, as well as the conditions under which it might be morally justified. As stated in that chapter, terrorism is the attempt to achieve (or prevent) political, social, economic or religious change by the actual or threatened use of violence against other persons or other persons' property; the violence (or threat thereof) employed in terrorism is aimed partly at destabilizing the existing political or social order, but mainly at publicizing the goals or cause espoused by the terrorists or by those on whose behalf the terrorists act; often, though not always, terrorism is aimed at provoking extreme counter-measures which will win public support for the terrorists and their cause. It is clear, then, that terrorism correctly construed involves a political, social, religious and/or economic motivation on behalf of the terrorist or on behalf of those on whose behalf the terrorist acts.

Furthermore, in the previous chapter the conditions of morally justified terrorism were enumerated, expounded, and defended: S is morally justified in employing terrorism, T, in a certain circumstance, C, and at a given time, t_1, to the extent that:

> (1') S, being morally innocent, is defending herself or another morally innocent individual or group of moral innocents in the face of a significant form of injustice in C at t_1 and concerning which injustice S [or the one(s) defended by S] is innocent;
>
> (2') S is as conscientiously selective as possible in her choice of terrorist targets in C at t_1-t_n;
>
> (3') In C at t_1, S directs terrorist activity proportionately and only against those clearly guilty of committing acts of significant injustice;[1]

---

[1] This condition renders implausible the objection that according to (1')-(6) war qualifies as terrorism. However, terrorism may be an "act of war."

(4) If time and circumstance permit, S attempts other non-violent means of political, social, economic, or religious change in good faith;
(5) S plans T so as to best achieve the cessation of the conditions of injustice which might justify the use of T in the first place; and
(6) It is morally justified for others in relevantly similar circumstances to engage in T.

Now it is important to note that nothing in my analysis is committed to the *a priori* view that terrorism *per se* is morally justified, or that any *particular* act of terrorism is. (1')-(6) is a philosophical *analysis* of the conditions that, *to the extent that they are satisfied*, justify an act of terrorism on moral grounds. And it is helpful to discuss and analyze some specific recent cases of terrorism in order to discern to what extent, if any, they are morally justified, and why. This provides us with an opportunity to apply the moral principles that ought to govern our assessments of particular acts of terrorism. I will consider the recent cases of the bombing of the Federal Building in Oklahoma City, and the Unabomber, respectively, in the United States, as well as the case of the Tupac Amuru Revolutionary Movement's (MRTA's) takeover of the Japanese Embassy in Lima, Peru in 1997, the even more recent cases of the Nairobi and Tanzania bombings of U.S. Embassies in 1998, and the 11 September 2001 terrorist attacks on the World Trade Center and U.S. Pentagon building. These five examples of terrorism provide us with an array of methods of and motives for terrorism, not to mention varying degrees to which terrorist acts might be morally justified.

THE BOMBING OF THE FEDERAL BUILDING IN OKLAHOMA CITY

In 1995, Timothy McVeigh, acting in concert with others, successfully targeted for terrorism the Federal Building in Oklahoma City, Oklahoma. Hundreds of people, including citizens and children, were injured and almost 200 persons were killed. The perpetrators indicated at one point of the investigation that they wanted a "body count" to make their "point" against the U.S. government. They used a fertilizer bomb to carry out their deed, and McVeigh has since been apprehended, tried, convicted, sentenced and executed. That the act in question was an act of terrorism seems plain, given the fact that what motivated it, according to the perpetrator's own testimony, was revenge against a political entity, namely, the U.S. government.

Is this act of terrorism morally justified? It would seem rather obvious that it was not, and for the following reasons. First, on the conditions that are necessary and sufficient to justify terrorism [(1')-(6)], McVeigh and his cohorts failed to even attempt to employ any non-violent means of confronting political authority, such as protest, public debate and discussion, etc. It appears that they became frustrated with what they perceived as being problematic actions on behalf of the U.S. federal government, and they hastily employed politically violent means of "revenge" rather than addressing in good faith the very problems. It would not appear that the circumstances warranted an immediate employment of violence, especially of the terroristic variety, in order to address the perceived problem. Assuming that McVeigh was sincere when he stated that his terrorism was in response to the excesses of the Bureau of Alcohol, Tobacco and Firearms unit of the U.S. government, it is noteworthy that certain changes were made in that division of law enforcement not long after the events of Ruby Ridge, ID and Waco, TX.

In reply to this criticism, supporters of McVeigh might argue that they construed themselves as being, not merely reformers, but revolutionaries, and that they were simply claiming their right to revolt (guaranteed them by the Declaration of Independence) against the government which they saw as intruding on the rights of citizens, especially in light of the Waco and Ruby Ridge incidents. They might add that just as John Rawls would admit that some cases of injustice call for immediate militancy rather than long-term reformist activity, what the terrorism in Oklahoma City represents is precisely such a case. Thus what happened there was at least somewhat morally justified in light of its revolutionary nature, and it is not to be judged in terms of reformist criteria.

However, even assuming that the reformist criterion of employing non-violent means of political change is inappropriate for the case of the Oklahoma City bombing, there is yet another reason that counts against its moral justification. It is that the perpetrators *intentionally* and *knowingly* targeted innocent parties (e.g., infants and ordinary U.S. citizens who had no obvious or direct causal responsibility for the alleged wrongs of the U.S. government). Now on the analysis provided above [(1')-(6)], even the *un*intentional bombing of innocent parties is morally unjustified. And the sentencing of such wrongdoers might be mitigated in light of their not intending to target innocents, and even more if they had gone out of their way to avoid harming innocents. But the fact that the perpetrators of the Oklahoma City bombing knew full well that they would kill innocent children and others and intended, for purposes of a "body count," to do so makes their act of terrorism morally unjustified in a rather obvious and strong sense, violating the moral dictum that the innocent ought never to suffer harm in that they do not deserve it. Moreover, it violates a version of Kant's Categorical Imperative which states that we ought never to treat human as mere means to ends, but as ends in themselves. Furthermore, no respectable form of utilitarianism could justify such willful disregard for human life. Even if some existentialist notion of collective moral liability were plausible, a plausible principle of proportionality would never permit the killing of those who were in no way directly responsible, causally at least, for significant wrongdoing. Thus the Oklahoma City terrorist bombing runs afoul of (3') of my analysis of morally justified terrorism. And these points count against McVeigh's act of terrorism whether or not it is construed as either retaliatory and/or revolutionary terrorism. Thus the moral condemnation of the bombing in Oklahoma City is nonpartisan, ethically speaking. Unless it can be plausibly argued that each of those who were harmed by the bombing in question were in some significant way deserving of their harm, the Oklahoma City bombing is best seen as an instance of morally *un*justified terrorism, plain and simple. It is an example of how a disgruntled person with political motives places a great deal of effort in destroying what he hates, yet not nearly sufficient energy into evaluating the situation on *moral* grounds. It is a case of some terrorists acting in concert with one another against a society. A moment's reflection on what would count as genuine collective moral responsibility would render a rather clear verdict that most, if not all, of those victimized in Oklahoma City terrorist bombing did not deserve it.

THE "UNABOMBER"

Assuming that Theodore Kaczinsky, the "Unabomber," wrote and believes sincerely all or significant portions of the "Unabomber's Manifesto," the following facts become apparent concerning his terrorist activities over the past decade or so in the U.S. Basically, Kaczinsky targeted specific individuals who he believed were responsible for certain perceived problems, often pertaining to certain technological "advances," leaving or mailing them letter and package bombs and such. Some were killed or otherwise harmed by his acts of terrorism. And indeed these were acts of terrorism in the sense that they were motivated by a political reason, namely, one which states that technologies of certain kinds are morally wrong and ought to be stopped. At least, this would be one reason for his terrorist acts that could be supplied by the "Unabomber's Manifesto."

But were the Unabomber's actions morally justified? Whereas the bombing of the U.S. Federal Building in Oklahoma City was obviously wrong on various moral grounds, as stated above, it is not as clear that the Unabomber's terrorism was totally unjustified. Although there seems to be no evidence that the Unabomber graduated his political action from non-violent to violent means of confronting political authority, he did target specific individuals (or *kinds* of individuals) who might well be, morally speaking, legitimate and primary targets of political violence. In the Unabomber's mind, and perhaps even objectively speaking, it might be the case that circumstances were such that more protracted means of non-violent social reform were not feasible, thus supporting (somewhat) the morality of what the Unabomber did. For these reasons, then, the Unabomber's terrorism was *more morally justified* than what happened in the Oklahoma City case. Even if it turns out that none of the Unabomber's targets deserved, all things considered, to be targeted, the Unabomber's victims were not intentionally targeted indiscriminately as in the case of the Oklahoma City bombing. Thus the Unabomber represents a case of an individual terrorist's targeting other individuals for political reasons and in a *more discriminating manner* than in the case of the Oklahoma City bombing.[2] Furthermore, the number of those killed or otherwise harmed by the Unabomber's terrorism is significantly less than those killed or otherwise harmed by McVeigh's terrorist act. Because moral justification, desert, moral responsibility and related concepts are degree-laden ones, it seems plausible to argue that Kaczinsky's terrorism was *more morally justified* than McVeigh's. For specific individuals were the targets of Kaczinsky's terrorism, and comparatively few innocents were killed or harmed in the process. From both the Kantian standpoint of intent and the utilitarian standpoint of consequences, then, the Unabomber's terrorism, taken as a series of acts, was *more morally justified* than the Oklahoma City terrorist bombing.

THE U.S. EMBASSIES IN NAIROBI AND TANZANIA

On 7 August 1998, the U.S. embassies in Nairobi and Tanzania were bombed, resulting in more than 200 deaths and thousands injured. Most who were injured were Kenyans and Tanzanians, though a few U.S. diplomats/citizens were killed or injured. On the assumption that the bombings were terroristic because political in nature and are aimed at the U.S. because, say, of U.S. foreign policy, what is their moral status?

Unless it can be plausibly argued first that the terrorism in question followed at least some non-violent attempts to achieve social and political betterment, and secondly, that individuals at those embassies were primarily responsible and deserving of such serious harm, then it would appear that there is not even a *prima facie* case for the moral justification of these cases of terrorism. Indeed, it would appear that these cases bear a striking resemblance to the case of the Oklahoma City bombings in that undeserving or morally illegitimate targets were victimized by the terrorism. If the morally legitimate targets of the violent terrorism in question were, say, U.S. foreign policy legislators/politicians in Washington, D.C. or even certain U.S. diplomats, then *those and only those* persons are morally justified targets of political violence. And the difficulty in targeting successfully such

---

[2] This seems true even though some of the Unabomber's victims ended up not being those he actually targeted.

persons by terrorists in no way justifies on moral grounds the targeting of innocents, which seems to be what happened in the cases of Nairobi and Tanzania. If it is the U.S. government that the terrorists want to stop, and let us even grant for the sake of argument that the U.S. is an "evil empire" with its own "axis of evil" consisting of, say, the President, the Congress, and the Pentagon, then only those in the U.S. government who are truly and directly responsible for the harms to which the terrorism in question is a response are legitimate targets of the terrorism. Otherwise, at least two moral principles are violated. First, there is a violation of the principle that innocent parties, human or nonhuman, ought never to suffer harm because they do not deserve it. Secondly, there is the violation of the moral principle that humans guilty and deserving of harm should suffer harm only in proportion to the harm(s) caused knowingly, intentionally, and voluntarily by their wrong doing. In both cases, conditions (2') and (3') of the analysis of morally justified terrorism are violated.

On behalf of the terrorists in the cases of Nairobi and Tanzania, respectively, it might be argued that the circumstances of U.S. perpetrated injustice were such that the terrorism was justified, all things considered. Desperate circumstances call for desperate measures, it might be argued. And the bombings of the U.S. embassies in Nairobi and Tanzania were in the end morally justified because they were the only feasible means to get the attention of the world and of the U.S., thereby perhaps deterring the U.S. from perpetrating further wrongs.

However, it must be kept in mind that of those who were killed or otherwise harmed by the blasts in Nairobi and Tanzania, most were innocent Africans, not U.S. governmental officials or even diplomats. Once again, it would also need to be shown that such victims were indeed somewhat directly responsible for whatever might justify terrorism against them, making them deserving of such harm. Yet if it is the U.S. government that the terrorists seek to bring down or otherwise punish or harm, then using as secondary targets U.S. diplomats in a foreign country hardly strikes to the core of what might end up effecting those ends. So even strategically the bombings were dubious. Perhaps political assassination of key political or business figures in the U.S. who are indeed responsible for the injustices that (we are assuming in this case) are caused by them by way of, say, corporate-lobbied and controlled legislative action and such might be a more morally justified politically violent response than simply targeting U.S. officials so far removed, causally speaking, from the wrong doing that we are assuming requires serious rectification. Assuming that the violent terrorism in question was performed by a group, it serves as an example of for the most part morally unjustified group terrorism against a country. This holds true even if the terrorist act is construed as merely an act of vengeance.

THE TUPAC AMURU REVOLUTIONARY MOVEMENT'S SEIZURE
OF THE JAPANESE EMBASSY IN LIMA, PERU

In 1997, The Tupac Amuru Revolutionary Movement (MRTA) seized the Japanese Embassy in Lima, Peru. The dual purpose of the terrorist act was to liberate political prisoners from Peruvian jails, and to secure significantly improved economic conditions for Peruvians nationwide. Soon after seizing the compound, MRTA soon released several hostages unharmed in that they were not deemed to be politically important, e.g., those who might be responsible for the conditions of Peru. Subsequent to several weeks of pleading for then Peruvian dictator Alberto Fujimori to negotiate in good faith with them about the two stated issues, Fujimori negotiated with MRTA for a short time, then without warning had his military storm the compound and murdered the terrorists, even though none of them had harmed a hostage.

Although Fujimori and some others would deem his response to MRTA's terrorism a huge success, there are several moral questions that emerge here. First, does the fact that Fujimori never warned MRTA of the storming of the Embassy for a counter-terrorist attack count against the morality of Fujimori's action? In defense of Fujimori's counter-terrorism, it might be argued that its not being pre-announced is just as justified as the seizure of the compound by MRTA weeks previously. Nonetheless, Fujimori's tactic does represent a kind of bad faith negotiating tactic. And it is precisely such a tactic that would never justify a terrorist's similar actions, morally speaking. For recall that MRTA has been attempting to win the minds and hearts of Peruvians for years prior to its seizing the embassy, and MRTA's tactics of negotiating and seizing the embassy led to no violence on their part, just hostage taking (likely, of course, with a *threat* of violence as MRTA representatives were armed). In fact, the actions of MRTA during that incident hardly even suggested that MRTA would do violence to the hostages. Instead, MRTA's actions spoke significantly in favor of their repeated assurances that no hostages would be harmed. And *none were harmed by MRTA during the entire terrorist encounter*. Thus it appears that Fujimori's negotiations were not made in good faith, hardly suggesting that his actions were on the moral high ground. And no amount of self-justification by Fujimori in light of MRTA's previously violent history will suffice here, as historical relations serve as nothing better than a *prima facie* reason for action. What Fujimori did must be judged morally in light of the entire context of MRTA's behavior, not just in light of MRTA's violent past. So Fujimori's tactics, though prudentially adequate, are morally suspect in that he did not negotiate with MRTA in good faith once he agreed to negotiate with MRTA.

But even if it was morally justified for Fujimori to launch such a counter-terrorist attack on MRTA, the details of his attack are morally suspect in serious ways. First, Fujimori's counter-terrorist attack violated a legal (in the U.S.) and moral rule that only enough force as it necessary to apprehend a legal criminal is to be used. Fujimori's counter-terrorist agents were given no orders to capture MRTA's members alive. This leads to a second moral problem facing Fujimori's counter-terrorist response to MRTA's non-violent terrorist activity at the Japanese embassy in Lima. For Fujimori's response left no possible room for due process of MRTA's terrorists. This is a rather serious miscarriage of justice, as the facts show that the MRTA terrorists were caught by surprise playing soccer and such, and could have been relatively easily taken into custody alive rather than murdered without due process. So not only did Fujimori's counter-terrorism violate a moral principle of negotiating in good faith, but it failed to provide an opportunity for due process of such criminals when such an opportunity clearly presented itself. This casts serious doubt on the seriousness with which the Fujimori regime took justice and ethics.

The foregoing becomes increasingly obvious when one considers the steps that MRTA took in perpetrating its terrorism there at the compound in Lima. After initially capturing the hostages, MRTA released several of them because they were simply not involved with the political structure of Peru, making them undeserving of being a hostage. Moreover, MRTA released other hostages due to physical illness or because they needed minor medical attention or medications, including some persons who did have political authority in Peru. Clearly, then, MRTA sought terrorist targets in a rather morally conscientious manner, satisfying condition (2')-(3') of the analysis of morally justified terrorism. Their terrorism was hardly indiscriminate, as in the cases of the Oklahoma City, Nairobi and Tanzanian cases. Moreover, as the weeks passed, it was MRTA that wanted to negotiate in good faith toward a fair and non-violent resolution to the stated problems. And indeed, MRTA harmed no hostage during the entire incident, and it is unclear that MRTA would have even if provided with an opportunity to do so. Given the facts of the case, then, it would appear that MRTA was morally justified in what it did and did *not* do (There seems to be no evidence that MRTA harmed anyone in the process), assuming that Fujimori's dictatorship was significantly responsible for sustaining and perhaps even worsening the poor economic conditions of most Peruvians and for the capture and detainment of political prisoners in Peru. Yet it is Fujimori's counter-terrorism that bespeaks of a kind of moral insensitivity and fundamental injustice, violating principles of fairness and due process.

Thus it is evident that there are degrees to which an act of terrorism is morally justified, all things and persons considered. And this holds true whether the terrorism is perpetrated by an individual such as the Unabomber or a larger organization such as the MRTA. In the end, the moral status of an act of terrorism, like any other act having moral implications, is to be judged according to how well it is supported by the balance of reason. In the case of MRTA in Lima, Peru, the terrorists were morally justified in what they did (at the time in question), as their actions satisfied the conditions of morally justified terrorism [(1')-(6)]. Their terrorism was one act in a long line of protests against the Peruvian government's seemingly indifferent attitude toward the massive numbers of Peruvian poor, consistent with (1') and (4). The terrorists, moreover, were conscientiously selective in their targets of terrorism [satisfying (2') and (3')], and employed non-violent, though armed, means of protest, calling the Peruvian government to the negotiating table [consistent with (3') and (4)]. And there is no question that the terrorism was very well-planned in an attempt to rid Peru of its massive poverty and to free political prisoners under Fujimori's dictatorship, consistent with (5) and (6). So not only was the act of terrorist hostage taking itself morally justified at least for the most part, so were the terrorists themselves. Ironically, it was the Peruvian government's counter-terrorism that was morally unjustified. For there were no signs indicating that members of MRTA were out for violence, but instead the release of political prisoners, etc. Yet MRTA's non-violent terrorism was met with a denial of due process, a breach of good faith negotiations, and finally death.

THE WORLD TRADE CENTER AND THE U.S. PENTAGON

On 11 September 2001, terrorists hijacked four commercial airliners belonging to U.S. companies. Two were flown as suicide attacks into the twin towers of the World Trade Center killing over four thousand people and destroyed the buildings, another was flown as a suicide attack into the U.S. Pentagon building killing about 200 persons, and another was thwarted in its attempt to hit another strategic target. Almost 300 passengers (total) died, thousands more died in the buildings attacked by the terrorists, and hundreds of millions of dollars worth of damage was wrought on buildings, and the U.S. economy tumbled downward. There is no question that terrorists had made their mark on perhaps the most economically powerful country in the world. An entire society, even millions of persons globally, were economically and psychologically devastated by the attacks. Given the magnitude of the terrorist acts (or terrorist event), it is important to attempt to arrive at a rational and reasonable understanding of the moral status of them (it).

Let us assume for the sake of argument that the terrorists in this case genuinely believe the U.S. to be what Rawls would term an "outlaw society" based on years of perceived evils perpetrated by the U.S., domestically and globally. Let us also assume that the far majority of U.S. citizens have little or no idea of U.S. foreign policies over the generations, much less an idea of their effects, positive and negative, on other countries and peoples around the world. Indeed, the terrorist attacks might even be (at least in part) retaliation for the U.S.-ordered retaliation against Afghanistan for the 1998 U.S. embassy terrorist bombings in Tanzania and Nairobi.

Was the set of attacks in question morally justified? The answer to this question depends in large part on whether or not the U.S. is guilty of committing acts of tremendous injustice against others, whether intentionally or not. In other words, were the terrorist attacks of 11 September 2001 *deserved*? If the answer to this question is negative, then the answer to the question of the justifiability of the terrorist attacks in question is, of course, negative as such acts would violate (1') of my analysis of morally justified terrorism.

But what if it turns out that, for instance, the longstanding U.S. support of, say, Israeli and Colombian governments (to name only two cases) is morally wrong, even morally evil since in either case thousands of lives have been lost due to Israeli oppression of Palestinians and the oppression of U'was by Colombian armed forces in their protection of the interests of Occidental Petroleum, a U.S.-based oil company? Or perhaps it is U.S. capitalism and its colonialist globalization tactics that have caused the seething resentment, even hatred, of the U.S. government (as it is, by and large, lobbied or controlled by certain U.S. business interests) by such terrorists. If it is true that these serve as motives or reasons for the terrorist attacks in question, then the terrorists seem to be *prima facie* morally justified from the standpoint of revolutionary and/or retributive motives. That is, there is *prima facie* moral justification for their terrorist attacks to the extent that their alleged evil policies, actions, omissions and/or attempts of the U.S. government that motivate the terrorists are indeed grounded in reality. Thus, it might be argued, there is at least a *prima facie* case in favor of the moral justification of the attacks on the U.S. on 11 September 2001 insofar as the attacks served as retribution against the U.S. for U.S.-perpetrated injustices. But even if the terrorists of that fateful day had in mind no reason of the sort that might serve as even a *prima facie* moral justification for the terrorist attacks in question, the terrorist attacks *themselves might* have been morally justified on the grounds that, the terrorist's intentions and beliefs notwithstanding, the U.S. genuinely deserved to be targeted by terrorism in the ways (i.e., to the degree) perpetrated on that morning.

Now these might seem to be baldly false claims given the horrendous nature of the attacks. Most importantly, it might be argued, though one attack targeted successfully the Pentagon building, hardly a haven for morally innocent folk (with the possible exception of *some* custodial and other office staff, etc.) given the ethically "challenged" nature of many U.S. military operations over the past few decades, the World Trade Center towers and the airline passengers are innocent, as well as others who perished or were injured in various phases of the attacks. Moreover, the economic reverberations adversely effected the entire country, even various other countries. Certainly it is implausible to think that all such persons are guilty of something that would make morally justifiable such terrorist attacks! How could such terrorist attacks be morally justified given that they targeted innocent persons, thereby violating (2') and (3') of the conditions of morally justified terrorism discussed above? Rawls reminds us that the *citizens* of even outlaw regimes are not deserving of violence (given the soundness of Just War Theory).[3] So even on the assumption that the U.S. is an outlaw regime, it is unclear that the typical U.S. citizen deserves to be targeted by terrorists in such violent ways as were employed on 11 September 2001.

In reply to this concern, some, like Ted Honderich, might argue that:

> . . . we were partly responsible and can be held partly responsible for the 3,000 deaths at the Twin Towers and at the Pentagon. We are rightly to be held responsible along with the killers. We share in the guilt. Those who condemn us have reason to do so. Did we bring the killing at the Twin Towers on ourselves? Did we have it coming? Did we ask for it? Those offensive questions, and their offensive answers *yes*, do contain a truth. We did play a part, our politicians at our head.

> For the 3,000 deaths there are lines of responsibility into the past, as real as chains of command, containing earlier and later perpetrators. We in our democracies are in them, and in particular those of us who have got themselves into our governments. We are there with those who aided the killers and with Osama bin Laden. The killers and those who aided them and bin Laden are not alone. We have to escape the long illusion that those of us who are ordinary are innocent.

> . . . We were not just scene-setters. President Bush and Mr. Blair and their predecessors were not just scene-setters. It is true, if not the only truth, that we did *immeasurably more* than the killers of September 11, over a greatly longer time. Our contribution to September 11 was no single monstrous act.[4]

Honderich's incisive words *claim* that "we" share responsibility for the terrorist attacks of 11 September 2001. From such a claim it might be further

---

[3] John Rawls, *The Law of Peoples* (Cambridge: Harvard University Press, 1999), pp. 94-5.
[4] Ted Honderich, *After the Terror* (Edinburgh: Edinburgh University Press, 2002), pp. 125-26.

inferred that U.S. citizens are deserving of such terrorist attacks.[5] But what argumentation might be adduced to support the claim that U.S. citizens in general are to one degree or another morally responsible (liable to blame and/or retribution) for and deserving of such terrorist attacks?

It might be argued that, though the conditions of morally justified terrorism [(1')-(6)] are themselves sound, they are not violated in the way suggested by the terrorist attacks of 11 September 2001. In Chapter 4, we learned that J. S. Mill cautioned those contemplating the use of revolutionary violence that most citizens are not the types who think critically about social change and that an account of such violence ought not to demand too much of citizens, morally speaking. Now if what Mill argues concerning revolutionary violence also applies to retributive violence of the terroristic variety, then perhaps ordinary citizens should not be held to high moral and epistemic standards that would make them liable to severe harm for evils wrought by their own government. The idea here is that it is quite often true that ordinary citizens quite typically lack significantly high levels of voluntariness and power to effect meaningful change in their society, and they also typically lack the knowledge of many of the evils perpetrated by their own government. And it would, the argument goes, be a moral stretch to insist that such citizens are morally responsible (liable) to severe harm that their government commits.

But *if it is reasonable to hold adult humans in a society to a reasonably high standard, morally to know their government's foreign and domestic policies and to seek to correct them when or even before they harm others illegitimately, then it is less legitimate to distinguish sharply between military and civilian targets, as civilians are required to know and correct bad foreign policies of their government.* Should they refuse to do so, or simply become slothful in their living up to the moral and epistemic responsibilities they have, then they are hardly morally innocent (though, in the main, they are more morally innocent than others who have contributed more directly and substantially to the harms to which the terrorism is a morally justified response). Instead, they are morally irresponsible citizens, either because they are bad Samaritans in not requiring significant revision of bad foreign policies that harm others unduly, or because they are egoistically unconcerned, apathetic as to the horrible implications of such policies on others. In either case, the attacks would not be made (as they were) on morally innocent persons, but on those who are in significant ways morally responsible (liable to harm) for what their representative democratic government has perpetrated throughout the world. This is especially the case given that the U.S. is somewhat of a democratic society in at least the sense that it fosters and seeks to protect the responsible freedoms (including the

---

[5] This further inference is not, of course, Honderich's point.

freedom to act responsibly) of its citizenry. Indeed, the attacks can be construed, on this view, as "chickens coming home to roost." The only innocent victims in the attacks would be children, and perhaps adults who vehemently protest the U.S. perpetrated evils in question. If this is true, then *U.S. citizens who are significantly morally liable (for whatever reasons) for harms caused to others by their own government are in no moral position to complain to terrorists or others who harm them for what turns out to be a morally justified terrorist response to such harms that generate such terrorism.*

In the end, it should be noted, this line of argument seems to be only as plausible as the reasonableness of its somewhat high moral and epistemic standards for citizens. It also assumes that the U.S. government and some of its most influential and controlling business interests are morally responsible for rather significant loss of life and injustice to others prior to the terrorism in question. Otherwise, proportionality, a requirement of (3') of my analysis of morally justified terrorism, would fail to obtain concerning the 11 September 2001 terrorist attacks. In any case, *wherever terrorism is morally justified, it is justified only to the extent that it succeeds in targeting only those most deserving of it in proportion to the seriousness of the harms for which they are responsible and blameworthy, pursuant to (2')-(3'), above.*

So even if it is correct that ordinary U.S. citizens and the citizenries of other governments supportive of the U.S. are partly to blame for supporting in various ways the governmental policies that would morally justify terrorism of the magnitude of 11 September 2001, it does not follow logically that the events of that fateful day are indeed morally justified. For not only did the terrorists fail, as far as I am aware, to satisfy (4), but there is good reason to believe that the terrorism in question failed to satisfy (3') in that it was not directed "proportionately and only against those clearly guilty of committing acts of significant injustice." For even if it were true that ordinary citizens share responsibility for the terrorism in question, it hardly follows from this logically that each member of the collective (e.g., the U.S.) ought to be treated with equal force and violence – especially of the kind meted out on 11 September 2001. Would we not think that those who have (*de facto*) the most power to effect change and who are most causally responsible for whatever might morally justify the terrorism ought to be the primary and most heavily targeted for terrorism? Are we to think that all persons, regardless of their role responsibility or actual power to effect change in a circumstance, are legitimate targets of the same kinds and levels of political violence? Would not condition (3') lend clarity to our otherwise troublesome thinking here? While otherwise insightful in not excusing those who think they have no responsibility whatsoever for the wrongs that might morally justify the terrorism of 11 September 2001, Honderich's otherwise incisive reasoning seems to lend itself to a kind of fallacy in thinking that because each member of the group of ordinary citizens seems to share responsibility for the terrorist attacks in question that each such citizen deserves to be violated so harshly as was done on that day and to so many persons who at most had varying degrees of responsibility for such circumstances of injustice that might morally justify the terrorism. Yet those most responsible for the circumstances that might morally justify the terrorism were, as far as I know, unscathed. It is for this reason that it does not follow logically from the supposition that citizens of a country share responsibility for injustice that they share such responsibility at such similar levels that they deserve to treated by terrorists in the same ways, without due moral regard for the vast differences in responsibility they share.

What is reasonable clear, however, is that if unrectified evil is evil still, and if those persons and agencies having the power to effect positive change in rectifying past evils continue to perpetrate new ones, such persons *themselves* qualify quite obviously as those deserving of the bloodiest kinds of terrorism, terrorism so horrendous that the depths of hell would appear to them a welcomed respite.[6]

The typical attitude in response to terrorism is to react violently in punishing the perpetrators. As I pointed out, this was precisely the attitude put into action by Fujimori against terrorists rebels who non-violently captured and held hostages at a party for dignitaries in Lima, Peru in 1997. It was also the reaction of former U.S. president Bill Clinton in reaction to the 1998 U.S. embassy attacks in Kenya and Tanzania, respectively. And it is precisely the current attitude of not only most self-avowed "patriotic" U.S. citizens, but of the military and other advisors to the current U.S. president as they react to the 11 September terrorist attacks on the World Trade Center and the U.S. Pentagon building by declaring a "war on terrorism."

It is of course natural for a society or an individual to react in such ways when being attacked. But this is hardly a reasonable or reflective position to take, unless, of course, the regime in power seeks to rebuild by the billions each year its military budget that has been slashed since the new cold war and the restructuring of the USSR a decade ago, and/or unless it seeks to hide its own role in the attacks and/or its foreknowledge of them by blaming and demonizing someone else for them, and/or it desires to keep secret the precise business controlling interests that not only contribute to unjust foreign policies but also drive the U.S. "war on terrorism." For a counter-attack of such measures assumes that all of the targets of terrorist attacks are undeserving of the violence, or that the U.S. government is innocent of the charges made against it by billions of persons globally.

But if ethics is to be taken seriously, then a society must not make such assumptions. Rather, it must consider such attacks in light of *reason*, giving

---

[6] Assumed here is the notion that evildoers deserve and ought to receive their just deserts.

due weight to all of the available evidence concerning politics, including foreign policies, economics (including controlling business interests), *and moral principles (objectively construed)*. One such moral principle is embedded deeply in the structure of U.S. society itself: due process and the presumption of innocence until an accused person is proven guilty. And not even a context of war precludes democratic principles such as due process (Recall that even in Post-World War II Europe, Nazis were provided some significant form of due process, however controlled by U.S. and allied interests, as others are today in the International War Crimes Tribunal). This is especially important now given the recent establishment of the International Criminal Court. For it is only via due process that an objective, fair and non-interest-driven search for the facts can even hope to be attempted and accomplished. Short of that, a society responding to a terrorist attack ends up being a rogue society, bent on meting out what it thinks is justice, when in fact it is simply reacting out of self-interested egoistic, self-serving emotion. Only via due process can the facts of a case even hope to be heard from all sides of a problem or issue. And if a society seeking to become or remain democratic is to take rights seriously, it must take seriously *every human's right to due process of law*, whether international law by way of, say the International War Crimes Tribunal or the International Criminal Court, or some similar organization which can and ought to handle such cases. In contrast, international due process assists in guarding against any one country's attempt to hide its evil actions toward others.[7] It can well yield a sufficiently objective examination and evaluation of the facts of the case taking into consideration arguments from both sides. This due process system would require, of course, that the terrorists voice be heard, but in the non-violent context of a legal courtroom. Only by way of such a process can it be decided fairly whether or not and, if so, how and to what extent terrorists ought to be punished. For if their cause was such that the terrorism perpetrated by them satisfied the conditions of morally justified terrorism set forth and defended in Chapter 5, then the terrorists ought not, of course, to be punished. For they ought to be punished, if they are punished at all, only to the extent that they violated those conditions, (1')-(6). One such condition that might be violated is (4) which requires, among other things, that non-violent means of social, political, religious and/or economic change be attempted in good faith, if time and circumstance permit.

---

[7] After all, terrorist attacks often provide opportunities for governments to dupe their citizens into believing propaganda designed to divert attention away from foreign or domestic policy issues which are said by terrorists and others to lie behind the terrorist attacks to instead have citizens rally behind a blind patriotism which sees no possible way in which their own government might have had some responsibility in causing the terrorist attacks in that, perhaps, such policies had eventuated in the understood and horrific oppression of certain other groups or societies beyond imagination or moral justification.

On the other hand, if terrorists are morally justified in their terrorism, then surely the targets of their terrorist activities are hardly in moral positions to strike out against the terrorists. Instead, if the targets of the terrorism are themselves at fault, or if it is their government which is at fault in its significant oppression of others (either the terrorists or of those on whose behalf the terrorist act), then that society must itself deal with the genuine causes of (or reasons for) the terrorism. It must, then, *blame its own government and its most influential and controlling business interests for placing the lives of its relatively innocent citizenry in terrorists' harm's way.* In such a case, *the government would serve at least as a contributory cause of the shared responsibility for the harm caused by the terrorism.* But in order for terrorism to be morally justified, it must satisfy, among other things, condition (4) wherein non-violent methods of change attempted in good faith. In the context of the International War Crimes Tribunal and the International Criminal Court, this implies that representative parties of terrorists' concerns ought to attempt to attain justice against a particular party prior to engaging in acts of terrorism against it. And the International War Crimes Tribunal and the International Criminal Court are becoming forums, however imperfect, to hear such cases.

What is clear is that a blanket condemnation of terrorism is a facile and incorrect as a universal approval of it. For there are various kinds of terrorism and motivations for it. These factors require, then, a more complex and reasoned assessment of it. Each case of it must be assessed, and according to a wide array of principles and factors. One truth that begins to emerge from this analysis is that, as history reveals, no country has ever achieved lasting peace by fighting terrorism head on, on a "tit for tat" basis. Israel, being both a target of Palestinian terrorism (lately of the suicide bombing variety), and an example of state-sponsored terrorism against Palestinians, is a paradigmatic instance here. Nor has one achieved solace fighting it covertly. So the real and lasting answer to terrorism and other forms of political violence involves *dialogue*, not just military self-defense or some business- and/or self-serving "war on terrorism." Dialogue will include good faith negotiations, unlike Fujimori's trickery and violation of due process as regards to the case of MRTA in 1997. For by means of authentic dialogue, a country stands a reasonable chance of reducing the probability that it will have many enemies, including terrorist ones.[8] As one writer puts it, "If we try to eradicate terrorism but refuse to consider its roots

---

[8] Robert Holmes suggests that we ought to first try to understand terrorists and communicate with them instead of refusing to deal with them at all. We need to understand what it is that leads terrorists to do such things, and to try to bring a measure of justice to the world so that terrorism becomes unnecessary [See Robert Holmes, "Terrorism and Violence: A Moral Perspective," in Joseph C. Kunkel and Kenneth C. Klein, Editors, *Issues in War and Peace: Philosophical Inquiries* (Wolfeboro: Longwood Academic, 1989), pp. 123-24].

because we don't want to contemplate the possibility that we might share responsibility, we are doomed to frustration in our quest."[9]

Perhaps those serious about understanding the problems of terrorism need to attempt to adopt, for at least a moment's reflection, the perspective of the terrorist. In so doing, they might better understand why many terrorists risk, *even sacrifice*, their lives for a particular reason or cause. The rationale for certain acts of terrorism might well emerge, thereby creating in the minds of those supporting the status quo a genuine understanding of terrorism. Without such an understanding, reactions to it will not likely be effective, nor will countries be able to proactively resolve the general problem of political violence. *For understanding that there are indeed circumstances in which political violence of various kinds are morally justified better enables a government to realize that it has a responsibility to everyone (not simply to its own citizens) to ensure against its creating such conditions, and it better enables its citizens to serve as guardians against their own government's perpetration of deeds that would deserve retributive political violence against their own government and its most influential and controlling business interests.*

TO NEGOTIATE, OR NOT TO NEGOTIATE, WITH TERRORISTS?

Current U.S. government policy in dealing with terrorism is "... to deny hostage takers the benefits of ransom, prison releases, policy changes, or other acts of concession."[10] The basic argument against negotiating with terrorists is that if you do so, you court a kind of policy that breeds a proliferation of terrorist acts in the future, seriously threatening social and political stability and well-being. Certainly this is an important concern, as social and political stability and well-being are essential to a well-ordered society.

Yet there lies a difficulty with the view that we ought never to negotiate with terrorists. If we do not live in a well-ordered society, then we cannot simply ignore the rights and needs and complaints, especially legitimate ones, of minority groups, whether those minority groups are ethnic, social, political or religious ones. To say that we ought never to negotiate with terrorists would be to ignore the (potentially terrorist) forces of our unjust society that might well be trying to improve the social order toward justice and away from injustice. If we say that we ought never to negotiate with terrorists, then are we not implying that there is a limit to the extent to which

---

[9] Trudy Govier, *A Delicate Balance: What Philosophy Can Tell Us About Terrorism* (Boulder: Westview Press, 2002), p. 95.
[10] United States Department of State, "Patterns of Global Terrorism, 2001," May, 2002, pp. 142-43.

we really want to strive toward justice? For what if in such an unjust society there is a group that is indeed correct about what needs to be changed, and has for years tried to appeal to our sense of justice by non-violent means in good faith and has failed to do so due to our ignoring their pleas? If we do not even want to negotiate with terrorists *in such cases*, are we not saying that we have resigned ourselves to the injustice that precipitates that terrorism in the first place?[11] For we have not listened to the cries for justice from the voices of non-violence, and we also do not want to even negotiate with those who have courageously placed their own lives on the line by taking their case for justice to the levels of terrorism.

My point is not that terrorism is always morally right, for it is often morally wrong as I have argued in the cases of the Oklahoma City, Nairobi and Tanzania bombings. Nor is my point that we ought always to negotiate with terrorists. For some acts of terrorism might be perpetrated by those who, for instance, have no moral case at all, much less a rightful moral case, all things considered. Those who seek to overthrow a government for the sake of installing a new government, for example, that would discriminate unjustly against, say, Native Americans is hardly a case we need to consider for negotiation.

What I have in mind instead is a rather select set of cases where the lines of moral right and wrong are not so easy to draw, or where the terrorists have at least a partially correct point that might indeed do us well to listen to and implement. Palestinian terrorism in response to decades of severe oppression by the Israeli government is an example here. But this point is predicated on a certain view of society that sees us as human brothers and sisters living together in a world where we are each treated as equals and whose voices are taken seriously. As Rawls notes,[12] not every view or lifestyle can be respected, as there are disagreements of some kinds that force us to choose for or against each other where there exist no areas of agreement. In such cases, there can be no fruitful or successful negotiation that might in the end lead us to implement the requested changes by the terrorists.

Nonetheless, even in such cases where a government disagrees completely with the terrorists regarding the moral, political or religious motives of the terrorism, it does not have to agree to implement the requested changes in order to gain at least some significant measure of respect from the terrorist such that the terrorist feels a sense of being a part of the process of political participation. In fact, if a government does negotiate with at least some terrorists, such groups might begin to feel a

---

[11] That is, in the instances where terrorism is a response to perceived and even actual injustice, pursuant to (1'), above.

[12] John Rawls, *Political Liberalism* (New York: Columbia University Press, 1993).

growing sense of being much more a part (or at least not hateful) of democratic (or other legitimate political) processes, and assuming that those of us who are invested in such political process are unlikely to seek to destroy it, we can to some extent assume that terrorists will in many cases begin to feel the same way.[13] I submit (without being overly idealistic) that we can infer that my suggestion represents a change in the right direction away from the position that we ought never to negotiate with terrorists. For our not negotiating with any terrorists seems to draw an absolute line between "us" and "them," as if somehow the U.S. is the moral arbiter of the world, as if the U.S. has no history of horrendous oppression toward domestic and foreign parties, as if the U.S. is never on the wrong side of justice.

Moreover, I am not averring that a government is to necessarily or always "give in" to terrorist demands, but that it is to listen carefully to what the terrorists have to say, and then make the morally right (best) decision, *all things and persons considered.* Sometimes this will morally require a government to revise its policies, discontinue to "obey" some of its most influential and controlling business interests, and cease being causally and morally responsible for significant injustice domestically and/or internationally. I argue that it is this attitude toward terrorism that will in some cases draw terrorists back into the folds of domestic or global political reform, making them less likely to engage in terrorism. What is the alternative? We can continue to refuse to negotiate with terrorists, and watch incidents of terrorism against, say, the U.S. increase qualitatively and quantitatively as they already have in the U.S. and elsewhere in the world, which is what sound social cognitive psychology would predict. For if those who feel alienated from a society (be that society global or not) feel they have no other means by which to be heard than to commit terrorist acts are continually alienated by a policy of non-negotiation, then the chances that such persons would engage in terrorism clearly increase rather than decrease. Witness the terrorist response (in part) to Clinton's intentional killing (bombing) of certain targets in Afghanistan in reaction to the terrorist bombings of U.S. embassies in Nairobi and Tanzania: the 2001 terrorist attacks on both the World Trade Center and the Pentagon! These and other terrorist activities certainly render dubious the alleged success of the current attitude of unleashing military attacks on terrorists and their supporters without negotiation. If the "no negotiating with terrorists" policy were reasonably successful, then it would seem that those governments employing such a strategy would reduce, rather than increase, the numbers and intensities of terrorist attacks on the societies governed by them. However,

---

[13] I have in mind here domestic terrorists, though a similar point might be made in regard to international terrorism and the global communities.

the opposite has proven true in the U.S., as exemplified on 11 September 2001. The same seems to be holding true regarding Israel's use of the same policy, as almost constantly there are reports of suicide and other bombings and attacks in Israel by Palestinian terrorists who appear to intensify their efforts with every Israeli counter-terrorist response.

Thus one way, it seems, to attempt to decrease the incidents of terrorism is not to ignore it, but to address the problem directly by listening to what terrorists have to say, and then make a decision as to what to do about the matter on a case-by-case basis. However, this kind of strategy assumes that societies are sufficiently open to and concerned with matters of ethics, rather than being concerned, presumptuously, with the fulfillment of their egoistic desires. One must remember that one of the worst terrorist groups in U.S. history is the Ku Klux Klan, a conglomeration of groups that the U.S. government to this day refuses to bring even remotely close to a full measure of justice, and this in light of some of the KKK's well-publicized bloody terrorist activities, albeit mostly in the past. And we know that the U.S. government and various state governments not only tolerated such terrorism, mostly against African Americans, but sometimes negotiated with leaders of the KKK to end the violence. Given these and related facts of history, then, the U.S. is nothing short of morally hypocritical in tolerating *for generations* violent and inhumane forms of terrorism against African Americans by the KKK as it now refuses to negotiate with international terrorists. That the international terrorists are often persons of color makes one wonder precisely how blatant the U.S. governmental tolerance of white terrorism is when it is directed specifically at harming persons of color. Then one wonders, perhaps, whether or not it is a racist kind of policy of terrorist tolerance here, or if it is a mere "coincidence." The point here is that if it is correct to never negotiate with terrorists, then the U.S. government should have attacked and killed KKK terrorists everywhere in the U.S. with impunity, precisely as it is waging a war on an entire country in order to "bring Osama Bin Laden to 'justice.'" Of course, there is no statute of limitations in the U.S. on murder, and the U.S. government, in conjunction with various state and local governments, could (if it wanted to) bring to justice some of the aged klanspersons who engaged in terrorist murders, dragging them from the rest homes, porched and shaded rocking chairs, and death beds in order to "bring *them* to justice!" But that would require a country and a judicial system with at least a minimal moral conscience, moral virtue, and moral fortitude. Given this level of moral hypocrisy, the U.S. government should either abandon its questionable policy of not negotiating with terrorists and declaring war on them, or retain the policy and enforce it with remaining KKK terrorist murderers who can be successfully hunted and killed like the evil[14] terrorists they are. After all, the U.S. criminal justice system has already put to death one domestic terrorist who, it turns out, killed far fewer people than did the KKK during its virtually unchecked reign of terror.

I have hardly endorsed terrorism *per se*. In fact, the previous chapter indicates that *I hold the terrorist to a mighty high moral standard for justificatory purposes, a standard perhaps stronger than any other philosopher holds the terrorist to without begging the moral question against terrorism*. The reality of terrorism is a sad fact, but terrorism is often a response to previous oppression and violence, except that innocent people are victimized like political pawns in a game played by those seeking economic and political power more than justice. In some recent cases, the words of terrorists like Osama Bin Ladin claim that it is not U.S. citizens whom he seeks to harm, but their government and its policies that are oppressive to various peoples throughout the world. If this is plausible, then those whom the terrorists seek to "punish" most are those on whom it is most difficult to inflict their retribution. Yet if terrorism is a response to severe injustice of a government, then there may be a real sense in which those most blameworthy for the innocents harmed by terrorism are those *governmental officials and their influential and controlling business interests most responsible for the oppression* that motivated the (justified) terrorism in the first place. And *it is they, rather than relatively innocent citizens, who ought to be most directly targeted by terrorists*.

THE PROBLEM OF COLLECTIVE MORAL RESPONSIBILITY

This raises another moral issue concerning terrorism, namely, the problem of collective moral responsibility.[15] Perhaps the primary objection to the employment of terrorism is that, it is argued, it inflicts harm on innocents. Or, to put the point more precisely in light of discussions of previous chapters, terrorism is morally wrong to the extent that it harms innocents. There is a distinctly humanistic consideration before us here, namely, *that no human being deserves to be treated in a way that would be unjust or undeserved*. This is surely not the only variety of humanistic principle with which we might work. However, it is one with which we

---

[14] For a discussion of the concept of evil, see Joel Feinberg, *Problems at the Roots of Law* (Oxford: Oxford University Press, 2003), Chapter 6.

[15] For analyses of the nature of collective moral responsibility, see J. Angelo Corlett, *Responsibility and Punishment* (Dordrecht: Kluwer Academic Publishers, 2001), Chapter 7; Peter French, *Collective and Corporate Responsibility* (New York: Columbia University Press, 1984); Larry May, *The Morality of Groups* (Notre Dame: Notre Dame University Press, 1987); *Sharing Responsibility* (Chicago: University of Chicago Press, 1990); Burleigh Wilkins, *Terrorism and Collective Responsibility* (London: Routledge, 1992).

might begin. The principle implies that innocent people or things ought not to be treated, for example, as guilty and blameworthy ones. It further implies the Kantian notion *that it is morally wrong to treat moral agents as mere means to ends*. In the context of this discussion, such ends would be terroristic ones.

This humanistic principle relates well to the matter of who or what counts as a legitimate target of terrorism and who or what does not. Now there are, as noted in the previous chapter, primary and secondary targets of terrorism. *Primary targets of terrorism* are those persons to whose sense of justice the terrorist attempts to appeal and who are directly responsible for the problems that need to be changed, according to the terrorists. Paradigmatic cases of primary targets would be government officials of high rank who have principal decision-making power as regards a certain policy that is deemed by the terrorists in need of revision. A *secondary target of terrorism* is a person or thing that the terrorist wants to use as a means of appealing to the sense of justice of a primary target. Secondary targets are often used when primary targets are, for whatever reason, unavailable to the terrorists. In many cases civilians are often used to make a point by terrorists. The bombing of the federal building in Oklahoma City, if it truly was politically motivated as many news media suggest, would be a case in point where secondary targets are used as mere means of making a political point that, in the terrorists' view, the U.S. government is evil.

But it is precisely here where terrorism, of *this* variety, goes morally wrong and in a horrible way! It is *this* sort of terrorism that gives terrorism a bad name. Not all terrorism is (nor need it be) done out of a disregard for the various degrees of guilt and innocence in the world. That which is done out of such disregard cannot be morally justified, while that which places an essential regard for such innocence might be morally justified, depending on the circumstances. For example, to cause the deaths or injuries of children and innocent adults for the sake of anti-governmental sentiment, right or left-wing (or otherwise), smacks of political dogmatism without moral heart to feel or eyes to see what morality permits or requires in a given circumstance. *That* kind of terrorism the world must do without. Terrorism in its best case scenario already involves a great deal of moral courage and fortitude on behalf of the terrorist, not to mention a clear-headed decision to combat evil *without* harming innocent persons or non-persons. Given that terrorism is no less rational than acceptable forms of warfare, then it is no less moral.[16] From within the just war tradition, a fair moral assessment of terrorism often shows as much justification for terrorism as for the widely accepted killing of civilians in war,[17] except that the terrorist is often much more morally

---

[16] Holmes, "Terrorism and Violence: A Moral Perspective," p. 119.
[17] Holmes, "Terrorism and Violence: A Moral Perspective," p. 120.

conscientious than the typical soldier or military officer.[18] In short, and other conditions obtaining, an act of terrorism is morally justified to the extent that it succeeds in targeting those most deserving of the harm caused by the terrorism, those most responsible for the severe injustice to which the terrorism is a response.

What has any of this to do with, say, the 11 September 2001 terrorist attacks on the World Trade Center and the U.S. Pentagon building? Let us assume, for the sake of argument, that whomever was responsible for the terrorism (and we may never know unless there is adequate due process in the matter) was motivated by a hatred of the U.S. government and genuinely sought to change matters in the world for the better. Let us further assume, for the sake of the terrorist's argument, that the U.S. government was indeed guilty of atrocious acts of domestic civil liberties violations and, beyond that, significant violations of human rights globally. Even with these assumptions made, we must demand of the terrorist answers to the following crucial questions: How does it logically follow that it is morally justified to perform an act which would kill any innocent person? Moreover, how is it morally justifiable to *intentionally* kill an innocent person? Furthermore, how is it morally justified to intentionally kill *several* persons, including children? I argue that terrorism can *never* be fully morally justified when it involves the intentional or unintentional harming of innocent persons. So *the real issue with terrorism is not whether or not it is terrorist by nature (and thereby morally wrong) as many would have us think. Rather, it is the extent to which the victims of the terrorism are genuinely significantly innocent, morally speaking.* Are they innocent of significant harms to others, say, in the form of oppressive rights violations? Or, are they supportive of an oppressive regime that deserves to become a target of terrorist violence? If so, how strongly and in what ways do they support the regime?

What makes things even worse, morally speaking, is that the terrorists targeting the World Trade Center and U.S. Pentagon buildings did not, as far as I know, first employ peaceful methods of political change, openly and in good faith prior to resorting to terrorism of the most drastic kind. This also counts against the moral justifiedness of that act of terrorism in that it is a violation of condition (4) of my analysis of morally justified terrorism. Furthermore, the terrorists had no regard for human life. Why could they not have simply bombed some important landmark or building without anyone in it? That would surely have sent the same message. After all, it would cost millions of dollars to rebuild the landmark or building, and citizens would have been rather frightened yet would not likely ignore what the terrorists have to say. And if the terrorists' concerns were even partially legitimate,

---

[18] Holmes, "Terrorism and Violence: A Moral Perspective," p. 121.

citizens would likely have thought a bit more seriously about their message of political change than they currently do.

If, on the other hand, the terrorists were out simply to avenge U.S. evils, then the moral justifiedness of their actions nonetheless fails to satisfy robustly (2') and (3') of my analysis of morally justified terrorism. Unless it is true that those most victimized by the terrorist violence were truly deserving of it, the actions were not fully morally justified. However, it is precisely this point where the moral case for such terrorism becomes weakest. For when applied to terrorism, *the principle of proportionality requires that the amount of harm inflicted by terrorist violence be commensurate with the deserved harm of the target(s)*. It would seem that, given the various degrees in which U.S. citizens are blameworthy for U.S. wrongs compared to those having the direct power to effect change in U.S. policies, that this principle of proportionality was not honored in the case of 11 September 2001. The terrorists should have been much more concerned about the morality of their actions, *targeting only those most responsible and blameworthy for the making and enforcement of harmful U.S. policies (including certain influential and controlling business interests)*. In the main, this would make the targeting of the U.S. Pentagon significantly more morally justified than the targeting of the World Trade Center. Moreover, it would imply that it is more morally justified to target [pursuant to (2') and (3')] the White House, Pentagon and U.S. Capitol Buildings than it would be to target the World Trade Center in light of the fact that those who are most directly responsible for U.S. foreign and domestic policy making and enforcement are typically found in the former buildings rather than in the World Trade Center. In some cases, it would seem to be morally legitimate to target certain primary decision-makers of powerful corporations, companies, firms that lobby, influence and/or control U.S. government officials for the sake of self-enhancing profits while simultaneously serving as primary contributory causes in the violation of basic human rights. Again, responsibility, whether collective or individual, admits of degrees, as does moral justification. And some acts of terrorism are more morally justified than others, *ceterus paribus*. *What the terrorist ought to consider prior to her actions is the extent to which she will minimize or avoid harming innocent persons while targeting those who are most directly responsible for severe injustices. All the while, the terrorist ought to act according to a sound principle of proportionality in exacting harm on those deserving of it. For even enemies deserving of horrendous harm ought to receive proportional treatment. Even evildoers should receive their just deserts.* Once again, however, one of the fundamental concerns here is the extent to which it is plausible to hold regular citizens of a country morally responsible (liable to blame and punishment) for not understanding or knowing and/or attempting to change their government's policies that are, let us say, causally responsible for the terrorism in the first place. For it is the answer to this intractable problem that will determine to a large extent the moral justifiability of acts of terrorism that target, as most do, a wide range of persons, many or most of whom seem to have no causal connection to injustices that might justify terrorism.

NON-VIOLENCE EDUCATION

Having argued that there are certain (highly demanding) conditions under which some terrorism is morally justified, and having also argued that some terrorist acts are more morally justified than others contingent on the extent to which the conditions of morally justified terrorism are satisfied, it is helpful to note the role of non-violence education in decreasing the overall incidents of terrorism. What can be done to decrease incidents of terrorism? I have already mentioned a selective negotiating with some terrorists as a partial answer. But there is an even more important answer to the problem, and it involves careful moral education. Most, if not all, societies do poor jobs of educating our children from pre-school through college of the virtues and wonderful successes of non-violent political change. I insist that critical moral education is a major component to decreasing acts of terrorism. The violence in U.S. society, for instance, is at an all time high, and it should therefore not surprise any of us that terrorism has come home to roost right in its heartland. But if the system diligently teaches the virtues of non-violence, then perhaps U.S. society will go a long way toward decreasing violence in general, including political violence and terrorism.

But moral education entails something far more extensive than the education of youth and adults in morally satisfactory ways and teachings. It involves that a society actually engage in the Socratic practice of knowing itself, and of the epistemic and moral responsibility[19] of asking itself continually whether or not it itself is morally right, or if it needs to revise its ways because its policies, foreign or domestic, harm others unwarrantedly by way of exploitation, oppression, etc. Surely a society that is blind to how its policies adversely affect others is in no moral position to complain about its victims' developing a seething resentment toward it. And where such a society inflicts devastating harms on others, the perpetrating society is in no moral position to complain about various forms of others confronting its authority: whether by means of non-violent direct action, civil disobedience, or even terrorism (contingent on the extent to which such political actions

---

[19] For philosophical analyses of these concepts, see J. Angelo Corlett, *Analyzing Social Knowledge* (Totowa: Rowman and Littlefield Publishers, 1996), pp. 98-104; "Epistemic Responsibility," forthcoming.

are meted out according to the conditions of morally justified terrorism, above).

The real questions here pertain to how badly and in what sorts of ways and under what conditions did a society harm others. Depending on these and related factors, a society that has caused tremendous harm to others might well be the morally legitimate victim of terrorism of even the most horrendous varieties. For terrorism is not wrong in and of itself. Rather, as we have seen, it is morally justified or not contingent on the extent to which it satisfies the conditions discussed above. And where terrorism is morally justified, not negotiating with terrorists is often a sign of the recalcitrance that might well have led to the terrorism in the first place, a resilient evil that has entrenched itself in a society bent on an egoistic behavior in the world, come what may. In order to genuinely understand terrorism, we must realize that it is not mere criminal behavior, rather, it is a form of political address.

But those interested in averting terrorist violence must not ignore the ugly realities that spell terrorist doom for the future of countries such as the U.S. For there are problems looming which, if not rectified, might well bring further terrorism to the U.S. in that of the implementation of some of its foreign and domestic policies.

Justice must accrue for peace to become real and lasting. But where justice is significantly lacking due to human evils, the threat of terrorist violence often hovers silently, waiting for its opportunity to effect retributive justice where reparative justice is continually refused by oppressors. Of course, *non-violence is the preferred path to peace and tranquility*. But this path must be cleared of the rubble of injustices in order for us to walk that path with the confidence that accompanies only authentic peace. For as Thomas Jefferson penned: "The tree of liberty must be refreshed from time to time with the blood of tyrants." And we must never forget that tyranny often seeks to disguise itself in self-proclaiming "democratic" leadership, supported by certain ill-motivated business and military interests each of which purports to serve and protect the well-being of the unwary.

CHAPTER 7

TERRORISM, SECESSION,
AND THE UNITED STATES:
AN INDIGENOUS PERSPECTIVE

"The final political end of society is to
become fully just and stable for the right reasons."[1]

Previous chapters of this book have laid the groundwork for the analyses of the natures and moral justification of terrorism and secession, respectively. The neutral conditions of what amounts to terrorism have been set forth and defended, along with the rather demanding (on terrorists) conditions of morally justified terrorism. Prior to that "secession" was defined and a Territorialist Rights-Based (Indigenous) Theory of Secession was articulated and defended. Now it is important to ask if there exist conditions which, morally speaking, might justify terrorism against and/or secession from the United States, and if so, why? In this regard, we want to know if (1')-(6) of morally justified terrorism (set forth and defended in Chapter 5) might be satisfied concerning the U.S. government and/or its citizens. Yet we also want to know whether the conditions that would justify, on moral grounds, secession can be satisfied in the case of Native Americans in the U.S. Along the way, it is helpful to know whether or not secession *and* terrorism might be morally justified in the case of the U.S. It is to these complex issues that I now turn, beginning with secession and the U.S.

From Lithuania to Spain, from Quebec to Czechoslovakia and beyond, claims to the right to secede ring loudly, demanding rational and reasonable analyses of under what conditions, if any, secession might be morally justified. When it seems that secession *is* morally justified, it is sometimes the case that secessionist movements are unable to effect secession because the governments from which they seek to secede block their respective secessionist moves. Moreover, some secessionist movements face (or would face) oppression of untold horrors, and require (it might be argued) timely intervention in cases where genocidal or other seriously oppressive acts are perpetrated against their people. Where there is a moral right of a particular group to secede, then there is a moral duty of its government to *not* prohibit the secession so long as the conditions of justified secession are satisfied.

---

[1] John Rawls, *The Law of Peoples* (Cambridge: Harvard University Press, 1999), p. 119.

This follows from the correlation of rights and duties.[2] But what about cases of justified or rightful secession which are blocked by a government, thereby illicitly denying secessionists their exercise and enjoyment of their moral right? Is this not, at least in some cases, a significant violation of a basic human right to sovereignty? Are there *rights* to humanitarian intervention under such conditions of severe injustice (e.g., gross human rights violations) facing those who would be the targets of the intervention? Furthermore, are there third party duties of humanitarian intervention under serious circumstances of injustice? If so, what kinds of humanitarian intervention are open to third party interveners under such circumstances? It is important to separate the questions of humanitarian intervention moral rights and duties in that it is possible for there to be a moral humanitarian right to intervene in the affairs of, say, a secessionist context without there being a duty to do so.

HUMANITARIAN INTERVENTION

By "humanitarian intervention" is meant third party (typically state) intervention into the affairs of one or more states in order to provide assistance to a significantly politically oppressed group whose basic human rights are disrespected (consonant with John Rawls' sixth principle of justice among free and democratic peoples).[3] Such intervention might take either violent or non-violent forms, depending on what is necessary to achieve the liberation of a seriously violated people. In either case, it is forceful intervention into the affairs of another country for humanitarian reasons. What is common to all instances of humanitarian intervention is that the intervening nation uses its armed forces coercively to cause some effect in the internal affairs of another country and once the humanitarian aim is achieved, the intervening force is withdrawn.[4]

One commonality between civil disobedience, terrorism, secession and humanitarian intervention is that it is important in each case to distinguish carefully between their respective natures, on the one hand, and their respective conditions of moral justification, on the other. In addition to the question of definition, there are at least two questions regarding humanitarian intervention. One might be referred to as the "question of justification." It asks whether or not it is morally justified or permitted to engage in humanitarian intervention. This question concerns whether or not a certain individual or group has a moral right to intervene humanitarianly in

[2] On the correlation of rights and duties, see Carl Wellman, *A Theory of Rights* (Totowa: Rowman and Littlefield Publishers, 1985), pp. 54, 57-8, 74-5.
[3] Rawls, *The Law of Peoples*, p. 37.
[4] Paul Christopher, *The Ethics of War and Peace* (Englewood Cliffs: Prentice-Hall, 2000), p. 193.

the affairs of others. But as with other rights, the moral right to humanitarian intervention is not a right that must be exercised. It may be exercised or enjoyed (as the case may be) when one desires to do so, though some contexts provide more justified scenarios than others in which to exercise the right. As with rights in general,[5] the right to humanitarian intervention can be either a *prima facie* right, or not. It might be argued that every society has a *prima facie* moral right to humanitarian intervention, though context and circumstance will determine, all things considered, whether or not the proper exercise of that right will be outweighed by certain competing rights, values and more general considerations. However, the moral right to humanitarian intervention is unlikely to be an absolute right (i.e., one that is always morally correct to exercise, no matter what the circumstances), as there are certainly scenarios in which, if a society chose to exercise its moral right to intervene humanitarianly in the affairs of others, that society would place itself in grave danger.

There is also the "question of duty" which asks whether or not there is a moral obligation of one or more parties to intervene in a humanitarian way in the affairs of others.[6] In the parlance of Immanuel Kant, duties are either perfect or imperfect. Using this categorization of moral duties, the moral duty of humanitarian intervention might be perfect, wherein it is a duty which obtains for the duty-bearer at all times and in all circumstances. Alternatively, the moral duty of humanitarian intervention might obtain only in certain cases, largely determined by context and circumstance. I shall assume that where there is a moral duty of humanitarian intervention, that the duty is an imperfect one.

Following John Stuart Mill, Michael Walzer argues that, in light of rights to sovereignty and self-determination, humanitarian intervention is

---

[5] For philosophical analyses of the various views of rights, see Ronald Dworkin, *Taking Rights Seriously* (Cambridge: Harvard University Press, 1977); Joel Feinberg, *Rights, Justice, and the Bounds of Liberty* (Princeton: Princeton University Press, 1980); *Freedom and Fulfillment* (Princeton: Princeton University Press, 1992), Chapters 8-10; Wesley Hohfeld, *Fundamental Legal Conceptions* (New Haven: Yale University Press, 1919); Loren Lomasky, *Persons, Rights, and the Moral Community* (Oxford: Oxford University Press, 1987); Robert Nozick, *Anarchy, State, and Utopia* (New York: Basic Books, 1974); Joseph Raz, *The Morality of Freedom* (Oxford: Clarendon Press, 1986); L. W. Sumner, *The Moral Foundation of Rights* (Oxford: Oxford University Press, 1987); Judith Jarvis Thomson, *The Realm of Rights* (Cambridge: Harvard University Press, 1990); Jeremy Waldron, *Liberal Rights* (Cambridge: Cambridge University Press, 1993); Carl Wellman, *A Theory of Rights* (Totowa: Rowman and Littlefield, 1985); *Real Rights* (New York: Oxford University Press, 1995); *The Proliferation of Rights* (Boulder: Westview Press, 1999). A special issue on rights and justice is found in *The Journal of Ethics*, 4 (2000), pp. 1-165.
[6] I assume for present purposes no distinction between duties and obligations, a distinction that has been made in Richard B. Brandt, "The Concepts of Obligation and Duty," *Mind*, 73 (1964), pp. 374-93; E. J. Lemmon, "Moral Dilemmas," *The Philosophical Review*, 71 (1962), pp. 139-58.

sometimes justified or permitted on moral grounds on the condition that ". . . intervening states must demonstrate that their own case is radically different from what we take to be the general run of cases, where the liberty or prospective liberty of citizens is best served if foreigners offer them only moral support."[7] Even when the moral case for humanitarian intervention, or counter-intervention, can be made, the point of the former is to balance out the powers between the opposing parties, and the goal of the latter is not to win the conflict, but to rescue.[8] Moreover, humanitarian intervention is justified, avers Walzer, "when it is a response (with reasonable expectations of success) to acts 'that shock the moral conscience of mankind.'"[9] Furthermore, he argues:

> . . . states can be invaded and wars justly begun to assist secessionist movements (once they have demonstrated their representative character), to balance the prior interventions of other powers, and to rescue peoples threatened with massacre. In each of these cases we permit or, after the fact, we praise or don't condemn these violations of the formal rules of sovereignty, because they uphold the values of individual life and communal liberty of which sovereignty itself is merely an expression.[10]

The basic "formula" here, according to Walzer, is one of a moral prerogative or permission, not a requirement or duty. But it is one with certain constraints.[11] Although it is true that having a moral justification or permission to do something is hardly the same as having a moral right to do so, moral justification can serve as a basis of moral rights.

Rawls proffers three "guidelines" for carrying out the "*duty* of assistance," ones which might well be taken to yield those for humanitarian intervention as understood above without contradicting his fourth principle of non-intervention.[12] First, "a well-ordered society need not be a wealthy society."[13] The aim of the duty of assistance in the "Law of Peoples" within an international community of states is to "realize and preserve just (decent) institutions...."[14] Secondly, the political culture of the society is "all-important," and the mere dispensing of funds in such assistance does not always suffice to rectify severe injustices ("though money is often

---

[7] Michael Walzer, *Just and Unjust Wars*, Third Edition (New York: Basic Books, 2000), p. 91.

[8] Walzer, *Just and Unjust Wars*, p. 104.

[9] Walzer, *Just and Unjust Wars*, p. 107.

[10] Walzer, *Just and Unjust Wars*, p. 108.

[11] A critical discussion of Michael Walzer's ideas on these and related matters is found in *Ethics and International Affairs*, 11 (1997), pp. 1-104.

[12] Rawls, *The Law of Peoples*, p. 37.

[13] Rawls, *The Law of Peoples*, p. 106.

[14] Rawls, *The Law of Peoples*, p. 107.

essential").[15] Thirdly, the aim of such assistance is to "help 'burdened' societies to be able to manage their own affairs reasonably and rationally and eventually to become members of the Society of well-ordered Peoples."[16] To object to my interpretation of Rawls' guidelines for assistance as those which are applicable to humanitarian intervention is a merely verbal point. For my main argument does not depend for its plausibility on these particular Rawlsian guidelines. In the end, my argument is that terrorism may, for all Walzer says about humanitarian intervention and Rawls says about intervention and assistance, count as a form of intervention for humanitarian purposes.

However, the very notion of the duty of humanitarian intervention seems problematic for political liberalism. With such high regard for personal and social freedom, how can a liberal society, or a society of peoples, have either a right or a duty to intervene in the affairs of others without violating fundamental human freedoms such as the right to sovereignty? Perhaps part of the answer lies with Mill's Harm Principle. Within a liberal state, state interference into the lives of citizens is justified only "to prevent harm to others."[17] Thus the prevention of harm to others is a reason, and the only good reason, for the state to restrict human freedom, and, I infer, to intervene into the lives of citizens. If Mill's Harm Principle is applied more globally to matters of humanitarian intervention, then it might state that the only good reason to justify the humanitarian intervention into the affairs of a society would be to prevent serious harm to persons, say, due to severe injustice. But even if this application of the Millian Harm Principle is correct, it seems only to ground a Walzerian moral *right* to humanitarian intervention, but it is insufficient to serve as a foundation for a Rawlsian moral *duty* of humanitarian intervention as Rawls insists exists at least in some cases.

Can there be a moral *duty* of humanitarian intervention? If so, under what conditions would it obtain, and why? In general, and excluding severe emergency situations, a third party has a moral duty of humanitarian intervention to the extent that: (1) that party has permitted sufficient time to elapse for the two parties which are at odds with one another to at least engage in good faith negotiations with each other in order to resolve their fundamental conflicts; (2) that party has allowed enough time to elapse for it itself to offer itself as a (hopefully) neutral agent of negotiations between the parties at odds with each other; (3) that party has strong evidence that there is severe injustice regarding basic human rights within the borders of the two

---

[15] Rawls, *The Law of Peoples,* pp. 108-09.
[16] Rawls, *The Law of Peoples,* p. 111.
[17] John Stuart Mill, *On Liberty* (Indianapolis: Hackett Publishing Company, 1978), p. 9. The Harm Principle is discussed in Joel Feinberg, *Harm to Others* (Oxford: Oxford University Press, 1984).

parties; (4) that party has strong evidence that a peaceful resolution between the two parties at odds with each other is highly unlikely (perhaps the results of good faith peaceful protests and negotiations are unsuccessful); (5) that party has strong reason to think that no (other) third party offers to resolve the problems between the two parties at odds with each other is likely; (6) that party is strongly justified in believing that only humanitarian intervention will stop (or at least contribute to the stoppage), say, the severe injustice in question; (7) that party seeks and obtains the uncoerced permission of the oppressed people to intervene in the situation; (8) that party uses only as much force as is necessary to stop the injustice in question (that the party does not act, as Walzer states, to "win the war," but to restore a context of humanitarian civility); (9) that party takes steps to ensure as best it can (practically speaking) that innocents (on both sides) are unharmed by the intervention; (10) that party refuses, unless requested at a later date by the parties involved in the conflict, to allow itself to get involved in the political processes of those parties subsequent to the intervention; (11) that party is not placing its constituents, or constituents of other third parties, in significant danger of societal survival; and (12) that party, if it did not engage in humanitarian intervention, would serve as a causal factor in the further harm of the oppressed.

Clarificatory comments on these conditions are in order. (1)-(5) convey the idea that sincere attempts to resolve the problem of oppression are made in good faith, but nonetheless fail. However, since the oppression continues, action is required. Given that non-violent means of social change are either not viable options (due to time urgency restrictions, for example), political violence might become an unfortunate option. Rather than continue to stand by and know that oppression will continue, intervention of a violent nature might be called for (6). (7) requires that the third party intervenor must seek and obtain the permission of the oppressed party. Insofar as violent means to end the problem are justified, the third party intervenor must target only those most responsible for the severe injustice, and avoid harming innocents even at significant cost to themselves [(8)-(9)]. But after the intervention subsides and is hopefully successful in ceasing the oppression, then the intervening party must step aside and refuse to allow itself to play a role in the politics of the situation, unless it is asked to do so by the oppressed party (perhaps even by both parties) [(10)]. (11)-(12) hold that not only must the intervening party guard against placing its own constituents in significant danger of life, but it must also be a fact of the matter that should the intervening party not intervene, then it would indeed serve as a significant causal factor (by way of negligence) in the ongoing harm of the oppressed party. (12) is based on the Millian claim that where "grave danger" or "grave peril of life, person or health" obtain, then good Samaritanism is morally required:

... certain acts of individual beneficence, such as saving a fellow creature's life, or interposing to protect the defenceless against ill-usage, things which whenever it is obviously a man's duty to do, he may rightfully be made responsible to society for not doing. A person may cause evil to others not only by his actions but by his inaction, and in either case he is justly accountable to them for the injury.[18]

This implies a moral duty to intervene under conditions where our non-intervention would contribute to the grave danger of others. And this holds for both individuals and collectives. This explication of (12) guards against the objection that the above analysis, even if plausible, provides us with conditions which, if satisfied, point to a moral justification (or perhaps a right) to humanitarian intervention, but not to a moral duty of intervention.

TERRORISM, SECESSION, AND HUMANITARIAN INTERVENTION

Now to the extent that justice via reparations to Native Americans are denied by the U.S. government and amount to a severe injustice to Native Americans, secession and in some cases, terrorism, are morally justified not only by Native Americans in defense of their own sovereignty and self-determination (and that these are goods for a people to have[19]), and in search of criminal justice, but by third party states engaging in humanitarian intervention or counter-intervention on behalf of Native Americans. Assumed here is what I have argued fully elsewhere, namely, that Native Americans are indigenous peoples to North America (or that their acquisition to the lands they inhabited was generally on just terms), and that reparations to Native Americans are morally justified.[20] Also assumed herein is what I have argued in Chapter 4, namely, that Native Americans have a moral right to secede from the U.S. (e.g., to claim the territory on which it resides, or another, within the U.S., as its own, and to live as sovereign nations), and that, as noted in Chapter 5, there are certain conditions which, if satisfied, would justify terrorism on moral grounds. The cases for Native American rights to reparations and secession are separate matters, as is the matter of morally justified terrorism. But I shall treat them as related for purposes of this chapter.

---

[18] Mill, *On Liberty*, pp. 10-1.

[19] Rawls, *The Law of Peoples,* p. 85. Whatever rights to sovereignty and self-determination amount to, they are restricted rights, as Rawls avers, ones involving, among other things, autonomy and a cluster of rights protecting it.

[20] J. Angelo Corlett, "Reparations to Native Americans?" in Alexandar Jokic, Editor, *War Crimes and Collective Wrongdoing* (London: Blackwell, 2000), pp. 236-69; *Responsibility and Punishment* (Dordrecht: Kluwer Academic Publishers, 2001), Chapter 9; and *Race, Racism, and Reparations* (Ithaca: Cornell University Press, 2003), Chapter 8.

When history is replete with instances where Native Americans and some of their supporters have filed numerous legal suits against the U.S. government (over the course of *generations*) for U.S. wrongs against Native Americans, and where generation after generation of Native Americans and their sympathizers have protested publicly the massive evils (of genocidal proportions) perpetrated against Native Americans by the U.S. government, there is no question that the U.S. has refused to award reparations to them in any adequate form.

Under conditions in which for generations of their being denied reparations for genocidal acts against them, some Native Americans might make a more radical attempt at sovereignty and self-determination that they so richly deserve. That attempt might take the form of secessionist movements from the U.S., which has been their most ardent, though not their sole, oppressor. As we saw in Chapter 4, secession is the right to self-determination[21] or sovereignty by a political collective. It involves, among other things, the collective's claiming territory as its own. It does not seek to overthrow the government. Instead, it attempts to break away from its authority. It need not become physically violent (As noted earlier, Brasil's secession from Portugal in 1822 was not violent), though it often leads to violence where severe conflicts arise concerning territorial boundaries, alleged human rights violations, etc.[22] Whether or not secession is morally justified is contingent, among other things, on the extent to which the secessionists have a *valid* moral interest and/or claim (i.e., a moral right) concerning the territory they claim as their own.

At first blush, it might be thought that nothing much would change or need to be changed if Native Americans seceded from the U.S. Perhaps all this would really amount to is that a thicker geographical line would be drawn around current Native American reservations, and a few stricter laws might be passed (by the U.S., of course) to better ensure Native American power over such lands. However, such a state of affairs would hardly amount to sovereignty for Native Americans. And if true sovereignty is what Native American nations want, no such "deal" would suffice. If sovereignty

---

[21] For an analysis of the right to self-determination, see Allen Buchanan, "The Right to Self-Determination: Analytical and Moral Foundations," *Arizona Journal of International and Comparative Law*, 8 (1991), pp. 41-50.

[22] Both "secession" and the "right to secede" are defined in Allen Buchanan, *Secession* (Boulder: Westview, 1990); "Theories of Secession," *Philosophy and Public Affairs*, 26 (1997), pp. 31-61; "Self-Determination and the Right to Secede," *Journal of International Affairs*, 45 (1992), pp. 347-65; "Federalism, Secession, and the Morality of Inclusion," *Arizona Law Review*, 37 (1995), pp. 53-63; David Copp, "International Law and Morality in the Theory of Secession," *The Journal of Ethics*, 2 (1998), pp. 219-45; J. Angelo Corlett, "The Right to Civil Disobedience and the Right to Secede," *The Southern Journal of Philosophy*, 30 (1992), pp. 19-28; "The Morality and Constitutionality of Secession," *Journal of Social Philosophy*, 30 (1998), pp. 120-29; "Secession and Native Americans."

is not gained, then Native American nations would continue to wither away without even an opportunity for self-determination, a political right that can only be realized if genuine Native American sovereignty obtains. Indeed, if Native Americans are ever to have the genuine sovereignty they deserve,[23] they must make a clean break from the dominion of the U.S. This would involve, it would appear, secession.

Now the matter of Native American secession is distinct from the issue of Native American reparations.[24] For the former can occur without the latter, and vice-versa. However, I am imagining a case whereby Native Americans are not awarded anything akin to the reparations they deserve from the U.S. and where this U.S. failure of justice serves as one justificatory reason why Native Americans want to secede from the U.S., as the refusal over several generations by the U.S. to pay anywhere akin to adequate reparations for the genocide it perpetrated against Native Americans surely bespeaks volumes of the fundamental disrespect the U.S. and its citizenry have for the basic human rights of Native Americans. As Thomas Nagel writes, "We have always known that the world is a bad place. It appears that it may be an evil place as well."[25] Perhaps few peoples, if any, understand this more than do Native Americans. So rather than continue to exist, mostly in squalor and under U.S. dominion, Native Americans, let us say, would prefer to live and die (as did several of the Apache nation, for example) in complete segregation from those who oppress them even today. This move requires, it appears, secession from the U.S. by Native Americans, especially in light of the history of Native American-U.S. relations.

Native American secession, like other cases of secession,[26] would be justified to the extent that the following conditions are satisfied. First, Native Americans would no longer desire to remain under the dominion of the U.S. Second, Native Americans would have a valid moral claim to and/or valid moral interest in the territories on which they reside and seek to claim as theirs independently of U.S. rule. Thirdly, Native Americans would agree to pay "exit costs" of secession, should they owe any. It is obvious that Native Americans qualify as those who satisfy each of these conditions, though if any party owes exit costs to another, it would be the U.S. which owes

---

[23] I assume here a plausible notion of moral desert. For discussions of desert, see J. Angelo Corlett, "Making *More* Sense of Retributivism: Desert as Responsibility and Proportionality," *Philosophy*, forthcoming; *Resposibility and Punishment*, Second Edition (Dordrecht: Kluwer Academic Publishers, 2003) Chapter 5. Louis Pojman and Owen McLeod, Editors, *What Do We Deserve?* (Oxford: Oxford University Press, 1999).

[24] See note 20, above.

[25] Thomas Nagel, *Mortal Questions* (Cambridge: Cambridge University Press, 1979), p. 74.

[26] See Chapter 4 of this book.

substantial exit costs to Native Americans.[27] And given that they are the ones who have *valid* claims to most all of the territories in the Americas, then *they* qualify as those satisfying the contents of the "Territoriality Thesis."[28] Native American claims to secede from the U.S., then, would impose on the U.S. a duty of non-interference with Native Americans concerning the exercise of their right to secede from the U.S. Of course, that the U.S. would genuinely respect the Native American right to secede from it is quite another question.

It does not take but a moment of serious reflection, however, to see what some of the implications of this political divorce might be. For if the Native American nations as a coalition turn to the United Nations, the International War Crimes Tribunal, and the International Criminal Court in order to seek justice along these lines, it might be the case that these bodies of international political power might well decide that both reparations and secession are legal rights to which Native Americans have valid claims against the U.S. government. As David Copp states,

> . . . the right to secede of territorial political societies could be implemented as an international legal right by adding disputes over secession to the jurisdiction of the International Court. On a request either by a secessionist group or by the larger state, the Court would have jurisdiction to rule on whether a secessionist group actually qualifies as a territorial political society and therefore has the liberty to conduct a plebiscite on secession.[29]

Moreover, it might be decided that those bodies would support any and all Native American secessionist movements within U.S. boundaries. Obviously, Native American secession from the U.S. is not contingent on the U.S. government's not paying adequate reparations to Native American nations, though the U.S. government's refusal to pay adequate reparations to Native American nations surely supports in a substantial way a Native American right to secede.[30] For Native American secession might well be justified on independent grounds.[31]

This scenario presents at least two kinds of questions, assuming that the U.S. would continue its history of neglect in honoring and respecting these and certain other Native American rights. One question is the extent to

---

[27] For those who might be tempted to think that Native Americans owe exit costs to the U.S. government for, say, protective services and the like, it needs to be recalled that such "services" were and are not only coerced, but they were also the very "services" (in the form of the U.S. Army) that committed genocidal acts against Native Americans by the millions, and created many of the conditions that stand to oppress many Native Americans even today.
[28] See Chapter 4 of this book.
[29] Copp, "International Law and Morality in the Theory of Secession," p. 235.
[30] This does not assume, however, a fault model of secession as fault is not a necessary condition of secession, though fault might be a sufficient condition of justified secession.
[31] Corlett, "Secession and Native Americans;" Chapter 4 of this book.

which humanitarian intervention and counter-intervention by third parties is allowed (or even required) in support of various Native American secessionist movements should they develop; another is the extent to which both Native Americans and intervening states and groups are morally permitted (or even required) to intervene. Options here include, but are not limited to, a formal decision to "side" with Native American rights to, say, reparations and secession from the U.S., public protests of U.S. policies regarding Native American human rights violations both on U.S. soil and elsewhere throughout the Americas (thereby raising international consciousness concerning the matter), other traditional methods of non-violent direct action and civil disobedience, provision of arms to Native Americans in order to assist in their secessionist goals, provision of UN troops to assist in the same, provision of arms and/or troops by non-UN states as well, and even terrorism against the U.S. government both within and outside of U.S. borders.[32] I shall focus on terrorism as a mode of humanitarian intervention in order to liberate Native Americans from U.S. dominion, assuming the satisfying of condition (7) of the duty of humanitarian intervention, above.

TERRORISM AS HUMANITARIAN INTERVENTION

Is terrorism ever morally justified against the U.S. as a mode of humanitarian intervention to assist Native American secessionists? To suggest that such terrorism is never morally justified[33] is simply to beg the question in favor of a status quo that seems to be riddled with historical evils that can hardly be outweighed by even the harshest forms of terrorism. So the hyperbolically conservative and self-serving suggestion (by most U.S. citizens, for instance) that terrorism under such circumstances can never be morally justified is just as wrongheaded as the exaggerated view that it is always justified under the conditions imagined. Intuitively, what seems most plausible is the position that *some* forms of physically violent response to U.S.'s neglect to rectify its genocidal evils and continued oppression of

---

[32] Examples of terroristic activities against the U.S. away from U.S. soil includes the Revolutionary Armed Forces of Colombia (FARC) and its incessant bombing of oil pipelines operated by U.S.-based Occidental Petroleum in Colombia, an oil company which is controlling land taken by the U'wa nation. Indeed, these bombings increased in protest of former U.S. President Bill Clinton's visit to Colombia on 31 August 2000. While these might be instances of FARC's morally justified terrorism, while instances of its unjustified terrorism include its kidnappings of thousands of Colombians many of whom are children who are undeserving targets of such terrorist activities.

[33] See R. M. Hare, *Essays on Political Morality* (Oxford: Oxford University Press, 1989), pp. 34-44; Igor Primoratz, "What is Terrorism?" *Journal of Applied Philosophy*, 7 (1990), p. 133; Carl Wellman, "On Terrorism Itself," *Journal of Value Inquiry*, 13 (1979), pp. 250-99.

Native Americans are justified. Terrorism is one such violent response, under certain conditions.

As I have argued in Chapter 5, terrorism is, generally, the attempt to achieve or prevent political, social, economic or religious change by the actual or threatened use of violence against other persons or other persons' property. The violence, or threat thereof, employed in terrorism is aimed partly at destabilizing the existing political or social order, but mainly at publicizing the goals or cause espoused by the terrorists or of those on behalf the terrorists act. Often, though not always, terrorism is aimed at provoking extreme counter-measures which will win public support for the terrorists and their cause. It is clear that this definition of "terrorism" neither rules out the justification of it on *a priori* grounds, nor makes it such that terrorism cannot be a species of humanitarian intervention.

Walzer defines the method of terrorism as the "random murder of innocent people,"[34] though he recognizes that there are examples of terrorists who refuse to target the innocent.[35] It is clear, then, that justified terrorism needs to distinguish between combatants and non-combatants,[36] and more specifically, between those who deserve and those who do not clearly deserve to become the victims of the violence of terrorism. Perhaps it can be argued with some plausibility that the U.S. citizens who in general really do or should know the history of genocidal acts of their own government against Native Americans are deserving of the terror that accompanies terrorism, though *the violence that is visited by terrorism ought to be reserved for those who hold primary positions of political and/or economic power and who could and should have at least supported Native American reparations and other forms of justice for Native Americans.* Even if Walzer were correct in his (presumably) descriptive claim that terrorists kill anybody,[37] it does not follow that *morally justified terrorism* is permitted to have such a policy. And even though it is true, as Walzer points out, that terroristic armed struggles for freedom might be "necessary" (Indeed, he argues that "it is at least possible to imagine oppression so severe that terrorism . . . might be morally defensible"[38]), this need not and ought never to include children.[39] It is for these and other reasons why it is argued that

---

[34] Walzer, *Just and Unjust Wars,* p. 197.

[35] Walzer, *Just and Unjust Wars,* pp. 198-99.

[36] The distinction between combatants and noncombatants is found in Richard Brandt, "Utilitarianism and the Rules of War," *Philosophy and Public Affairs,* 1 (1972), pp. 1f.; Nagel, *Mortal Questions,* Chapter 5 (see also Hare, *Essays on Political Morality,* Chapter 5, which is a commentary on Nagel, *Mortal Questions,* Chapter 5); and Walzer, *Just and Unjust Wars,* though neither philosopher applies the distinction to acts of terrorism as is found in Chapter 5 of this book.

[37] Walzer, *Just and Unjust Wars,* p. 203.

[38] Michael Walzer, *Obligations* (Cambridge: Harvard University Press, 1970), p. 67.

[39] Walzer, *Just and Unjust Wars,* p. 205.

political violence such as terrorism must exercise restraint in not targeting innocents.[40]

Under what conditions would terrorism be a justified mode of political response to the U.S. and its recalcitrant attitude toward justice concerning Native Americans? These conditions must, of course, be consistent with those articulated and defended in Chapter 5. First, *whatever injustice is at the root of Native American-U.S. relations here must be significant*. It must be a violation of one or more of the Rawlsian principles of justice.[41] This condition is satisfied in that there is a clear record of generations of legal suits, non-violent protests and general consciousness-raising campaigns by Native Americans which would easily satisfy this necessary condition of the employment of terrorism. In fact, most every U.S. citizen is of the opinion that what the U.S. did to Native Americans (genocide) in order to steal the land on which they reside as U.S. citizens was somehow "justified" so that the U.S. could become the "greatest country in the world." Thus it is unlikely that further campaigns of consciousness-raising would do any good to change the tide of public support for manifest destiny and U.S. imperialism when it comes to Native Americans and their rights. It appears that the only thing to which most U.S. citizens might take heed is something of a violent nature, such as terroristic violence. Thus the basic reason for the terrorist activity would certainly be a morally adequate one. This condition assumes that *those who are justified in employing terrorism are not themselves guilty of unrectified and severe injustice.*

Second, there must be a *highly conscientious selection of targets* in order for terrorism to be a morally justified form of response. *No random or indiscriminate terrorism is ever morally justified.* On the contrary, the most deserving of severe harm in a society must be the targets, and the only targets, of morally justified terrorism. Often, but not always, this will eliminate the general population of non-combatant civilians from the terrorists' legitimate aim.

I should hasten to add, though, to the previous point the fact that the U.S. is populated (and always has been populated) by a citizenry fewer than 50% of whom (at any given time slice of history) have a college education, and far fewer than that number have received a good quality university education. This fact, coupled with the fact that pre-college "education" in the U.S. (public or private) typically amounts to ideological propaganda (rather than a critical inquiry into problems) especially in terms of moral and social

---

[40] Walzer, *Just and Unjust Wars*, pp. 205-06; Chapter 5 of this book.
[41] John Rawls, *A Theory of Justice* (Cambridge: Harvard University Press, 1971); *Political Liberalism* (New York: Columbia University Press, 1993); *Collected Papers*, Edited by Samuel Freeman (Cambridge: Harvard University Press, 1999); *The Law of Peoples*. Also see Burleigh T. Wilkins, "A Third Principle of Justice," *The Journal of Ethics*, 1 (1997), pp. 355-74.

issues, matters of the U.S. genocidal acts and land theft against Native Americans hardly receives sufficient attention, if indeed they receive attention at all, in U.S. pre-college social studies and history courses. Moreover, if they do receive attention, it is highly unlikely that such issues are taught from anything but a greatly distorted perspective (e.g., the goodness of manifest destiny, the unparalleled greatness of U.S. society, etc.), thereby mis-educating U.S. youth about the moral foundations of U.S. society. This being the case, it is unclear that U.S. citizens, even most who are putatively university educated, would have anything but a distorted understanding of the moral character and/or status of U.S. society. Such ideological poison pervades the very core of U.S. social life at almost every turn, making it difficult to draw the inference that U.S. citizens truly support the continual oppression of Native Americans. How can they be said to support (or condemn) that about which they genuinely do not have adequate knowledge? It is for this reason that I believe there is insufficient reason to think that the U.S. attitude toward the Native American experience amounts to a "considered judgment." If this is true, then there is good reason to think that a comprehensive educational campaign must be directed at the U.S. public, one which outlines the facts of history, the grounds for reparations to Native Americans by the U.S. government, the grounds for the U.S. government's respecting a peaceful secession of Native Americans from the U.S. which grants Native American nations full rights to sovereignty. Once these cases are made and heard by nearly every U.S. citizen, then and only then can this second condition of morally justified terrorism as humanitarian intervention be satisfied in a robust sense. Perhaps even more importantly, this effort provides the U.S. *one final opportunity* to do the right thing in paying adequate reparations to Native Americans for both the genocidal acts, inactions and attempted actions against Native Americans, and for the coercive and fraudulent ways in which millions of acres of Native American lands were acquired or transferred from Native Americans to others. It also gives the U.S. *one last opportunity* to do the right thing concerning Native American sovereignty by way of granting peaceful secessions of Native American nations from the U.S. This would fulfill the moral duty of the U.S. to not interfere with Native Americans' exercise and enjoyment of their moral right to secede.

Third, *whatever terrorism is employed must target only those most guilty of significant injustices only, never children or obviously innocent persons or other sentient beings.*[42] Moreover, the employment of *terrorism*

---

[42] See Chapter 5 of this book. This point is based on what is said about just war doctrine in Hare, *Essays on Political Morality*, p. 55, Nagel, *Mortal Questions*; and Walzer, *Just and Unjust Wars*. It is also consistent with John Rawls' seventh principle of justice among "free and democratic peoples" (Rawls, *The Law of Peoples*, pp. 37, 94-5).

must always be proportional to the harm caused to those suffering and in need of humanitarian intervention.[43] Here the costs to innocents are relevant. Targeting an entire civilian population with terrorism is justified in the case under consideration only to the extent that that population is collectively liable (not necessarily causally responsible) for harms to Native Americans in question. However, that most U.S. citizens are morally blinded to the facts of history and that their own government owes reparations to Native Americans is insufficient reason to make such citizens direct targets of violent forms of terrorism. But it is enough reason to target directly the U.S. government and those existing businesses that benefit(ed) from the oppression of Native Americans, and to provide fair notice to all civilians of the history of the problem and any impending terrorist activity aimed at the U.S. government and its controlling business interests. This final warning to U.S. citizens makes them aware that severe danger lies ahead for them. This third condition, then, raises the complex issue of collective moral responsibility. Although an analysis of collective moral responsibility is beyond the scope of this book, such an analysis is unnecessary to claim plausibly that terrorism is morally justified against certain persons and/or institutions in the U.S. who and/or which are most culpable, provided that the three conditions of justified terrorism are satisfied.[44] As Walzer writes, "Assuming that the regime is in fact oppressive, one should look for agents of oppression and not simply for government agents."[45] Moreover, Walzer's position about liberatory armed struggles is applicable to terrorism also:

> . . . The mark of a revolutionary struggle against oppression, however, is not the incapacitating rage and random violence, but restraint and self-control. The revolutionary reveals his freedom in the same way that he earns it, by directly confronting his enemies and refraining from attacks on anyone else. It

---

[43] A similar point is made in Haig Katchadourian, *The Morality of Terrorism* (New York: Peter Lang Publishers, 1998), pp. 26f.; "Terrorism and Morality," *Journal of Applied Philosophy*, 5 (1988), pp. 131-45.

[44] For some discussions of the concept of collective moral responsibility, see J. Angelo Corlett, "Collective Responsibility," in Patricia Werhane and E. Freeman, Editors, *Encyclopedic Dictionary of Business Ethics* (London: Blackwell, 1997), pp. 120-25; "Corporate Punishment and Responsibility," *Journal of Social Philosophy*, 28 (1997), pp. 86-100; "Collective Moral Responsibility," *Journal of Social Philosophy*, 32 (2001), pp. 573-84; *Responsibility and Punishment*, Chapter 7; Joel Feinberg, *Doing and Deserving* (Princeton: Princeton University Press, 1970), Chapter 9; Peter French, *Corporate and Collective Responsibility* (New York: Columbia University Press, 1982); *Responsibility Matters* (Lawrence: University Press of Kansas, 1992), Chapters 6-7; Margaret Gilbert, *Sociality and Responsibility* (Lanham: Rowman and Littlefield, 2000); *The Journal of Ethics*, 6 (2002), pp. 111-98; Larry May, *The Morality of Groups* (Notre Dame: Notre Dame University Press, 1987); Larry May and Stacey Hoffman, Editors, *Collective Responsibility* (Totowa: Rowman and Littlefield, 1991); Burleigh T. Wilkins, *Terrorism and Collective Responsibility* (London: Routledge, 1992).

[45] Walzer, *Just and Unjust Wars*, p. 202.

was not only to save the innocent that revolutionary militants worked out the
distinction between officials and ordinary citizens, but also to save themselves
from killing the innocent.[46]

Although these words are not referring to terrorism *per se*, they ought to be
the guidance of terrorism, especially of the humanitarian interventionist
variety. As there are kinds of terrorism, from non-violent kidnappings to
airline highjackings to bombings of various sorts, perhaps the terrorist who
is engaging in humanitarian intervention ought to be bound to the same rules
of the use of force to which *morally justified terrorism* in general is bound:
*Only   as   much   force   is   needed   to   achieve   the   legitimate
liberatory/humanitarian aim of intervention is justified.* This might in many
cases require only non-violent forms of terrorism, while in some cases it
might justify the use of even the worst kinds of terroristic violence. In any
case, *terrorism as humanitarian intervention must target only the most
guilty, and never innocents.* Indeed, it must go out of its way to do so in
order to be morally justified, as was argued in Chapter 5.

Of course, since terrorism is morally justified only to the extent that it is
a response to significant forms of injustice, terrorism will typically be harsh.
But it ought not ever to become overly harsh. Nonetheless, there are some
injustices that are so longstanding, so evil, that no kind or amount of
terrorism seems to be overly harsh. A few instances here would be any
terrorist response to Nazi Germany in the height of its power, or to Stalin's
Soviet Union during his years of terrorist persecution, or to Andrew
Jackson's U.S. as it deliberately committed continuous and heinous acts of
genocide against dozens of Native American nations as it simultaneously
and brutally created and sustained race-based slavery against millions of
Native Americans and Africans. Indeed, if it is true that unrectified evil is
evil still, then certain examples of unrectified evil might well qualify as
legitimate targets of terrorism of even the harshest varieties.

Fourth, *where time and circumstance permit, other forms of political
change must have been attempted in good faith, and failed.* Humanitarian
intervention of the terroristic variety need not be a "last resort," for there are
always "other" modes of address. Nonetheless, this condition is satisfied to
the extent that other (non-violent) modes of change have been attempted in
good faith, but have failed and there is no significant indication that further
such attempts will fare better. In this regard, the use of terrorism as a means
of humanitarian intervention is similar to the moral justification of civil
disobedience, as we saw with the farm workers example in Chapter 2. Of
course, U.S. history is replete with instances of Native Americans
approaching U.S. presidents, the U.S. Congress, and the U.S. Supreme Court

---

[46] Walzer, *Just and Unjust Wars*, pp. 205-06.

in attempts, often in vain, to gain justice for past evils that the U.S. perpetrated against them. So even though I have argued that U.S. *society* ought to be given *one final opportunity* to understand and rectify such matters before terrorists justifiably intervene to bring justice to the U.S., it is important to know that this condition has already been satisfied by Native Americans in most obvious ways.

Fifth and sixth, *terrorists must plan their actions well in order to best ensure the cessation of the injustices to which their terrorism is a legitimate response, and any other person or group of persons in relevantly similar circumstances as the terrorists would also be morally justified in engaging in terrorism.* The satisfaction of these conditions would attest to the terrorists' rationality and reasonableness, delimiting the extent to which they would act from unreasoned passion.

The line of reasoning in favor of Native American (or those third parties who support Native American nations) *terrorism as a form of humanitarian intervention against the U.S. government runs as follows: such terrorism is morally justified to the extent that the above six conditions of morally justified terrorism and the above twelve conditions of morally justified and dutiful humanitarian intervention are satisfied.* Just as "decent peoples have a [moral] right to war in self-defense,"[47] so too do decent folk like Native Americans have a (moral) right to terrorism as a means of war in self-defense, provided that the above conditions obtain. Rawls argues that "*any* society that is nonaggressive and that honors human rights has the right to self-defense"[48] against "outlaw regimes."[49] Certainly Native Americans satisfy the description of a set of "decent peoples" who are justified in employing terrorism against the U.S., and the U.S. government fits the description of being an outlaw regime.[50] Given that terrorism can in some cases be a mode of self-defense,[51] Native Americans would be morally justified in employing terrorism as a means of self-defense against certain leaders in the U.S. government and relevantly deserving business leaders in accordance with the conditions above. Given that terrorism can in some cases be a mode of defense of others in danger of serious rights violations, certain third parties would be morally justified in employing terrorism as a

---

[47] Rawls, *The Law of Peoples,* p. 92.

[48] Rawls, *The Law of Peoples,* p. 92.

[49] The nature of outlaw states is described in Rawls, *The Law of Peoples,* pp. 80f.

[50] The latter point seems to hold in light of at least two factors: (a) the clear history of U.S. oppression of Native American nations; and (b) the blatant disregard that the U.S. often demonstrates toward organs of international justice such as the United Nations, and its unsupportive attitude regarding the recently established International War Crimes Tribunal and the International Criminal Court.

[51] For a discussion of the notion of the justification of the use of terrorism as a means of self-defense, see Wilkins, *Terrorism and Collective Responsibility*, Chapter 1.

means of self-defense against the U.S. government in accordance with the conditions above. Thus even if there is no moral duty to commit terrorist acts against the U.S. because of, say, U.S. evils against Native Americans that have gone unrectified for generations, there might well be a moral *right* to do so. And if there is such a moral right, then those who choose to exercise that right against the U.S. and its relevantly deserving business leaders are morally justified in doing so, and neither the U.S. nor any other party would be in a moral position to prevent the terrorism that would ensue. For a terrorist's having a moral right to commit terrorist acts against a party implies a moral duty of other parties to not interfere with the exercise of that valid moral claim and/or interest.

But *prior to engaging in terrorist activity against the U.S. government and its relevantly deserving business leaders*, would-be terrorists might see that a coalition of states might be formed to lend support to the Native American alliance in terrorist activities against the U.S. government and its relevantly deserving business leadership for their failure to pay reparations to Native Americans and to secure secession from the U.S. should the U.S. resist such a move. As Rawls states,

> For well-ordered peoples to achieve this long-run aim, they should establish new institutions and practices to serve as a kind of confederative center and public forum for their common opinion and policy toward non-well-ordered regimes. They can do this within such institutions as the United Nations or by forming separate alliances of well-ordered peoples on certain issues. This confederative center may be used both to formulate and to express the opinion of the well-ordered societies. There they may expose to public view the unjust and cruel institutions of oppressive and expansionistic regimes and their violations of human rights.[52]

Once fair notice has been given, then Native Americans and their supporters have an opportunity to *approach the U.S. government, its relevantly deserving business sectors, and its citizenry one final time* to rectify the problem of its injustices against Native Americans. As Rawls avers,

> ... Gradually over time, then, well-ordered peoples may pressure the outlaw regimes to change their ways; but by itself this pressure is unlikely to be effective. It may need to be backed up by the firm denial of economic and other assistance, or the refusal to admit outlaw regimes as members in good standing in mutually beneficial cooperative practices.[53]

Thus to the extent that certain leaders in the U.S. government, its relevantly deserving business sectors, and its citizens show a continued disregard for Native American rights to compensation, then the terrorism may begin in

---

[52] Rawls, *The Law of Peoples,* p. 93.
[53] Rawls, *The Law of Peoples,* p. 93.

accordance with the above conditions for purposes of effecting and sustaining Native American secession from the U.S.[54] Although no innocents may be targeted directly,[55] certain U.S. officials of the highest ranks are obvious targets of justified terrorism, as was suggested in the previous chapter. In general, certain of those with the greatest power to effect change but refuse to rectify past evils of the U.S. government are the most justified targets here.[56]

Although it is unlikely that more than (at most) a few Native Americans would engage in terrorist activities like these, there are certainly third party states and others who would consider it their moral duty to cause harm to the U.S. and its relevantly deserving business leadership, given their long history of oppressive relations globally. So as the U.S. faces terrorism from external parties, it would be forced to reconsider its policy of avoidance behavior regarding its refusal to pay reparations for its genocidal acts against Native Americans. And it would be coerced to fulfill its duty of non-interference with regard to the Native Americans' right to secede.

OBJECTIONS, AND REPLIES

There are objections that might be raised to the above argument for terroristic humanitarian intervention against the U.S. government and its deserving business leadership. I will consider three such objections: one concerning the claim that there is a moral duty to humanitarian intervention, another pertaining to the claim that the duty involves terroristic intervention in the case of Native Americans, and a third concerning putative rights to territory which might be said to ground humanitarian intervention on behalf of Native Americans.

First, it might be argued that, though there might be a moral prerogative (entailing a moral justification or a right) of humanitarian intervention toward others, there is no such moral *duty*. This is especially true given quality of life considerations that seem always to exist in a society and stand as reasons for non-intervention. Our projects, individual and social, assist in defining ourselves without which utilitarian concerns would intrude into our

---

[54] On my no-fault model of secession, U.S. unrectified evils serve as a sufficient, not a necessary, condition of justified secession.

[55] Indeed, on my analysis, terrorists must go out of their way to not target innocents if they are to be morally justified in employing terrorism, as argued in Chapter 5.

[56] This proportional view of acts of political violence targeting certain wrongdoers is not inconsistent with that found in Nagel, *Mortal Questions*, p. 64. The proportionality of terrorism regards both those who are legitimate targets of it, and what sorts of levels and kinds of terrorism might be employed against them.

lives in ways that would undermine human autonomy.[57] A duty of
humanitarian intervention, as opposed to a moral justification of or a moral
right to the same, would (if it is not unwarrantedly paternalistic) tend to at
least sometimes undermine human autonomy in the pursuit of our projects
that define who we are as individuals and as social beings. If anything,
humanitarian intervention is a moral prerogative, not a duty: we are
permitted but not required to perform it.[58] Thus Rawls is incorrect to insist
that there is a duty of humanitarian intervention, though Walzer is correct to
argue that there are times when humanitarian intervention is morally
justified.

In reply to this objection, it must be pointed out that it is excessively
individualistic – even to the point of being egoistic. Even if it were true that
on some occasions the personal autonomy of some afflicted with the dire
need of others for basic human rights to be respected when they are denied
or violated, there is no good reason (save an egoistic one) to think that my
pursuing my own projects is a right that trumps, all things considered, the
moral requirement that I in some cases assist others in serious need of human
rights being respected. This is especially the case when our assisting others
in severe need does not threaten in a serious way our basic autonomy.
Although the moral duty to humanitarian intervention is not an absolute one,
it is at least a *prima facie* one. And perhaps this is what Rawls has in mind
when he discusses the matter in *The Law of Peoples*.

Furthermore, even if it turns out that there is no moral duty of terroristic
humanitarian intervention against the U.S. for its long-standing unrectified
evils against Native Americans, there might well be either a moral right, or a
permission, to the same. This is consistent with my proposed argument
which is not contingent on there being a moral duty to terroristic intervention
against the U.S.

Second, it might also be objected that, though the above analyses of
morally justified and dutiful humanitarian intervention (on the one hand) and
morally justified terrorism (on the other hand) might well have been satisfied
in the distant past when the U.S. government perpetrated numerous human
rights violations (including a genocide!) against Native Americans, such
conditions do not exist today. Whatever injustices that the U.S. government
is currently committing against Native American nations hardly qualifies as
those which would justify humanitarian intervention, much less of the
terroristic variety.

---

[57] An incisive discussion of autonomy is found in Keith Lehrer, "Freedom, Preference, and
Autonomy," *The Journal of Ethics*, 1 (1997), pp. 3-25.
[58] For a discussion of moral prerogatives and consequentialism, see Samuel Scheffler, *The
Rejection of Consequentialism* (Oxford: Oxford University Press, 1982); Samuel Scheffler,
Editor, *Consequentialism and Its Critics* (Oxford: Oxford University Press, 1988).

In reply to this objection, it must be pointed out that the objection wrongly assumes a "time slice" perception of historical injustice in regard to the U.S. genocide of Native Americans. The difficulty here is in assuming that unrectified (or grossly insufficiently rectified) human rights violations of genocidal proportions can be "made better" or simply lose moral significance over time, by the evolutionary process of unrectified wrongs becoming "right," say, by a society's overall positive moral development. That the U.S. government no longer commits genocidal acts against Native American nations and steals their lands is most likely because there are so few Native American lives to take and so little land (of value to the U.S.) remains to steal. Those tasks have already been realized on the path toward manifest destiny. But as long as adequate reparations to Native Americans go unpaid, so long as the U.S. government remains willful sovereign over Native American nations, both the unrectified genocidal human rights violations and the refusal of the U.S. to grant Native American sovereignty stand as good reasons why Native American secession and terrorism (by and/or on behalf of Native Americans) are morally justified given the satisfying of the above conditions. The "time slice" view of Native American-U.S. relations ignores these facts, and hence cannot serve as a reasonable challenge to my argument.

Finally, it might be argued that there is a moral statute of limitations on Native American claims to lands taken from them by the U.S. government and its citizens by force or fraud such that what were once valid moral claims of Native Americans to (occupy, not necessarily own) lands currently occupied by U.S. citizens and their government are now replaced by what have become valid moral claims to such lands by U.S. citizens and their government.[59] Thus Native Americans have no valid moral claims to and/or valid moral interests in what are arguably U.S. lands, and so have no right to secede in a way that would make claims to such lands. Moreover, third parties have no rights or duties to intervention on behalf of Native Americans to assist in such secessionist moves, especially by way of terrorism. If this objection is plausible, then it would further tend to counter much of what was argued in Chapter 4 regarding Native American nations' putative moral right to secede.

In reply to this objection, it must be asked if there is a *sound*, non-question-begging and non-self-serving argument which would ground a

---

[59] Similar views are found in Buchanan, *Secession*, pp. 88f; "Democracy and Secession," in Margaret Moore, Editor, *National Self-Determination and Secession* (Oxford: Oxford University Press, 1998); "Self-Determination, Secession, and the Rule of Law," in Robert McKim and Jeff McMahan, Editors, *The Morality of Nationalism* (Oxford: Oxford University Press, 1997), pp. 311f; David Lyons, "The New Indian Claims and Original Rights to Land," *Social Theory and Practice*, 4 (1977), pp. 249f.; Jeremy Waldron, "Superceding Historic Injustice," *Ethics*, 103 (1992), pp. 15f.

moral statute of limitations on rectification of the human rights violations in question. Surely the convenience of the U.S. legal system hardly serves as an adequate ground for the moral statute of limitations on Native American land claims to what was taken by them by force and fraud. Neither do the adverse economic, political and geographical impacts that respecting Native American claim rights along these lines imply for the U.S. socio-economic and political system serve as adequate grounds for the moral statute of limitations on Native American claim rights to the lands in question. *It stretches to the breaking point the bounds of credulity to imagine how a plundering nation's genocide of millions of Native Americans and violent and fraudulent theft of most of their lands can somehow justify an emergent right of the wrongdoers and their descendents to what were once lands occupied my moral right by Native American nations.* Much less is it plausible to hold to a moral statute of limitations on genocide, as U.S. law posits no statute of limitations on murder. And we must bear in mind in light of this information that it is *those who insist that there is a moral statute of limitations on such injustices who have the burden of argument here.* It is difficult to imagine precisely how that burden can be satisfied adequately. Yet until it has been satisfied, there is no adequate reason to accept a moral statute of limitations on injustice as being plausible.

If sound arguments for a moral statute of limitations on the American genocide and its implications are *not* forthcoming,[60] then there is good reason to think that Native Americans have not somehow lost, in the dreadful mire of U.S. genocidal acts of land theft, their moral claim rights to the lands in question and reparations for such wrongs. In light of the fact that there is in U.S. law no statute of limitations on murder, and given the fact that the U.S. Army (often under the orders of its then Commander in Chief, Andrew Jackson) was responsible for numerous acts of genocide against dozens of Native American nations, Native American secession might assist in Native American sovereignty given that adequate reparations by the U.S. government for the genocidal acts are not forthcoming due to the recalcitrant attitude of the U.S. government and its citizenry. But Native American secession would be justified because Native Americans still possess, lacking some *sound* argument for a moral statute of limitations on Native American claim rights to the lands of North America, moral claim rights (of occupation, not necessarily ownership) to U.S. lands. Recall that the "Territoriality Thesis"[61] is a necessary condition for justified secession, and it requires (among other things) that the seceding group have a valid moral

---

[60] My thinking on this point of reply is congruent with that found in Rodney C. Roberts, "The Morality of a Moral Statute of Limitations on Injustice," *The Journal of Ethics*, 7 (2003), pp. 115-38.

[61] See Chapter 4.

claim to the territory which it seeks to make its own by way of its break from the government. If Native American secession is justified on these grounds, then third party interventions, even terroristic ones which seek to assist Native American secessionist movements from the U.S. should the U.S. attempt to block the secessions, are justified to the extent that the conditions of justified terrorism obtain. Moreover, such interventions are morally dutiful (or at least permitted) to the extent that conditions (1)-(12) obtain.

In sum, subsequent to expounding on the notions of there being moral justifications for rights and duties to humanitarian intervention, I provided an analysis of the conditions under which it would be morally justified and dutiful for third parties to engage in terrorism against the U.S. government and its relevantly deserving business sectors for the purposes of effecting Native American sovereignty and/or reparations. In conclusion, we do have a *prima facie* moral justification and a duty of humanitarian intervention, and this justification or duty increases in strength to the extent that our failure to intervene would serve as a genuine causal factor in the further or continual harm to Native Americans. In the case of Native American nations in the U.S., it seems clear that there is a moral justification, at the very least, to engage in terrorism in order to effect reparations to and/or secession of Native Americans, on the condition (among others) that third party intervenors are given permission by Native American nations to intervene in their affairs and without unwanted subsequent political participation by the third party intervenor. After all, Native Americans might well experience reprisals from the U.S. government and its citizens should such terrorism be traced to Native American nations. So Native Americans might, as I noted earlier, be quite reluctant to either employ or request violence of any sort in order to achieve justice under U.S. dominion.

It is undoubtedly unfortunate that the moral arguments have reached this juncture. But it is equally certain that the fault for this moral failure lies primarily with the U.S. government and part of its business community, and secondarily, though not insignificantly, with its citizenry by way of its bad Samaritanism concerning Native Americans. That the employment of terrorism in order to effect reparations to Native Americans and/or secession of Native Americans from the U.S. is morally justified does not imply that such terrorism is necessarily a moral duty. However, whether or not such terrorism amounts to a moral duty, it is hardly inevitable, though the fact of its moral justifiedness alone sounds as a sharp pre-notification to those of us who understand that rectified injustice would ward-off even the very thought of such political violence.

A "call to arms" this is not. Rather, it is a recognition of the rather poor moral position in which the U.S., many of its business sectors, and most of its citizens find themselves given the facts of their past and present oppression of Native Americans, and the moral permission the latter have to secede and, if blocked from seceding, to inflict various and gradual forms of political violence on the former consistent with the conditions of morally justified terrorism outlined above. Should such violence erupt because of injustices against Native Americans, the U.S. is hardly in a moral position to object (or even to engage in self-defense via a "war on terrorism"), as it has had a history of centuries in which to right its wrongs against them. *The better solution for everyone, of course, is the non-violence that only reparations of an adequate nature and full sovereignty which can only be effected by peaceful secession can effect for Native American nations.*[62] Perhaps the U.S. (both its leadership and its self-avowed citizen-patriots) will listen to the voices of ethics and do the right things by way of Native Americans. For only then does it have even a minute opportunity, to use Rawls' words from the commencement of this chapter, to "become fully just and stable for the right reasons."

---

[62] See J. Angelo Corlett, *Race, Racism, and Reparations* (Ithaca: Cornell University Press, 2003).

CONCLUSION

Throughout this book, I have set the conceptual framework for discussions of terrorism and secession, each of which is more often than not a form of actual or threatened political violence. Explored were various complexities of the putative moral obligation to obey the law, pacifism, the nature and justification of civil disobedience (as construed by traditionalists such as John Rawls), non-violent direct action, the natures and moral justifications of political violence in general, and of terrorism and secession in particular.

If Joel Feinberg is correct in arguing that there is not even a *prima facie* moral obligation to obey the law, then Immanuel Kant is incorrect in thinking that there is an absolute moral obligation to obey the same. It would follow that to the extent that certain conditions obtain, disobedience to the law is sometimes justified. Few would deny that pacifistic disobedience to political authority is at least sometimes justified on moral grounds, and the same might be said of non-violent direct action and civil disobedience.

Problems arise, of course, when certain other methods of social change are at issue. After discussing the nature of political violence and conditions under which it is morally justified, I turned my attention to analyzing the nature of secession and the conditions under which *it* is morally justified. I provided an indigenous perspective on secession based on the mainstream (relative to analytical political philosophy) acceptance of the "Territoriality Thesis" which is central to all major philosophical accounts of secession. That thesis implies that secession is justified to the extent that the secessionist group has a moral right to the territory sought by the secessionist group. But since virtually the only groups which have moral rights to, say, the lands that they might likely claim should they decide to secede in order to gain genuine sovereignty are indigenous peoples or Native Americans (in the Americas), only they (typically) have the moral right to secede.[1]

Having argued in favor of an indigenous paradigm of the right to secede, I analyzed the nature of terrorism and the conditions under which it is morally justified. A new conception of the nature of terrorism is provided and defended, along with a new analysis of the conditions under which terrorism is morally justified. A defense of these analyses is given before some recent cases of terrorism are discussed both in terms of what makes

---

[1] Although there are those societies that have acquired legitimately the land on which they reside that would also qualify as secession candidates, other conditions of morally justified secession obtaining.

them terrorist acts (events, or states of affairs), and in terms of whether or not (or to what extent) they were morally justified.

Elsewhere, I have argued that the experience of Native Americans at the hands of the United States requires adequate reparations sufficient to compensate Native American nations for the holocaust that the U.S. inflicted on them.[2] Whether or not such reparations are in fact forthcoming by the U.S., Native Americans are morally justified in seceding from the U.S. But refusal of the U.S. to pay adequate reparations to Native Americans for past evils serves as a sufficient condition that morally justifies Native American secession from the U.S. Furthermore, failure of the U.S. to pay adequate reparations to Native American nations or U.S. attempts to block peaceful Native American secessions would, under certain circumstances, warrant terrorism against the U.S. and its relevantly deserving business leadership by either Native Americans or third party sympathizers. Assuming the plausibility of the reparations argument concerning African Americans, and assuming the implausibility of the various objections raised to it,[3] it would seem that the failure of the U.S. to pay adequate reparations to African Americans also serves to bolster the case for terrorism against the U.S. and its supportive business interests that have benefited significantly from the enslavement of Africans in the U.S., as well as the subsequent Jim Crow oppression of thousands of African Americans still living in the U.S.

Not only are some past terrorist acts more or less morally justified, not only are certain other terrorist and/or secessionist scenarios morally justified, say, against the U.S. because of its unrectified severe injustices against various peoples, foreign and domestic, there is good reason to think that the U.S. continues to make and/or sustain enemies such that the terrorism against it for, say, severely harmful foreign policies might well be morally justified, contingent on certain conditions obtaining. Again, an indigenous perspective is provided with the assumption that *indigenous peoples possess the same basic human rights and duties of any other peoples,* including moral rights to reparations for past injustices wrought on them by the U.S. government.

What becomes increasingly clear from the contents of the chapters of this book is how egoistic pursuits of wealth and prosperity often bring terrorism on societies that wreak destruction on others by way of various forms of exploitation and oppression. Sometimes, though not always, such terrorism is deserved, at least to some degree or in certain respects. The U.S.

---

[2] A full defense of this claim is found in J. Angelo Corlett, *Responsibility and Punishment* (Dordrecht: Kluwer Academic Publishers, 2001), Chapter 9; "Reparations to Native Americans?" in Aleksandar Jokic, Editor, *War Crimes and Collective Wrongdoing* (London: Blackwell Publishers, 2001), pp. 236-69.
[3] A full defense of these claims is found in J. Angelo Corlett, *Race, Racism, and Reparations* (Ithaca: Cornell University Press, 2003), Chapter 8.

is one such country the leadership of which has through the enactment of various self-serving policies made several enemies at home and abroad, enemies that are sometimes (under certain conditions) morally justified in committing terrorist acts against certain leaders of the U.S. and its relevantly deserving business sectors. One hope is that the U.S. and certain other countries face the empirical fact that military wars on terrorism will only lead to more anti-U.S. terrorism and other violence against U.S. allied countries.

But if reason is more powerful than violence,[4] then perhaps the political leaders of various countries will begin to realize that certain policies have evil consequences for others. And if it is true that unrectified evil is evil still, then reparations are due to those who deserve them, such as Native Americans whose ancestors were victimized in the form of horrendous human rights abuses by the same U.S. government that exists today.[5] Moreover, any society worth having is one that can admit and rectify its significant immorality (when it has a record of such immorality). Failure or refusal to do this almost ensures that such a society is likely to continue down its path to harming others and remaining deserving of serious harm itself. And if this is true, then in some cases of severe oppression and injustice, terrorism might well be a morally justified method of bringing an end to the oppression. And the society victimized by the justified terrorism would in no way be in a moral position to complain about its own fate, a fate that has been, ironically enough, imposed on them by the very leadership it elected. This implies that the U.S. government, or at least various of its agents (as well as certain controlling business interests), serve as contributory causes of at least some terrorism directed at the U.S. in that it has provided the moral justification of terroristic responses to oppression to which at least some terrorism is a response. Yet it is precisely *that political and business leadership, in the case of the U.S., which incessantly demonizes terrorists as it continues to unwittingly (or even uncaringly) place U.S. and other citizens in harm's way*. Moral responsibility for terrorist harms is hardly a facile matter of blaming terrorists for what most victims of terrorism fail to either understand or even desire to understand. It is, rather, more complex. It is a shared responsibility between all persons who ought to have a joint commitment[6] for rooting out gross forms of exploitation and injustice globally. Yet such a concern cannot be shared genuinely by those

---

[4] Certainly reason is to be *preferred* over violence, as a general rule.

[5] The cases for reparations to both Native and African Americans is made in Corlett, *Race, Racism, and Reparations*, Chapters 8-9.

[6] On the concept of joint commitment and related concepts, see Margaret Gilbert, *Living Together* (Lanham: Rowman and Littlefield Publishers, 1996); *On Social Facts* (Princeton: Princeton University Press, 1992); *Sociality and Responsibility* (Lanham: Rowman and Littlefield Publishers, 2000).

who fail to fathom that they are indeed partners in the unjust treatment of others. However, until such concerns become more universal, countries like the U.S. can count on an ever-escalating frequency and kind of terrorist acts against it both at home and abroad, acts of terrorism that cannot be totally eradicated by even the most impressive display of military might.

SELECTED BIBLIOGRAPHY

Allen, E. L., F. E. Pollard and G. A. Sutherland, *The Case for Pacifism and Conscientious Objection* (London: Central Board for Conscientious Objectors, 1946).

Allen, R. E., "Law and Justice in Plato's *Crito*," *The Journal of Philosophy*, 69 (1972), pp. 557-67.

Allen, Wayne, "Terrorism and the Epochal Transformation of Politics," *Public Affairs Quarterly*, 6 (1992), pp. 133-54.

Anderson, William L., *Cherokee Removal* (Athens: University of Georgia Press, 1991).

Arenilla, Lewis, "The Notion of Civil Disobedience According to Locke," *Diogenes*, 35 (1961), pp. 109-35.

Arendt, Hannah, *Civil Disobedience* (New York: Penguin Books, 1973).

_____, *On Revolution* (New York: The Viking Press, 1963).

_____, *On Violence* (San Diego: Harcourt Brace Jovanovich, Publishers, 1970).

Aronovitch, Hilliard, "Why Secession is Unlike Divorce," *Public Affairs Quarterly*, 14 (2000), pp. 27-37.

Ashe, Geoffrey, *Gandhi: A Study in Revolution* (London: Heinemann, 1968).

Audi, Robert, "On the Meaning and Justification of Violence," in Jerome A. Shaffer, Editor, *Violence* (New York: McKay, 1971).

Baier, Annette, "Violent Demonstrations," in R. G. Frey and Christopher Morris, Editors, *Violence, Terrorism, and Justice* (Cambridge: Cambridge University Press, 1991), pp. 33-58.

Bailey, Garrick and Roberta Glenn Bailey, *A History of the Navajos* (Santa Fe: School of American Research Press, 1986).

Barlow, R. M., "Terrorism: Analysis and Response," *Contemporary Philosophy*, 16 (1994), pp. 16-20.

Bar On, Bat-Ami, "Why Terrorism is Morally Problematic," in Claudia Card, Editor, *Feminist Ethics* (Lawrence: University of Kansas Press, 1991).

Bayles, Michael, "The Justifiability of Civil Disobedience," *The Review of Metaphysics*, 24 (1970), pp. 3-20.

Bedau, Hugo Adam, Editor, *Civil Disobedience in Focus* (New York: Routledge, 1991).

_____, "Civil Disobedience and Personal Responsibility for Injustice," *Monist*, 54 (1970), pp. 517-35.

_____, "On Civil Disobedience," *The Journal of Philosophy*, 58 (1961), pp. 653-64.

_____, "Review of Carl Cohen, *Civil Disobedience: Conscience, Tactics, and the Law*," *The Journal of Philosophy*, 69 (1972), pp. 81f.

Beehler, Rodger, "Pacifism: A Note," *Dialogue*, 11 (1972), pp. 584-87.

Belliotti, Raymond A., "Are All Modern Wars Morally Wrong?" *Journal of Social Philosophy*, 26 (1995), pp. 17-31.

_____, *Seeking Identity* (Lawrence: University Press of Kansas, 1995).

Benjamin, Martin, "Pacifism for Pragmatists," *Ethics*, 83 (1973), pp. 196-213.

Berger, Fred R., "Law and Order and Civil Disobedience," *Inquiry*, 13 (1970), pp. 254-73.

Berkhoffer, Robert, Jr., *Salvation and the Savage* (New York: Athenum, 1965).

Betz, Joseph, "Can Civil Disobedience Be Justified?" *Social Theory and Practice*, 1 (1970), pp. 13-30.

Bigelow, John, Robert Pergetter and Robert Young, "Land, Well-Being, and Compensation," *Australasian Journal of Philosophy*, 68 (1990), pp. 330-46.

Black, Virginia, "The Two Faces of Civil Disobedience," *Social Theory and Practice*, 1 (1970), pp. 17-25.

Blackstone, William T., "Civil Disobedience: Is it Justified?" *The Southern Journal of Philosophy*, 8 (1970), pp. 233-50.

_____, "The Definition of Civil Disobedience," *Journal of Social Philosophy*, 2 (1971), pp. 3-5.

Bolin, Frederick, "Quebec Secession: How Should the National Debt be Divided? Should Quebec Secede?" *Public Affairs Quarterly*, 8 (1994), pp. 219-23.

Bondurant, Joan V., *Conquest of Violence, The Gandhian Philosophy of Conflict* (New Jersey: Princeton University Press, 1958).

Bostock, David, "The Interpretation of Plato's *Crito*," *Phronesis*, 35 (1990), pp. 1-20.

Boubia, Fawzi, "Hegel's Internationalism: World History and Exclusion," *Metaphilosophy*, 28 (1997), pp. 417-32.

Brandt, Richard B., "The Concepts of Obligation and Duty," *Mind*, 73 (1964), pp. 374-93.

_____, "Utilitarianism and Rules of War," *Philosophy and Public Affairs*, 1 (1972).

Brann, Eva, "The Offense of Socrates: A Re-reading of Plato's "Apology," *Interpretation*, 7 (1978), pp. 1-21.

Brock, Peter, *Twentieth-Century Pacifism* (London: Van Nostrand Rein, 1970).

Brown, Dee, *Bury My Heart at Wounded Knee* (New York: Henry Holt and Company, 1970).

Brown Jr., Stuart M., "Civil Disobedience," *The Journal of Philosophy*, 58 (1961), 669-80.

Bruening, William, "World Peace and Moral Obligation," *Journal of Social Philosophy*, 12 (1981), pp. 11-9.

Buchanan, Allen, "Democracy and Secession," in Margaret Moore, Editor, *National Self-Determination and Secession* (Oxford: Oxford University Press, 1998).

_____, "Federalism, Secession, and the Morality of Inclusion," *Arizona Law Review*, 37 (1995), pp. 53-63.

_____, "Quebec, Secession and Aboriginal Territorial Rights," *The Network* (March, 1992), pp. 2-4.

_____, "A Reply to Grand Chief Coon Come and Mr. David Cliché," *The Network* (May, 1992), p. 13.

_____, "The Right to Self-Determination: Analytical and Moral Foundations," *Arizona Journal of International and Comparative Law*, 8 (1990), pp. 41-50.

_____, "The Role of Collective Land Rights in a Theory of Indigenous Peoples' Rights," *Transnational Law and Contemporary Problems*, 3 (1993), pp. 90-108.

_____, *Secession* (Boulder: Westview Press, 1991).

_____, "Self-Determination and the Right to Secede," *Journal of International Affairs*, 45 (1992), p. 347-65.

_____, "Self-Determination, Secession, and the Rule of Law," in Robert McKim and Jeff McMahan, Editors, *The Morality of Nationalism* (New York: Oxford University Press, 1997), pp. 301-23.

_____, "Theories of Secession," *Philosophy and Public Affairs*, 26 (1997), pp. 31-61.

_____, "Toward a Theory of Secession," *Ethics*, 101 (1991), pp. 322-42.

_____, "What's So Special About Nations?" *Canadian Journal of Philosophy* (Supplementary Volume), 22 (1996), pp. 283-309.

Buckle, Stephen, *Natural Law and the Theory of Property* (Oxford: Oxford University Press, 1991).

Burke, Richard, "Epistemological Pacifism," in Kenneth H. Klein, Editor, *In the Interest of Peace: A Spectrum of Philosophical Views* (Wolfeboro: Longwood, 1990).

Burger, Fred R., "'Law and Order' and Civil Disobedience," *Inquiry*, 13 (1970), pp. 254-73.

Cady, Duane L., "Backing into Pacifism," *Philosophy and Social Criticism*, 10 (1984), pp. 173-80.

_____, "In Defense of Active Pacifists," *Journal of Social Philosophy*, 25 (1994), pp. 89-91.

_____, *Issues in War and Peace: Philosophical Inquiries* (Wolfeboro: Longwood, 1989).

_____, *From Warism to Pacifism: A Moral Continuum* (Pennsylvania: Temple University Press, 1989).

_____, "Pacifism, Duty and Superrogation," in Kenneth H. Klein, Editor, *In the Interest of Peace: A Spectrum of Philosophical Views* (Wolfeboro: Longwood, 1990).

Camus, Albert, "The Just Assassins," in *Caligula and Three Other Plays*, Translated by Stuart Gilbert (New York: Alfred A. Knopf, 1958).

Cane, Peter, *Responsibility in Law and Morality* (London: Hart Publishing, 2002).

Caney, Simon, "Self-government and Secession: The Case of Nations," *Journal of Political Philosophy* 5 (1997), pp. 351-72.

Carter, Alan, "In Defense of Radical Disobedience," *Journal of Applied Philosophy*, 15 (1998), pp. 29-47.

Childress, James, "Civil Disobedience, Conscientious Objection, and Evasive Noncompliance: Analysis and Assessment of Illegal Actions in Heath Care," *Journal of Medicine and Philosophy*, 10 (1985), pp. 63-84.

Chitty, Andrew, "On Humanitarian Bombing," *Radical Philosophy* 96 (1999), pp. 2-5.

Chomsky, Noam, *9/11* (New York: Seven Stories Press, 2001).

_____, *For Reasons of state* (New York: Vintage Books, 1973).

Christiano, Thomas, "Secession, Democracy, and Distributive Justice," *Arizona Law Review*, 37 (1995), pp. 65-72.

Christopher, Paul, *The Ethics and War and Peace* (Englewood Cliffs: Prentice-Hall, 2000).

Churchill, Ward, *From a Native Son* (Boston: South End Press, 1996).

_____, *Indians Are Us?: Culture and Genocide in Native North America* (Monroe: Common Courage Press, 1994).

_____, *Since Predator Came* (Littleton: Aigis, 1995).

_____, *Struggle for the Land* (Monroe: Common Courage Press, 1993).

Churchill, Ward, Editor, *Critical Issues in Native North America*, Volumes 1-2 (Copenhagen, 1988-91).

Coady, C. A. J., "The Idea of Violence," *Journal of Applied Philosophy*, 3 (1986), pp. 3-19.

_____, "The Morality of Terrorism," *Philosophy*, 60 (1985), pp. 47-70.

Cochran, David Carroll, "War-Pacifism," *Social Theory and Practice*, 22 (1996), pp. 161-80.

Cohen, Carl, *Civil Disobedience: Conscience Tactics, and the Law* (New York: Columbia University Press, 1971).

_____, "Defending Civil Disobedience," *Monist*, 54 (1970), pp. 469-87.

_____, "Militant Morality: Civil Disobedience and Bioethics," *Hastings Center Report*, 19 (1989), pp. 23-5.

Cohen, Marshall, "Civil Disobedience in a Constitutional Democracy," *Philosophic Exchange*, (1970), pp. 99-112.

_____, "Liberalism and Disobedience," *Philosophy and Public Affairs*, 1 (1972), pp. 283-314.

Colson, Darel D., "*Crito* 51 A-C: To What Does Socrates Owe Obedience?" *Phronesis*, 34 (1989), pp. 27-55.

Congleton, Ann, "Two Kinds of Lawlessness: Plato's 'Crito,' *Political Theory*, 2 (1974), pp. 432-46.

Copp, David, "Democracy and Communal Self-Determination," in Robert McKim and Jeff McMahan, Editors, *The Morality of Nationalism* (New York: Oxford University Press, 1997), pp. 277-300.

_____, "International Law and Morality in the Theory of Secession," *The Journal of Ethics*, 2 (1998), pp. 219-245.

Corlett, J. Angelo, *Analyzing Social Knowledge* (Totowa: Rowman and Littlefield Publishers, 1996).

_____, "Can Terrorism Be Morally Justified?" *Public Affairs Quarterly*, 10 (1996), pp. 163-84.

_____, "Collective Moral Responsibility," *Journal of Social Philosophy*, 32 (2001), pp. 573-84.

_____, Editor, *Equality and Liberty: Analyzing Rawls and Nozick* (London: Macmillan, 1990).

_____, "Latino Identity," *Public Affairs Quarterly*, 13 (1999), pp. 273-95.

_____, "Latino Identity and Affirmative Action," in Jorge J. E. Gracia and Pablo DeGrieff, Editors, *Ethnic Identity, Culture, and Group Rights* (London: Routledge, 2000), pp. 223-34.

_____, "Making Sense of Retributivism," *Philosophy*, 76 (2001), pp. 77-110.

_____, "Making *More* Sense of Retributivism: Desert as Responsibility and Proportionality," *Philosophy*, forthcoming.

_____, "The Morality and Constitutionality of Secession," *Journal of Social Philosophy* 29 (1998), pp. 120-8.

_____, "Political Integration, Political Separation, and the African American Experience," Martin Luther King, Jr. and Malcolm X on Social Change," *Humbodlt Journal of Social Relations*, 21 (1995), pp. 191-208.

_____, "The Problem of Collective Moral Rights," *Canadian Journal of Law and Jurisprudence*, 7 (1994), pp. 237-59.

_____, *Race, Racism, and Reparations* (Ithaca: Cornell University Press, 2003).

_____, "Reparations to Native Americans?" in Aleksandar Jokic, Editor, *War Crimes and Collective Wrongdoing* (London: Blackwell Publishers, 2000), pp. 236-69.

_____, *Responsibility and Punishment* (Dordrecht: Kluwer Academic Publishers, 2001).

_____, *Responsibility and Punishment*, Second Edition (Dordrecht: Kluwer Academic Publishers, 2003)

_____, "The Right to Civil Disobedience and the Right to Secede," *The Southern Journal of Philosophy,* 30 (1992), pp. 19-28.

_____, "Secession and Native Americans," *Peace Review,* 12 (2000), pp. 5-14.

_____, "What is Civil Disobedience?" *Philosophical Papers,* 27 (1997), pp. 241-59.

Cover, Robert M., *Justice Accused* (New Haven: Yale University Press, 1975).

Curtin, Deane, Editor, *Institutional Violence* (Amsterdam: Rodopi, 1999).

_____, "Making Peace with the Earth: Indigenous Agriculture and the Green Revolution," *Environmental Ethics,* 17 (1995), pp. 59-74.

Dalton, Dennis, Editor, *Mahatma Ghandi: Selected Political Writings* (Indianapolis: Hackett Publishing Co., 1996).

Danielson, Peter and MacDonald, Chris J., "Hard Cases in Hard Places: Singer's Agenda for Applied Ethics," *Dialogue,* 35 (1996), pp. 599-610.

Danley, John R., "Liberalism, Aboriginal Rights, and Cultural Minorities," *Philosophy and Public Affairs,* 20 (1991), pp. 168-85.

Dardis, Tony, "Primoratz on Terrorism," *Journal of Applied Philosophy,* 9 (1992), pp. 93-7.

Davion, Victoria, "Caring and Violence," *Hypatia,* 7 (1992), pp. 135-37.

_____, "Pacifism and Care," *Hypatia,* 5 (1990), pp. 90-100.

Davis, Stephen T., "Is Terrorism Ever Morally Justified?" in Creighton Peden and Y. Hudson, Editors, *Terrorism, Justice and Social Values* (Lewiston: The Edwin Mellen Press, 1990).

Debo, Angie, *A History of the Indians in the United States* (Norman: University of Oklahoma Press, 1970).

_____, *And Still the Waters Run* (Norman: University of Oklahoma Press, 1989).

Dixit, R. D., "Socrates on Civil Disobedience," *Indian Philosophical Quarterly,* 8 (1980), pp. 91-8.

Dixon, Nicholas, "The Morality of Anti-Abortion Civil Disobedience," *Public Affairs Quarterly,* 11 (1997), pp. 21-38.

Donaghy, John, "Pacifism and Revolution," in Kennith H. Klein, Editor, *In the Interest of Peace: A Spectrum of Philosophical Views* (Wolfeboro: Longwood, 1990).

Dooley, Patrick K., "Emerson on Civil Disobedience: The Question of an Immoral Law," *Journal of Thought*, 15 (1980), pp. 11-20.

_____., "Thoreau on Civil Disobedience: From Pacificism to Violence," *Journal of Thought*, 13 (1978), pp. 180-87.

Dougherty, Michael, *To Steal a Kingdom: Probing Hawai'ian History* (Waimanalo: Island Style Press, 1992).

Dworkin, Ronald, *Law's Empire* (Cambridge: Harvard University Press, 1986).

_____, "Review of Robert M. Cover, *Justice Accused*," *Times Literary Supplement*, 5 December 1975.

_____, *Taking Rights Seriously* (Cambridge: Harvard University Press, 1978).

Earle, William, "In Defense of War," *Monist*, 57 (1973), pp. 551-65.

Ehle, John, *Trail of Tears* (New York: Anchor Books, 1988).

Eller, Cynthia, *Conscientious Objectors and the Second World War: Moral and Religious Arguments in Support of Pacifism* (New York: Praeger, 1991).

Elliston, Frederick A., "Civil Disobedience and Whistleblowing: A Comparative Appraisal of Two Forms of Dissent," *Journal of Business Ethics*, 1 (1982), pp. 23-8.

Endres, Michael E., "Civil Disobedience and Modern Democracy," *Thought*, 43 (1968), pp. 499-506.

Ethics and International Affairs, 11 (1997), pp. 1-104.

Euben, Peter J., "Philosophy and Politics in Plato's "Crito," *Political Theory*, 6 (1978), pp. 149-72.

_____, "Walzer's Obligations," *Philosophy and Public Affairs*, 1 (1972), pp. 438-59.

Ewin, R. E., "Peoples and Secession," *Journal of Applied Philosophy*, 11 (1994), pp. 225-31.

Farrell, Daniel M., "Illegal Actions, Universal Maxims, and the Duty to Obey the Law: The Case for Civil Authority in the 'Crito,'" *Political Theory*, 6 (1978), pp. 173-89.

_____, "Paying the Penalty: Justifiable Civil Disobedience and the Problem of Punishment," *Philosophy and Public Affairs*, 6 (1977), pp. 165-84.

Feinberg, Joel, "Civil Disobedience in the Modern World," *Humanities in Society*, 2 (1979), pp. 37-59. Reprinted in Joel Feinberg and Hyman Gross, Editors, *Philosophy of Law*, Fifth Edition (Belmont: Wadsworth Publishing Company, 1995), pp. 121-33.

_____, *Doing and Deserving* (Princeton: Princeton University Press, 1970).

_____, "Duty and Obligation in the Non-Ideal World," *Journal of Philosophy*, 70 (1973), pp. 263-75.

_____, *Freedom and Fulfillment* (Princeton: Princeton University Press, 1992).

_____, *Harm to Others* (Oxford: Oxford University Press, 1984).

_____, *Harm to Self* (Oxford: Oxford University Press, 1986).

_____, *Harmless Wrongdoing* (Oxford: Oxford University Press, 1990).

_____, "The Moral and Legal Responsibility of the Bad Samaritan," in Joel Feinberg, *Freedom and Fulfillment* (Princeton: Princeton University Press, 1992), pp. 175-96.

_____, "The Nature and Value of Rights," *The Journal of Value Inquiry*, 4 (1970), pp. 243-57.

_____, *Offense to Others* (Oxford: Oxford University Press, 1985).

_____, *Problems at the Roots of Law* (Oxford: Oxford University Press, 2003)

_____, *Rights, Justice, and the Bounds of Liberty* (Princeton: Princeton University Press, 1980).

_____, *Social Philosophy* (Englewood Cliffs: Prentice-Hall, 1973).

Ferrarotti, Franco, "Terrorism and the Tradition of Intellectual Elitism in Italy," *Praxis*, 1 (1981), pp. 140-59.

Field, G. C., *Pacifism and Conscientious Objection* (Cambridge: Cambridge University Press, 1945).

_____, "Some Reflections on Pacifism," *Proceeding of the Aristotelian Society*, 44 (1944), pp. 43-60.

Foreman, Grant, *Indian Removal* (Norman: University of Oklahoma Press, 1932).

Fotion, Nicholas, and Gerard Elfstrom, *Military Ethics: Guidelines for Peace and War* (Boston: Routledge, 1986).

_____, "Reactions to War: Pacifism, Realism, and Just War Theory," in Andrew Valls, Editor, *Ethics in International Affairs: Theories and Cases* (Lanham: Rowman and Littlefield, 2000).

Frazier, Clyde, "Between Obedience and Revolution," *Philosophy and Public Affairs*, 1 (1972), pp. 315-34.

French, Peter, *Corporate and Collective Responsibility* (New York: Columbia University Press, 1984).

Frey, R. G. and Christopher Morris, Editors, *Violence, Terrorism, and Justice* (Cambridge: Cambridge University Press, 1991).

_____, "Violence, Terrorism, and Justice," in R. G. Frey and Christopher Morris, Editors, *Violence, Terrorism, and Justice* (Cambridge: Cambridge University Press, 1991), pp. 1-17.

Fuller, Lon, "Eight Ways to Fail to Make Law," in Joel Feinberg and Hyman Gross, Editors, *Philosophy of Law*, Fifth Edition (Belmont: Wadsworth Publishing Company, 1995), pp. 88-90.

Fuson, William M., "The Ethics of Pacifism: A Critique and a Reappraisal," *The Philosophical Review*, 52 (1943), pp. 494-98.

Gan, Barry, "Loving One's Enemies," in Kennith H. Klein, Editor, *In the Interest of Peace: A Spectrum of Philosophical Views* (Wolfeboro: Longwood, 1990).

Gandhi, M. K., *Non-Violent Resistance*, Bharatan Kumarappa, Editor (New York: Schocken Books, 1961).

Garver, Newton, "Philosophy and Pacifism," *Philosophy Today*, 2 (1967), pp. 142-7.

Gauthier, David, "Breaking Up: An Essay on Secession," *Canadian Journal of Philosophy,* 24 (1994), pp. 357-71.

Gewirth, Alan, "Civil Disobedience, Law, and Morality: An Examination of Justice Fortas," *Monist*, 54 (1970), pp. 536-55.

Gilbert, Margaret, *Living Together* (Lanham: Rowman and Littlefield, 1996).

_____, *On Social Facts* (Princeton: Princeton University Press, 1992).

_____, *Sociality and Responsibility* (Lanham: Rowman and Littlefield, 2000).

Gilbert, Paul, "Community and Civil Strife," *Journal of Applied Philosophy*, 7 (1990), pp. 3-14.

_____, "Just War: Theory and Application," *Journal of Applied Philosophy*, 4 (1987), pp. 217-22.

Ginsberg, Robert, Editor, *The Critique of War: Contemporary Philosophical Explorations* (Chicago: Regnery, 1969).

_____, "Institutional Violence as Systematic Evil," in Deane Curtin, Editor, *Institutional Violence* (Amsterdam: Rodopi, 1999).

Glover, Jonathan, "State Terrorism," in R. G. Frey and Christopher Morris, Editors, *Violence, Terrorism, and Justice* (Cambridge: Cambridge University Press, 1991), pp. 256-75.

Goldman, Alan H, "Reparations to Individuals or Groups?" *Analysis*, 35 (1975), pp. 168-70.

Goodin, Robert E., "Nuclear Disarmament as a Moral Certainty," *Ethics*, 95 (1985), pp. 641-58.

Gottlieb, Roger, "The Concept of Resistance: Jewish Resistance During the Holocaust," *Social Theory and Practice*, 9 (1983), pp. 31-50.

Gould, Carol C., "Group Rights and Social Ontology," *The Philosophical Forum*, 28 (1996-7), pp. 73-86.

Govier, Trudy, *A Delicate Balance: What Philosophy Can Tell Us About Terrorism* (Boulder: Westview Press, 2002).

Gracia, Jorge J. E., *Hispanic/Latino Identity* (London: Blackwell Publishers, 2000).

Gracia, Jorge J. E. and Pablo DeGrieff, Editors, *Ethnic Identity, Culture, and Group Rights* (London: Routledge, 2000).

Graham, Gordon, "Terrorists and Freedom Fighters," *Philosophy and Social Action*, 11 (1985), pp. 43-54.

Grand Council of the Crees, *Sovereign Injustice: Forcible Inclusion of the James Bay Crees and Cree Territory into a Sovereign Quebec* (Nemaska: Grand Council of the Crees, 1995).

Green, Michael D., *The Politics of Indian Removal* (Lincoln: University of Nebraska Press, 1982).

Greenawalt, Kent, *Conflicts of Law and Morality* (New York: Oxford University Press, 1987).

Griffin, James, "Welfare Rights," *The Journal of Ethics*, 4 (2000), pp. 27-43.

Grundmann, Reiner, "Fundamentalist Intolerance or Civil Disobedience?" *Political Theory*, (1991), pp. 572-605.

Guevara, Ché, *Bolivian Diary*, Translated by Carlos P. Hansen and Andrew Sinclair (London: Jonathan Cape/Lorrimer, 1968).

Gupta, R. K., "Defining Violent and Non-Violent Acts," *Journal of Indian Council of Philosophical Research*," 9 (1992), pp. 157-61.

_____, "Defining Violent and Non-Violent Acts: A Supplement," *Journal of Indian Council of Philosophical Research*," 10 (1993), pp. 109-11.

Gurr, Nadine and Benjamin Cole, *The New Face of Terrorism: Threats From Weapons of Mass Destruction* (London: I.B. Tauris Publishers, 2002).

Haksar, Vinit, *Civil Disobedience, Threats and Offers: Gandhi and Rawls* (New York: Oxford University Press, 1986).

_____, "Coercive Proposals (Rawls and Gandhi)," *Political Theory*, 4 (1976), pp. 65-79.

_____, "Rawls and Gandhi on Civil Disobedience," *Inquiry*, 19 (1976), pp. 151-92.

Hall, Robert, "Legal Toleration of Civil Disobedience," *Ethics*, 81 (1971), pp. 128-42.

Hancock, Roger, "Kant and Civil Disobedience," *Idealistic Studies*, 5 (1975), pp. 164-76.

Hare, R. M., *Essays on Political Morality* (Oxford: Oxford University Press, 1989).

_____, "On Terrorism," *Journal of Value Inquiry*, 12 (1979), pp. 241-9. Reprinted in Joe P. White, Editor, *Assent/Dissent* (Dubuque: Kendall/Hunt, 1984), pp. 242-50.

Harris, John, "The Marxist Conception of Violence," *Philosophy and Public Affairs*, 3 (1974), pp. 192-220.

Harris, Paul, Editor, *Civil Disobedience* (Lanham: University Press of America, 1989).

Hartmann, George W., "The Strength and Weakness of the Pacifist Position as seen by American Philosophers," *The Philosophical Review*, 52 (1944), pp. 125-44.

Hartney, Michael, "Some Confusions Concerning Collective Rights," *Canadian Journal of Law and Jurisprudence*, 4 (1991), pp. 293-314.

Hawk, William, "Must We Do What Right Requires?" *Journal of Value Inquiry*, 17 (1983), pp. 241-7.

_____, "Pacifism and Social Responsibility," in Creighton Peden, Editor, *Freedom, Equality and Social Change* (Lewiston: Mellen Press, 1989).

Held, Virginia, "Civil Disobedience and Public Policy," in E. Kent, Editor, *Revolution and the Rule of Law* (Englewood Cliffs: Prentice Hall, 1971).

_____, "The Media and Political Violence," *The Journal of Ethics* 1 (1997), pp. 187-202.

_____, "Terrorism, Rights, and Political Goals," in R. G. Frey and Christopher W. Morris, Editors, *Violence, Terrorism, and Justice* (Cambridge: Cambridge University Press, 1991), pp. 59-85.

_____, "Violence, Terrorism, and Moral Inquiry," *The Monist*, 67 (1984), pp. 605-26.

Herman, A. L., "Satyagraha: A New Indian Word for Some Old Ways of Western Thinking," *Philosophy East and West*, 19 (1969), pp. 123-42.

Herman, Barbara, "Murder and Mayhem: Violence and Kantian Casuistry," *The Monist*, 72 (1989), pp. 411-31.

Herr, William A., "Thoreau: A Civil Disobedient?" *Ethics*, 85 (1974), pp. 87-91.

Herrera, Christopher D., "Civil Disobedience and Plato's 'Crito,'" *The Southern Journal of Philosophy*, 33 (1995), pp. 39-55.

Hicks, Kathryn, "Illuminations of Terrorism," *Contemporary Philosophy*, 19 (1997), pp. 36-41.

Hill, Thomas, Jr. "A Kantian Perspective on Political Violence," *The Journal of Ethics*, 1 (1997), pp. 105-40.

_____, "Making Exceptions Without Violating the Principle: Or How a Kantian Might Think About Terrorism," in R. G. Frey and Christopher W. Morris, Editors, *Violence, Terrorism, and Justice* (Cambridge: Cambridge University Press, 1991), pp. 196-229.

Hohfeld, Wesley, *Fundamental Legal Conceptions* (New Haven: Yale University Press, 1919).

Holmes, Robert L., *Non-violence in Theory and Practice* (Belmont: Wadsworth Publishing Company, 1990).

_____, "On Pacifism," *The Monist*, 57 (1973), pp. 489-506.

_____, *On War and Morality* (Princeton: Princeton University Press, 1989).

_____, "Pacifism for Nonpacifists," *Journal of Social Philosophy*, 30 (1999), pp. 387-400.

_____, "Pacifism and Wartime Innocence: A Response," *Social Theory and Practice*, 20 (1994), pp. 193-202.

_____, "Terrorism and Violence: A Moral Perspective," in Joseph Kunkel and Kenneth H. Klein, Editors, *Issues in War and Peace: Philosophical Inquiries* (Wolfeboro: Longwood, 1989).

Honderich, Ted, *After the Terror* (Edinburgh: Edinburgh University Press, 2002).

_____, "After the Terror: A Book and Further Thoughts," *The Journal of Ethics*, 7 (2003), pp. 161-81.

_____, "Four Conclusions About Violence of the Left," in Joe P. White, Editor, *Assent/Dissent* (Dubuque: Kendall/Hunt, 2984), pp. 261-79.

_____, *Political Violence* (Ithaca: Cornell University Press, 1976).

Hoppe, Hans Hermann, "Small is Beautiful and Efficient: The Case for Secession," *Telos*, 107 (1996), pp. 95-101.

Horsburgh, Howard J. N., *Non-Violence and Aggression: A Study of Gandhi's Moral Equivalent of War* (Oxford: Oxford University Press, 1968).

Howlett, Charles F., *Troubled Philosopher: John Dewey and the Struggle for World Peace* (Port: Washington Kennikat Press, 1977).

Hughes, Graham, "Response to Marshall Cohen," *Philosophic Exchange*, (1970), 121-28.

Hughes, Martin, "Terrorism and National Security," *Philosophy*, 57 (1982), pp. 5-26.

Ihara, Craig K., "In Defense of a Version of Pacifism," *Ethics*, 88 (1978), pp. 369-74.

_____, "Pacifism as a Moral Ideal," *Journal of Value Inquiry*, 22 (1988), pp. 267-77.

Ingram, David, *Group Rights: Reconciling Equality and Difference* (Lawrence: Kansas University Press, 2000).

Jackson, Christine M., "The Fiery Fight For Animal Rights," *Hastings Center Report*, 19 (1989), pp. 37-9.

Jackson, M. W., "Justice and The Cave," in Creighton Peden, Editor, *Terrorism, Justice and Social Values* (Lewiston: Mellen Press, 1990).

Jaimes, M. Annette, "Federal Indian Identification Policy: A Usurpation of Indigenous Sovereignty in North America," in M. Annette Jaimes,

Editor, *The state of Native North America* (Boston: South End Press, 1992), pp. 123-38.

Jaimes, M. Annette, Editor, *The state of Native North America* (Boston: South End Press, 1992).

James, Gene G., "The Orthodox Theory of Civil Disobedience," *Social Theory and Practice*, 2 (1973), pp. 475-98.

_____, "Socrates on Civil Disobedience and Rebellion," *The Southern Journal of Philosophy*, 11 (1973), pp. 119-27.

Johnson, David L., "Breaking Stones with Water: Gandhi's Moderate Revolution," *Journal of Thought*, 9 (1974), pp. 244-51.

Johnson, James Turner and John Kelsay, Editors, *Cross, Crescent, and Sword* (Westport: Greenwood Press, 1990).

Jones, Gary E., "On the Permissibility of Torture," *Journal of Medical Ethics*, 6 (1980), pp. 11-3.

The Journal of Ethics, 1 (1997), pp. 105-208.

The Journal of Ethics, 4 (2000), pp. 1-165.

The Journal of Ethics, 5 (2001), pp. 197-267.

The Journal of Ethics, 6 (2002), pp. 111-98.

The Journal of Ethics, 8 (2004), pp. 1f.

Kalla, Sarala, "Hannah Arendt on Civil Disobedience," *Indian Philosophical Quarterly*, 13 (1986), pp. 261-69.

Kant, Immanuel, *The Metaphysical Elements of Justice*, John Ladd, Translator (Indianapolis: Bobbs-Merrill, 1965).

_____, *The Metaphysics of Morals*, Mary Gregor, Translator (Indianapolis: Hackett Publishing Company, 1996).

Kavka, Gregory, "Nuclear Hostages," in R. G. Frey and Christopher Morris, Editors, *Violence, Terrorism, and Justice* (Cambridge: Cambridge University Press, 1991), pp. 276-95.

Khatchadourian, Haig, *The Morality of Terrorism* (New York: Peter Lang, 1998).

_____, *The Quest for Peace Between Israel and the Palestinians* (New York: Peter Lang Publishers, 2000).

_____, "Terrorism and Morality," *Journal of Applied Philosophy*, 5 (1988), pp. 131-45.

_____, "Terrorism and Morality," in Brenda Almond, Editor, *Applied Philosophy* (New York: Routledge, 1992).

King, Martin Luther, Jr., "Letter from Birmingham Jail," in Paul Harris, Editor, *Civil Disobedience* (Lanham: University Press of America, 1989), pp. 57-71.

Klein, Kenneth H., Editor, *In the Interest of Peace: A Spectrum of Philosophical Views* (Wolfeboro: Longwood, 1990).

Kleinig, John, "Bad Samaritanism," in Joel Feinberg and Hyman Gross, Editors, *Philosophy of Law*, Fifth Edition (Belmont: Wadsworth Publishing Company, 1995), pp. 529-32.

Kohl, Marvin, "Toward Understanding the Pragmatics of Absolute Pacifism," in Kenneth H. Klein, Editor, *In the Interest of Peace: A Spectrum of Philosophical Views* (Wolfeboro: Longwood, 1990).

Kramer, Matthew H., *John Locke and the Origins of Private Property* (Cambridge: Cambridge University Press, 1997).

Kucheman, Clark A., "Morality and Coercion by Violence," in Creighton Peden, Editor, *Terrorism, Justice and Social Values* (Lewiston: Mellen Press, 1990).

Kunkel, Joseph C., Editor, *Issues in War and Peace: Philosophical Inquiries* (Wolfeboro: Longwood, 1989).

_____, "Just-War Doctrine and Pacifism," *The Thomist*, 47 (1983), pp. 501-12.

Kymlicka, Will, *Liberalism, Community, and Culture* (Oxford: Oxford University Press, 1989).

_____, *Multicultural Citizenship* (Oxford: Oxford University Press, 1995).

Lackey, Douglas P., *The Ethics of War and Peace* (Englewood Cliffs: Prentice-Hall, 1989).

Lang, Berel, "Civil Disobedience and Non-violence: A Distinction with a Difference," *Ethics*, 80 (1970), pp. 156-59.

Laqueur, Walter, *A History of Terrorism* (New Brunswick: Transaction Publishers, 2002).

_____, *Terrorism* (Boston: Little, Brown and Company, 1977).

Lawson, Bill, "Crime, Minorities, and the Social Contract," *Criminal Justice Ethics*, 9 (1990), pp. 16-24.

Leary, Lewis, Editor, *Henry David Thoreau: Selected Writings* (Arlington Heights: A.H.M., 1958).

Leber, Gary, "We Must Rescue Them," *Hastings Center Report*, 19 (1989), pp. 26-7.

Lehrer, Keith, "Freedom, Preference, and Autonomy," *The Journal of Ethics*, 1 (1997), pp. 3-25.

_____, *Theory of Knowledge*, (Boulder: Westview Press, 1990)

Lemmon, E. J., "Moral Dilemmas," *The Philosophical Review*, 71 (1962), pp. 139-58.

Lomasky, Loren, "Liberty and Welfare Goods: Reflections on Clashing Liberalisms," *The Journal of Ethics*, 4 (2000), pp. 99-113.

_____, *Persons, Rights, and the Moral Community* (Oxford: Oxford University Press, 1987).

_____, "The Political Significance of Terrorism," in R. G. Frey and Christopher W. Morris, Editors, *Violence, Terrorism, and Justice* (Cambridge: Cambridge University Press, 1991), pp. 86-115.

Luke, Timothy W., "Re-Reading the Unabomber Manifesto," *Telos*, 107 (1996), pp. 81-94.

Lynd, Staughton, "Civil Disobedience and Non-violent Obstruction," *The Humanist*, 28 (1968).

Lyons, David, "Moral Judgment, Historical Reality, and Civil Disobedience," *Philosophy and Public Affairs*, 27 (1989), pp. 31-49.

_____, "The New Indian Claims and Original Rights to Land," *Social Theory and Practice*, 4 (1977), pp. 249-72.

_____, *Rights, Welfare, and Mill's Moral Theory* (Oxford: Oxford University Press, 1994).

MacFarlane, Leslie, "Justifying Political Disobedience," *Ethics*, 75 (1965), pp. 103-11.

_____, "More About Civil Disobedience," *Ethics*, 77 (1967), pp. 311-13.

Mack, Eric, "In Defense of the Jurisdiction Theory of Rights," *The Journal of Ethics*, 4 (2000), pp. 71-98.

Madden, Edward H. and Hare, Peter H., "Reflections on Civil Disobedience," *Journal of Value Inquiry*, 4 (1970), pp. 81-95.

Margalit, Avishai and Joseph Raz, "National Self-Determination," *The Journal of Philosophy*, LXXXVII (1990), pp. 439-61.

Margolis, Joseph, "The Problem of Revolution," *Philosophy in Context*, 5 (1976), pp. 28-41.

Martin, Michael, "Ecosabotage and Civil Disobedience," *Environmental Ethics*, (1990), pp. 291-310.

_____, "On an Argument Against Pacifism," *Philosophical Studies*, 26 (1974), pp. 437-42.

Martin, Rex, "Civil Disobedience," *Ethics*, 80 (1970), pp. 123-39.

_____, "Socrates on Disobedience to the Law," *The Review of Metaphysics*, 24 (1970), pp. 21-38.

Marx, Karl, *On Freedom of the Press and Censorship*, Saul K. Padover, Editor and Translator (New York: McGraw-Hill, 1974).

May, Larry, *The Morality of Groups* (Notre Dame: University of Notre Dame Press, 1987).

_____, *Sharing Responsibility* (Chicago: University of Chicago Press, 1990).

McCloskey, H.J., "Justification and the Problems to Which it Gives Rise," *Philosophy and Phenomenological Research*, 40 (1980), pp. 536-57.

McGary, Howard, "Justice and Reparations," *Philosophical Forum*, 9 (1978), pp. 250-63.

_____, *Race and Social Justice*, (London: Blackwell Publishers, 1999).

McLaughlin, Robert J., "Socrates on Political Disobedience," *Phronesis*, 21 (1976), pp. 185-97.

McMahan, Jeff, "War and Peace," in Peter Singer, Editor, *A Companion to Ethics* (Cambridge: Blackwell, 1991), pp. 384-95.

Miguens, Jose Enrique, "Magical Aspects of Political Terrorism," *Diogenes*, 126 (1984), pp. 104-22.

Mill, John Stuart, "The Contest in America," in John M. Robson, Editor, *Essays on Equality, Law, and Education* (Toronto: University of Toronto Press, 1984).

_____, "The French Law Against the Press," in John M. Robson, Editor, *Collected Works of John Stuart Mill*, Volume 25 (Toronto: University of Toronto Press, 1982).

_____, *On Liberty* (Indianapolis: Hackett Publishing Company, 1978).

_____, "Radical Party in Canada," in John M. Robson, Editor, *Collected Works of John Stuart Mill*, Volume 25 (Toronto: University of Toronto Press, 1982).

Miller, David, "Secession and the Principle of Nationality," *Canadian Journal of Philosophy* (Supplementary Volume), 22 (1996), pp. 261-82.

Miller, Richard B., *Interpretations of Conflict: Ethics, Pacifism, and the Just-War Tradition* (Chicago: University of Chicago Press, 1991).

Mills, Claudia, "Should We Boycott Boycotts?" *Journal of Social Philosophy*, 27 (1996), pp. 136-48.

Moellendorf, Darrel, *Cosmopolitan Justice* (Boulder: Westview Press, 2002).

_____, "Liberalism, Nationalism, and the Right to Secede," *The Philosophical Forum*, 28 (1996-97), pp. 87-99.

Moore, Margaret, *National Self-Determination and Secession* (Oxford: Oxford University Press, 1998).

Moore, Terrence L., "The Nature and Evaluation of Terrorism," Ph.D. dissertation, University of Pittsburgh, 1987.

Morano, Donald V., "Civil Disobedience and Legal Responsibility," *Journal of Value Inquiry*, 5 (1971), pp. 185-93.

Morreall, John, "The Justifiability of Violent Civil Disobedience," *Canadian Journal of Philosophy*, 6 (1976), pp. 35-47.

Morris, Glenn T., "International Law and Politics: Toward a Right to Self-Determination for Indigenous Peoples," in M. Annette Jaimes, Editor, *The state of Native America* (Boston: South End Press, 1992), pp. 55-86.

Mosley, Albert, "Preferential Treatment and Social Justice," in Peden Creighton Editor, *Terrorism, Justice and Social Values* (Lewiston: Mellen Press, 1990).

Moss, Myra M., "The Verifiability of Ethical Judgments," in Creighton Peden, Editor, *Terrorism, Justice and Social Values* (Lewiston: Mellen Press, 1990).

Nagel, Thomas, *Mortal Questions* (Cambridge: Cambridge University Press, 1979).

Narveson, Jan, "Is Pacifism Consistent?" *Ethics*, 78 (1968), pp. 148-50.

_____, "Pacifism: A Philosophical Analysis," *Ethics*, 75 (1965), pp. 259-71.

_____, "Sterba's Program of Philosophical Reconciliation," *Journal of Social Philosophy*, 30 (1999), pp. 401-10.

_____, "Terrorism and Morality," in R. G. Frey and Christopher W. Morris, Editors, *Violence, Terrorism, and Justice* (Cambridge: Cambridge University Press, 1991), pp. 116-69.

Nathanson, Bernard, "Operation Rescue: Domestic Terrorism or Legitimate Civil Rights Protest?" *Hastings Center Report*, 19 (1989), pp. 28-32.

Nelson, Julianne, "Rational Altruism or the Secession of Successful?: A Paradox of Social Choice," *Public Affairs Quarterly* 7 (1993), pp. 29-46.

Nickel, James, "Ethnocide and Indigenous Peoples," *Journal of Social Philosophy*, 24 (1994), pp. 84-98.

_____, "Group Agency and Group Rights," *NOMOS*, 29 (1997).

_____, *Making Sense of Human Rights*, (Berkely: University of California Press, 1987).

Nielsen, Kai, "On Justifying Violence," *Inquiry*, 24 (1981), pp. 21-58.

_____, "Political Violence and Ideological Mystification," *Journal of Social Philosophy*, 13 (1982), pp. 25-33.

_____, "Remarks on Violence and Paying the Penalty," *Philosophic Exchange*, (1970), pp. 113-22.

_____, "Secession: The Case of Quebec," *Journal of Applied Philosophy*, 10 (1993), pp. 29-43.

Norman, Richard, "The Case for Pacifism," in Brenda Almond, Editor, *Applied Philosophy* (New York: Routledge, 1992).

_____, "A Reply to Dworkin's "Civil Disobedience and Nuclear Protest," *Radical Philosophy*, 44 (1986), pp. 24-7.

Oelschlaeger, Max, "A Neo-Hobbesian Perspective on Twentieth Century Terrorism," *Contemporary Philosophy* (1998), pp. 25-8.

Oruka, Odera H., "Legal Terrorism and Human Rights," *Praxis*, 1 (1982), pp. 376-85.

Peden, Creighton, Editor, *Terrorism, Justice and Social Values* (Lewiston: Mellen Press, 1990).

Parsons, Howard and Somerville, John, Editors, *Marxism, Revolution and Peace: From the Proceeding of the Society for the Philosophical Study of Dialectical Materialism* (Amsterdam: Gruner, 1977).

Paskins, Barrie and Michael Dockrill, *The Ethics of War* (Minneapolis: Minnesota University Press, 1979).

Peach, Lucinda J., "An Alternative to Pacifism? Feminism and Just War Theory," *Hypatia*, 9 (1994), pp. 152-72.

Phillips, Robert L., *War and Justice* (Norman: University of Oklahoma Press, 1984).

Philpott, Daniel, "In Defense of Self-Determination," *Ethics*, 105 (1995), pp. 352-85.

Piccone, Paul, "Secession or Reform? The Case of Canada," *Telos* 106 (1996), pp. 15-63.

Pincoffs, Edmund L., Editor, *The Concept of Academic Freedom* (Austin: University of Texas Press, 1975).

Pogge, Thomas, "Cosmopolitanism and Sovereignty," *Ethics*, 103 (1992), pp. 48-75.

_____, "Group Rights and Ethnicity," *NOMOS*, 39 (1997).

_____, "The International Significance of Human Rights," *The Journal of Ethics*, 4 (2000), pp. 45-69.

Pojman, Louis and Owen McLeod, Editors, *What Do We Deserve?* (Oxford: Oxford University Press, 1999).

Poole, Ross, "National Identity, Multiculturalism, and Aboriginal Rights: An Australian Perspective," *Canadian Journal of Philosophy* (Supplementary Volume), 22 (1996), pp. 407-38.

Primoratz, Igor, "The Morality of Terrorism," *Journal of Applied Philosophy*, 14 (1997), pp. 221-33.

_____, "What is Terrorism?" *Journal of Applied Philosophy*, 7 (1990), pp. 129-38.

Prosch, Harry, "Limits to the Moral Claim in Civil Disobedience," *Ethics*, 75 (1965), pp. 103-11.

_____, "More about Civil Disobedience," *Ethics*, 77 (1967), pp. 311-13.

_____, "Toward an Ethics of Civil Disobedience," *Ethics*, 77 (1967), pp. 176-92.

Pullman, Daryl, "Self-Respect, Morality, and Justice," in Creighton Peden, Editor, *Terrorism, Justice and Social Values* (Lewiston: Mellen Press, 1990).

Purtill, Richard L., "On the Just War," *Social Theory and Practice*, 1 (1971), pp. 97-102.

Ramsey, Paul, *The Just War: Force and Political Responsibility* (Lanham: University Press of America, 1983).

Rapaport, David C., *The Morality of Terrorism* (New York: Pergamon, 1982).

Rawls, John, *Collected Papers*, Samuel Freeman, Editor (Cambridge: Harvard University Press, 1999).

_____, *Justice as Fairness: A Restatement* (Cambridge: Harvard University Press, 2001).

_____, *The Law of Peoples* (Cambridge: Harvard University Press, 1999).

_____, *Lectures on the History of Moral Philosophy* (Cambridge: Harvard University Press, 2000).

_____, "Legal Obligation and the Duty of Fair Play," in Joe P. White, Editor, *Assent/Dissent* (Dubuque: Kendall/Hunt, 1984), pp. 45-56.

_____, *Political Liberalism* (New York: Columbia University Press, 1993).

_____, *A Theory of Justice* (Cambridge: Harvard University Press, 1971).

Raz, Joseph, *The Morality of Freedom* (Oxford: Oxford University Press, 1986).

Reader, Soran, "Making Pacifism Plausible," *Journal of Applied Philosophy*, 17 (2000), pp. 169-80.

Regan, Thomas, "A Defense of Pacifism," *Canadian Journal of Philosophy*, 2 (1972), pp. 73-86. Reprinted in Joe P. White, Editor, *Assent/Dissent* (Dubuque: Kendall/Hunt, 1984), pp. 98-110.

Reitan, Eric, "The Irreconcilability of Pacifism and Just War Theory: A Response to Sterba," *Social Theory and Practice*, 20 (1994), pp. 117-34.

Remini, Robert V., *The Legacy of Andrew Jackson* (Baton Rouge: Louisiana state University Press, 1988).

Robbins, Rebecca L., "Self-Determination and Subordination: The Past, Present, and Future of American Indian Governance," in M. Annette Jaimes, Editor, *The state of Native America* (Boston: South End Press, 1992), pp. 87-122.

Roberts, Rodney C., "The Morality of a Moral Statute of Limitations on Injustice," *The Journal of Ethics*, 7 (2003), pp. 115-38.

Roth, John K., "No Confusion: Some Reflections on TWA Flight 847," in Creighton Peden, Editor, *Terrorism, Justice and Social Values* (Lewiston: The Edwin Mellen Press, 1990).

Routley, Richard, "On the Alleged Inconsistency, Moral Insensitivity, and Fanaticism of Pacifism," *Inquiry*, 27 (1984), pp. 117-36.

Ryan, Alan, "state and Private: Red and White," in R. G. Frey and Christopher Morris, Editors, *Violence, Terrorism, and Justice* (Cambridge: Cambridge University Press, 1991), pp. 230-55.

Ryan, Cheyney C., "Self-Defense, Pacifism, and the Possibility of Killing," *Ethics*, 93 (1983), pp. 508-24.

Sandler, Todd and Lapan, Harvey E., "The Calculus of Dissent: An Analysis of Terrorists' Choice of Targets," *Synthese*, 76 (1988), pp. 245-61.

Santoni, Ronald E., "A Reply to Professor Garver on Pacifism," *Philosophy Today*, 2 (1967), pp. 147-50.

Sarala, Kella, "Hannah Arendt on Civil Disobedience," *Indian Philosophical Quarterly*, 13 (1986), pp. 261-99.

Schaff, Adam, "Marxist Theory on Revolution and Violence," *Journal of the History of Ideas*, 34 (1973), pp. 263-70.

Schlossberger, Eugene, "Civil Disobedience," *Analysis*, 49 (1989), pp. 148-53.

Schmidt, Karl, "Freedom and Democracy," *Journal of Philosophy*, 39 (1942), pp. 365-80.

Schwarz, Robert, "Disobeying the Law: A Critique of a Critique," *Journal of Social Philosophy*, 4 (1973), pp. 11-3.

Sher, G. *Desert* (Princeton: Princeton University Press, 1987)

_____, "Diversity," *Philosophy and Public Affairs*, 28 (1999), pp. 85-104.

_____, "Groups and Justice," *Ethics*, 87 (1977), pp. 174-81.

Shue, Henry, *Basic Rights* (Princeton: Princeton University Press, 1980).

_____, "Torture," *Philosophy and Public Affairs*, 7 (1978), pp. 124-43.

Sibley, Mulford O., "Conscience, Law, and Obligation to Obey," *The Monist*, 54 (1970), pp. 556-86.

Siegel, Steve, "Grassroots Opposition to Animal Exploitation," *Hastings Center Report*, 19 (1989), pp. 39-41.

Sievers, Bruce, "Civil Disobedience in Political Theory: The Classical Model Revisited," *Humanities in Society*, 2 (1979), pp. 61-8.

Simmons, A. John, *A Lockean Theory of Rights* (Princeton: Princeton University Press, 1992).

_____, "Makers' Rights," *The Journal of Ethics*, 2 (1998), pp. 197-218.

Singh, Nirmala, "A Note on the Concept of Satyagrah," *Indian Philosophical Quarterly*, 24 (1997), pp. 521-26.

Singer, M. S., "Justice in Preferential Hiring," *Journal of Business Ethics*, (1991), pp. 797-803.

Singer, Peter, *Democracy and Disobedience* (Oxford New York: Clarendon Press, 1973).

_____, "To Do or Not to Do?" *Hastings Center Report*, 19 (1989), pp. 42-4.

Sinnott-Armstrong, Walter, "On Primoratz's Definition of Terrorism," *Journal of Applied Philosophy*, (1991), pp. 115-20.

Sinnott-Armstrong, Walter, and Mark Timmons, Editors, *Moral Knowledge?* (Oxford: Oxford University Press, 1996).

Smart, Brian, "Defining Civil Disobedience," *Inquiry*, 21 (1978), pp. 249-69.

Smith, John E., "The Inescapable Ambiguity of Non-violence," *Philosophy East and West*, 19 (1969), pp. 155-58.

Smith, Steven A., "How To Respond To Terrorism," in Creighton Peden, Editor, *Terrorism, Justice and Social Values* (Lewiston: Mellen Press, 1990).

Smithka, Paula, "Are Active Pacifists Really Just Warists in Disguise?" *Journal of Social Philosophy*, 23 (1992), pp. 166-83.

_____, "Pragmatic Pacifism: A Methodology for Gaining the Ear of the Warist," in Kennith H. Klein, Editor, *In the Interest of Peace: A Spectrum of Philosophical Views* (Wolfeboro: Longwood, 1990).

Sparrow, Robert, "History and Collective Responsibility," *Australasian Journal of Philosophy*, 78 (2000), pp. 346-59.

Sreenivasan, Gopal, *The Limits of Lockean Rights in Property* (Oxford: Oxford University Press, 1995).

Stanage, Sherman M., Editor, *Reason and Violence: Philosophical Investigations* (Totowa: Rowman and Littlefield, 1974).

_____, "Violence and the New Terrorism," in Yeager Hudson, Editor, *Philosophical Essays* (Lewiston: Mellen Press, 1988).

Stannard, David, E., *American Holocaust* (Oxford: Oxford University Press, 1992).

Steele, Ian, *Warpaths* (Oxford: Oxford University Press, 1994).

Sterba, James P. "Five Commentators: A Brief Response," *Journal of Social Philosophy*, 30 (1999), pp. 424-37.

_____, *Justice for Here and Now* (Cambridge: Cambridge University Press, 1998).

_____, "Reconciling Pacifists and Just War Theorists," *Social Theory and Practice*, 18 (1992), pp. 21-38.

_____, "Reconciling Pacifists and Just War Theorists Revisited (Response to Reitan)," *Social Theory and Practice*, 20 (1994), pp. 135-42.

Stern, Jessica, *The Ultimate Terrorists* (Cambridge: Harvard University Press, 1999).

Stichler, Richard N., "The Right to Revolution: Locke or Marx?" in Creighton Peden, Editor, *Terrorism, Justice and Social Values* (Lewiston: Mellen Press, 1990).

Sumner, L. W., *The Moral Foundations of Rights* (Oxford: Oxford University Press, 1987).

Tawakley, I. D., "Socrates's Conception of Civic Duty and the Basic Principle of Civil Resistance," *Philosophical Quarterly (India)*, 20 (1944), pp. 118-28.

Teichman, Jenny, "How to Define Terrorism," *Philosophy*, 64 (1989), pp. 505-17.

_____, "Pacifism," *Philosophical Investigations*, 5 (1982), pp. 72-83.

_____, *Pacifism and the Just War* (London: Blackwell Publishers, 1986).

Thalberg, Irving, "Themes in the Reverse Discrimination Debate," *Ethics*, 91 (1980), pp. 138-50.

Thompson, Janna, "Historical Injustice and Reparation: Justifying Claims of Descendants," *Ethics*, 112 (2001), pp. 114-35.

_____, "Land Rights and Aboriginal Sovereignty," *Australasian Journal of Philosophy*, 68 (1990), pp. 313-29.

Thomson, Judith J., *The Realm of Rights* (Cambridge: Harvard University Press, 1990).

Thoreau, Henry David, *Walden and Civil Disobedience* (New York: Penguin Books, 1983).

Timmons, Mark, *Moral Theory* (Lanham: Rowman and Littlefield Publishers, 2002).

_____, *Morality Without Foundations* (Oxford: Oxford University Press, 1998).

Trafzer, Clifford E., *The Kit Carsen Campaign* (Norman: University of Oklahoma Press, 1982).

Trotsky, Leon, *Terrorism and Communism* (Ann Arbor: University of Michigan Press, 1961).

Tucker, Robert W., "Morality and Deterrence," *Ethics*, 95 (1985), pp. 461-78.

Tully, James, "Aboriginal Property and Western Theory: Recovering a Middle Ground," *Social Philosophy and Policy*, 11 (1994), pp. 153-80.

_____, *An Approach to Political Philosophy: Locke in Contexts* (Cambridge: Cambridge University Press, 1993).

Tuomela, Raimo, *A Theory of Social Action* (Dordrecht: D. Reidel Publishing Company, 1984).

United States Department of state, "Patterns of Global Terrorism, 2001," May, 2002.

Valls, Andrew, "Can Terrorism Be Justified," in Andrew Valls, Editor, *Ethics in International Affairs: Theories and Cases* (Lanham: Rowman and Littlefield, 2000).

_____, Editor, *Ethics in International Affairs: Theories and Cases* (Lanham: Rowman and Littlefield, 2000).

Van Der Burg, Wibren, "The Myth of Civil Disobedience," *Praxis International*, 9 (1989), pp. 287-304.

Vlacke, Catherine, "Civil Disobedience and the Rule of Law—A Lockean Insight," *Nomos*, 36 (1994), pp. 45-62.

Vlastos, Gregory, "Socrates on Political Obedience and Disobedience," *Yale Review* (1974), pp. 517-34.

Vorobej, Mark, "Pacifism and Wartime Innocence," *Social Theory and Practice*, 20 (1994), pp. 171-91.

Wade, Francis C., "In Defense of Socrates," *The Review of Metaphysics*, 25 (1971), pp. 311-25.

Wagoner, Jennings L., "The Dilemma of Civil Disobedience in a Lockean Perspective," *Journal of Thought*, 6 (1971), pp. 49-57.

Waldron, Jeremy, *Liberal Rights* (Cambridge: Cambridge University Press, 1993).

_____, "The Role of Rights in Practical Reasoning: 'Rights' Versus 'Needs,'" *The Journal of Ethics*, 4 (2000), pp. 115-35.

_____, "Superceding Historic Injustice," *Ethics*, 103 (1992), pp. 4-28.

_____, Editor, *Theories of Rights* (Oxford: Oxford University Press, 1984).

Wallace, G., "Area Bombing, Terrorism and the Death of Innocents," *Journal of Applied Philosophy*, 6 (1989), pp. 3-15.

_____, "The Language of Terrorism," *International Journal of Moral and Social Studies*, 8 (1993), pp. 123-34.

_____, "Terrorism and Argument from Analogy," *International Journal of Moral Social Studies*, 6 (1991), pp. 149-60.

_____, "War, Terrorism, and Ethical Consistency," in Brenda Almond, Editor, *Introducing Applied Ethics* (Cambridge: Blackwell, 1995).

Walter, Edward F., "Rawls on Act Utilitarianism and Rules," in Creighton Peden, Editor, *Terrorism, Justice and Social Values* (Lewiston: Mellen Press, 1990).

Walzer, Michael, *Just and Unjust Wars*, Third Edition (New York: Basic Books, 2000).

_____, "The Obligation to Disobey," *Ethics*, 77 (1967), pp. 163-75. Reprinted in Joe P. White, Editor, *Assent/Dissent* (Dubuque: Kendall/Hunt, 19840, pp. 57-72.

_____, *Obligations* (Cambridge: Harvard University Press, 1970).

_____, "Terrorism: A Critique of Excuses," in Steven Luper-Foy, Editor, *Problems of International Justice* (Boulder: Westview Press, 1988).

Warren, Karen J., "Peacemaking and Philosophy: A Critique of Justice for 'Here and Now,'" *Journal of Social Philosophy*, 30 (1999), pp. 411-23.

Washington, James M., Editor, *A Testament of Hope: The Essential Writings and Speeches of Martin Luther King, Jr.* (San Francisco: Harper San Francisco, 1986).

Wasserstrom, Richard, "The Obligation to Obey the Law," *UCLA Law Review*, 10 (1963). Reprinted in Joe P. White, Editor, *Assent/Dissent* (Dubuque: Kendall/Hunt, 1984), pp. 29-44.

Weiss, Paul, "The Ethics of Pacifism," *The Philosophical Review*, 51 (1942), pp. 476-96.

Wellman, Carl, *The Proliferation of Rights* (Boulder: Westview Press, 1999).

_____, *Real Rights* (Oxford: Oxford University Press, 1995).

_____, "On Terrorism Itself," *Journal of Value Inquiry*, 13 (1979), pp. 250-8. Reprinted in Joe P. White, Editor, *Assent/Dissent* (Dubuque: Kendall/Hunt, 1984), pp. 251-60.

_____, "Terrorism and Moral Rights," in John Howie, Editor, *Ethical Principles and Practice* (Carbondale: South Illinois University Press, 1987), pp. 128-53.

_____, *A Theory of Rights* (Totowa: Rowman and Littlefield Publishers, 1985).

Wellman, Christopher, "A Defense of Secession and Political Self-Determination," *Philosophy and Public Affairs*, 24 (1995), pp. 142-71.

Westra, Laura, "Environmental Racism and the First Nations of Canada: Terrorism at Oka," *Journal of Social Philosophy*, 30 (1999), pp. 103-24.

_____, "Terrorism, Self-Defense, and Whistleblowing," *Journal of Social Philosophy*, 20 (1989), pp. 46-58.

Whitman, M. Jay, "Is Pacifism Self-Contradictory?" *Ethics*, 76 (1966), pp. 307-08.

Whittaker, David J., *Terrorism: Understanding the Global Threat* (London: Longman, 2002).

_____, Editor, *The Terrorism Reader* (London: Routledge, 2001).

Wieck, David T., "Dissidence," *The Monist*, 54 (1970), pp. 587-601.

Wilkins, Burleigh T., "Secession," *Peace Review*, 12 (2000), pp. 15-22.

_____, *Terrorism and Collective Responsibility* (New York: Routledge, 1992).

_____, "Terrorism and Consequentialism," *Journal of Value Inquiry*, 21 (1987), pp. 141-51.

_____, "A Third Principle of Justice," *The Journal of Ethics*, 1 (1997), pp. 355-74.

Wilkinson, Paul, *Terrorism and the Liberal state* (New York: New York University Press, 1986).

Williams, Geraint, "J. S. Mill and Political Violence," *Utilitas*, 1 (1989), pp. 102-11.

Wit, Ernst Jan C., "Kant and the Limits of Civil Obedience," *Kant Studien,* 90 (1999), pp. 285-305.

Wolff,, Robert Paul, *In Defense of Anarchism* (New York: Harper and Row, 1970).

Wood, Peter H., Gregory A. Waselkov and M. Thomas Hatley, Editors, *Powhatan's Mantle* (Lincoln: University of Nebraska Press, 1989).

Woodward, Grace Steele, *The Cherokees* (Norman: University of Oklahoma Press, 1963).

Woozley, A.D., "Civil Disobedience and Punishment," *Ethics*, 86 (1976), pp. 323-31.

_____, *Law and Obedience: The Arguments of Plato's "Crito"* (London: Duckworth, 1979).

_____, "Socrates on Disobeying the Law," in Gregory Vlastos, Editor, *The Philosophy of Socrates* (New York: Anchor-Doubleday, 1971), pp. 299-318.

Young, Gary, "Socrates and Obedience," *Phronesis*, 19 (1974), pp. 1-29.

Young, Robert, "Revolutionary Terrorism, Crime, and Morality," *Social Theory and Practice*, 4 (1977), pp. 287-302.

INDEX

PHILOSOPHICAL STUDIES SERIES

PHILOSOPHICAL STUDIES SERIES

26. John D. Hodson: *The Ethics of Legal Coercion*. 1983   ISBN 90-277-1494-0
27. Robert J. Richman: *God, Free Will, and Morality*. Prolegomena to a Theory of Practical Reasoning. 1983   ISBN 90-277-1548-3
28. Terence Penelhum: *God and Skepticism*. A Study in Skepticism and Fideism. 1983
          ISBN 90-277-1550-5
29. James Bogen and James E. McGuire (eds.): *How Things Are*. Studies in Predication and the History of Philosophy of Science. 1985   ISBN 90-277-1583-1
30. Clement Dore: *Theism*. 1984   ISBN 90-277-1683-8
31. Thomas L. Carson: *The Status of Morality*. 1984   ISBN 90-277-1619-9
32. Michael J. White: *Agency and Integrality*. Philosophical Themes in the Ancient Discussions of Determinism and Responsibility. 1985   ISBN 90-277-1968-3
33. Donald F. Gustafson: *Intention and Agency*. 1986   ISBN 90-277-2009-6
34. Paul K. Moser: *Empirical Justification*. 1985   ISBN 90-277-2041-X
35. Fred Feldman: *Doing the Best We Can*. An Essay in Informal Deontic Logic. 1986
          ISBN 90-277-2164-5
36. G. W. Fitch: *Naming and Believing*. 1987   ISBN 90-277-2349-4
37. Terry Penner: *The Ascent from Nominalism*. Some Existence Arguments in Plato's Middle Dialogues. 1987   ISBN 90-277-2427-X
38. Robert G. Meyers: *The Likelihood of Knowledge*. 1988   ISBN 90-277-2671-X
39. David F. Austin (ed.): *Philosophical Analysis*. A Defense by Example. 1988
          ISBN 90-277-2674-4
40. Stuart Silvers (ed.): *Rerepresentation*. Essays in the Philosophy of Mental Representation. 1988   ISBN 0-7923-0045-9
41. Michael P. Levine: *Hume and the Problem of Miracles*. A Solution. 1989 ISBN 0-7923-0043-2
42. Melvin Dalgarno and Eric Matthews (eds.): *The Philosophy of Thomas Reid*. 1989
          ISBN 0-7923-0190-0
43. Kenneth R. Westphal: *Hegel's Epistemological Realism*. A Study of the Aim and Method of Hegel's *Phenomenology of Spirit*. 1989   ISBN 0-7923-0193-5
44. John W. Bender (ed.): *The Current State of the Coherence Theory*. Critical Essays on the Epistemic Theories of Keith Lehrer and Laurence BonJour, with Replies. 1989
          ISBN 0-7923-0220-6
45. Roger D. Gallie: *Thomas Reid and 'The Way of Ideas'*. 1989   ISBN 0-7923-0390-3
46. J-C. Smith (ed.): *Historical Foundations of Cognitive Science*. 1990   ISBN 0-7923-0451-9
47. John Heil (ed.): *Cause, Mind, and Reality*. Essays Honoring C. B. Martin. 1989
          ISBN 0-7923-0462-4
48. Michael D. Roth and Glenn Ross (eds.): *Doubting*. Contemporary Perspectives on Skepticism. 1990   ISBN 0-7923-0576-0
49. Rod Bertolet: *What is Said*. A Theory of Indirect Speech Reports. 1990
          ISBN 0-7923-0792-5
50. Bruce Russell (ed.): *Freedom, Rights and Pornography*. A Collection of Papers by Fred R. Berger. 1991   ISBN 0-7923-1034-9
51. Kevin Mulligan (ed.): *Language, Truth and Ontology*. 1992   ISBN 0-7923-1509-X

PHILOSOPHICAL STUDIES SERIES

52. Jesús Ezquerro and Jesús M. Larrazabal (eds.): *Cognition, Semantics and Philosophy*. Proceedings of the First International Colloquium on Cognitive Science. 1992 ISBN 0-7923-1538-3

53. O.H. Green: *The Emotions*. A Philosophical Theory. 1992   ISBN 0-7923-1549-9

54. Jeffrie G. Murphy: *Retribution Reconsidered*. More Essays in the Philosophy of Law. 1992
                                                                       ISBN 0-7923-1815-3

55. Phillip Montague: *In the Interests of Others*. An Essay in Moral Philosophy. 1992
                                                                       ISBN 0-7923-1856-0

56. Jacques-Paul Dubucs (ed.): *Philosophy of Probability*. 1993   ISBN 0-7923-2385-8

57. Gary S. Rosenkrantz: *Haecceity*. An Ontological Essay. 1993   ISBN 0-7923-2438-2

58. Charles Landesman: *The Eye and the Mind*. Reflections on Perception and the Problem of Knowledge. 1994   ISBN 0-7923-2586-9

59. Paul Weingartner (ed.): *Scientific and Religious Belief*. 1994   ISBN 0-7923-2595-8

60. Michaelis Michael and John O'Leary-Hawthorne (eds.): *Philosophy in Mind*. The Place of Philosophy in the Study of Mind. 1994   ISBN 0-7923-3143-5

61. William H. Shaw: *Moore on Right and Wrong*. The Normative Ethics of G.E. Moore. 1995
                                                                       ISBN 0-7923-3223-7

62. T.A. Blackson: *Inquiry, Forms, and Substances*. A Study in Plato's Metaphysics and Epistemology. 1995   ISBN 0-7923-3275-X

63. Debra Nails: *Agora, Academy, and the Conduct of Philosophy*. 1995   ISBN 0-7923-3543-0

64. Warren Shibles: *Emotion in Aesthetics*. 1995   ISBN 0-7923-3618-6

65. John Biro and Petr Kotatko (eds.): *Frege: Sense and Reference One Hundred Years Later*. 1995
                                                                       ISBN 0-7923-3795-6

66. Mary Gore Forrester: *Persons, Animals, and Fetuses*. An Essay in Practical Ethics. 1996
                                                                       ISBN 0-7923-3918-5

67. K. Lehrer, B.J. Lum, B.A. Slichta and N.D. Smith (eds.): *Knowledge, Teaching and Wisdom*. 1996   ISBN 0-7923-3980-0

68. Herbert Granger: *Aristotle's Idea of the Soul*. 1996   ISBN 0-7923-4033-7

69. Andy Clark, Jesús Ezquerro and Jesús M. Larrazabal (eds.): *Philosophy and Cognitive Science: Categories, Consciousness, and Reasoning*. Proceedings of the Second International Colloquium on Cogitive Science. 1996   ISBN 0-7923-4068-X

70. J. Mendola: *Human Thought*. 1997   ISBN 0-7923-4401-4

71. J. Wright: *Realism and Explanatory Priority*. 1997   ISBN 0-7923-4484-7

72. X. Arrazola, K. Korta and F.J. Pelletier (eds.): *Discourse, Interaction and Communication*. Proceedings of the Fourth International Colloquium on Cognitive Science. 1998
                                                                       ISBN 0-7923-4952-0

73. E. Morscher, O. Neumaier and P. Simons (eds.): *Applied Ethics in a Troubled World*. 1998
                                                                       ISBN 0-7923-4965-2

74. R.O. Savage: *Real Alternatives, Leibniz's Metaphysics of Choice*. 1998 ISBN 0-7923-5057-X

75. Q. Gibson: *The Existence Principle*. 1998   ISBN 0-7923-5188-6

76. F. Orilia and W.J. Rapaport (eds.): *Thought, Language, and Ontology*. 1998
                                                                       ISBN 0-7923-5197-5

PHILOSOPHICAL STUDIES SERIES

KLUWER ACADEMIC PUBLISHERS – DORDRECHT / BOSTON / LONDON